AUTHOR AND AGENT

BOOKS BY MICHAEL KREYLING

Eudora Welty's Achievement of Order
Figures of the Hero in Southern Narrative

AUTHOR AND AGENT

Eudora Welty and Diarmuid Russell

MICHAEL KREYLING

Farrar Straus Giroux

NEW YORK

*Published simultaneously in Canada by HarperCollins*CanadaLtd
Printed in the United States of America
Designed by Victoria Wong
First edition, 1991

Library of Congress Cataloging-in-Publication Data
Kreyling, Michael.
Author and agent : Eudora Welty and Diarmuid Russell / Michael Kreyling.—1st ed.
p. cm.
Includes bibliographical references.
1. Welty, Eudora. . 2. Russell, Dairmuid, d. 1973. 3. Welty, Eudora. —Friends and associates. 4. Authors, American—20th century—Biography. 5. Literary agents—United States—Biography. I. Title.
PS3545.E6Z74 1991 813'.52—dc20 [B] 90-48225 CIP

Grateful acknowledgment is made to the following for permission to reproduce photographs: of the Murray Hill Hotel party, reprinted from the November 22, 1941, issue of Publishers Weekly, *R. R. Bowker Company; of Herschel Brickell, Special Collections, John Davis Williams Library, University of Mississippi; of Kenneth Millar, Cordelia Editions, Santa Barbara, California. Photograph of William Maxwell courtesy of Mr. Maxwell. Photograph of Edward Weeks courtesy of Mr. Weeks. All other photographs courtesy of Eudora Welty*

For C. M. K.
and
L. M. K.

Contents

AUTHOR AND AGENT

Introduction

This book began several years ago when I observed to Eudora Welty that in interviews she had often mentioned her literary agent, Diarmuid Russell, as the trusted counselor of her writing career. I was particularly intrigued by his literary instincts and the "absolute" trust she placed in his judgment. He had spotted the novel *Delta Wedding* in a short story called "The Delta Cousins" and simply told her to go on and finish the potential novel. Welty's first novel actually seems to have been written at greater cost, as the letters testify, but Russell was crucial nevertheless. "Had anyone ever written about Russell and his literary career?" I asked. "No," Welty answered, and complained that he'd been remembered in only two scanty obituaries. "Why don't you? I have some letters you can use . . ."

She had saved, it turned out, several hundred letters from Russell beginning with his first query in May 1940 and ending with letters, in a shaky hand, confessing with bracing honesty and no self-pity that convalescing from cancer surgery had ruled out even part-time work at the office of Russell & Volkening, the literary agency he had co-founded more than thirty years before. Before he left the agency, he took her letters to him and passed them on to Welty a few months before he died. "Dear me, what a long association it has been," he wrote when he first looked into the archive in 1969. I had to buy a suitcase to carry just the first half of the correspondence home when Welty, hauling it downstairs in a plastic garbage bag, offered to let me use it for a book about herself and Diarmuid.

Fortunately for me, Welty almost always typed her letters and Russell his—although she often omitted dates beyond the day of the week (so often did they write) and he was idiosyncratic about spelling and punctuation. Anything fancier than a period seems to have been beneath his notice. I have identified undated letters with approximate dates and a parenthetical reference to the dated letter, if one exists, to which it serves as reply. I have tried to let the correspondents' voices create a dialogue. Where one correspondent seems to fall silent, the reason is usually that letters are not available.

There was a time—a long time—when Eudora Welty was not the eminent American writer she is today. Russell can take some credit for her success, although he would refuse it, for from the outset he expressed boundless faith in her art. Like all writers, Welty has had ups and downs, stretches of confidence and of doubt. Some of the stories we now think of as immediately recognizable were, Russell himself would be quick to point out, rejected by more than one prestigious journal and respected editor. A few were minutes from the incinerator. The rare ensemble or exhibition-like quality of Welty's collections, her reservations about the primacy of plot and the novel as a genre, her uneasy but career-long alliance with ambiguity as foe and as chosen ally—these have not been more clearly illustrated than in her correspondence with Russell. This book can add to our appreciation for Welty's work, to our understanding of what the author was trying to say by the *way* she chose to write. Subject matter—the South of Jackson, Mississippi, and the rural and small-town South of Mississippi, the territory of Welty's frequent travels, the character of family life—was so close as to be grasped without question. Russell and Welty did discuss *how* to communicate the material, and in this book I hope I relay the essentials of that dialogue.

For readers curious about American literary business, the view through Russell's eyes is special as well. Satellite figures around the canonical American writers are not unknown. In our century we have examples of editors: Maxwell Perkins, editor to Fitzgerald, Hemingway, and Wolfe; Saxe Commins to Faulkner; and others. What we lack are preeminent examples of author-agent relations, and by and large, our understanding of a writer's relationship with the first reader on the outside, typically the agent, is relegated to the side aisle of literary history and never fully lighted.

What precisely, or even approximately, is the daily work of the literary agent? Do all agents do the same work in the same way? Where is the line between business agent and creative collaborator? Is the pact one of "strictly business," or is there something more, something less tangible, that the intermediary supplies—something without which the writer would not be exactly the writer he or she is?

The partnership of Welty and Russell over the three decades from 1940, the year he opened his agency with Henry Volkening and John Slocum, to 1973 suggests some answers. It needs saying that Russell's first response was to a standard of past achievement and of future promise he held for each writer he represented, Eudora Welty not excepted. "His terms were not uncertain," Welty remembered in 1977, "you knew how well he liked something or how well he didn't. I just can't tell you what it meant to me to have him there. His integrity, his understanding, his instincts—everything was something I trusted" (Prenshaw, 185). From the writer's point of view, then, Russell's first allegiance was reciprocal—back to the writer before any thought of commerce.

The agent, as Russell knew well, was an intermediary or buffer between the artist and the marketplace, and once the question of literary quality was settled in the affirmative he went into the market fully convinced that good work would always sell. His early preparation for literary agency—even though he then held no conscious aims of such a career—took place under the tutelage of his father, George William Russell (A.E.), friend and early cohort of Yeats, poet, editor, artist. A.E. kept the spheres of art and commerce as far apart as he could; the lesson was not lost on his son, who wrote to Welty when she had been his client for about three years.

> I did another article for the Atlantic which I think was a good subject but which I think I did badly—I really should have read a lot of books to collect facts but I've had this article in my mind for so long and I never seemed to get time to even start it so I decided I'd better do it rather than keep on talking about it for the tongue wags away all energy and inspiration when one writes and all writers should keep their jaws shut. The idea was the difference between professional writers, those who have to write in order to live, and amateurs, those who earn their living by a job and write on the side. I'm all for the amateurs because it seems to me they will only write when forced to do so by internal feelings and not by the pressure of low bank balances and I think the majority of the odd, unique books have come from amateurs—Moby Dick, Alice in Wonderland, Seven Pillars, Uncle Tom's Cabin and so on. I think the pros as a result of the necessity of writing turn more and more towards fact—more books like historical novels or The Grapes of Wrath, which looks like a good reportorial job to me, or books which are more about the insides of different kinds of businesses like the hotel book that Lewis wrote—Arnold Bennett did one too or the innumerable books about doctors etc. I think there's something right to the idea and wish I had more time but there is little to spare in the office. . . . [DR to EW, January 20, 1943]

Welty agreed and championed Russell's manifesto:

> Your article sounds good to me—especially since I agree with it—and let me know its date. (Is it already sold?) I think too that the people who write for money always bring out the worst in the civilization that reads them—civilization is too big a word, but I mean in a material age readers will fasten onto books that are factual and reportorial just like the flies on over-ripe fruit, and all work together to hasten the decay. [EW to DR, January 24, 1943]

It must be remembered, in order to appreciate Welty's faith in her agent's stance, that until the publication of *Losing Battles* (1970) and

The Optimist's Daughter (1972), she could not live on her writing income alone (Prenshaw, 71).

Over time, the center shifted to the market. The techniques of marketing and of managing money overtook, it seemed to Russell, the preserve of the amateurs. Diarmuid grew restive as the shifting progressed. He was a literary man of very simple but not simplistic beliefs, prominent among which was the belief, closely resembling his father's, that the practice of literature is akin to the sacred. Woe to ye, writer, editor, publisher, or reviewer, who forgets that high precept. The letters record Diarmuid's growing alienation from an establishment he had known, and I have tried to supply as much of the antagonistic context as possible.

Russell was, at the same time, no mooncalf. Writers—like agents—required money to live, the more money the nicer the life, and he overlooked no opportunity to steer money toward the writer through his agency. Anthologists, for example, received undiminished scorn throughout his career: they usually wanted the writer's work for nothing. Yet, by the standards of the "superagents" of this decade, whose precursors were at work during Diarmuid's career, Russell never hit the megabook jackpot.

What emerges, I hope, from these pages is a complementary portrait—author and agent—against a thick background of changing literary tastes, impinging world events, some personal life history, literary critical trends, the fabric of Welty's fiction, and the course of American publishing. I have tried to prevent rashes of literary interpretation from breaking out; in a few cases I have allowed myself to scratch a little in the hope that I am illuminating some crucial aesthetic crossroads in the writer-agent partnership. Russell was there to talk or to listen as the writer made her way through growth and confusion and discouragement.

This book has taken more time to write than I had ever anticipated. Many people have heard me talk about it and will be pleased to know that they can now read it, or not, at their own leisure. Your encouragement kept me going, though, and helped me clarify my aims as I worked. You know who you are.

I acknowledge with gratitude the patience of the American Council of Learned Societies. The ACLS granted me a summer fellowship in 1985 for a project I sincerely thought would be finished by 1986. They understood immediately when I explained how the project had grown, and did not ask for their money back.

Material help and time have come from the people of the Interlibrary Loan Department of the Jean and Alexander Heard Library of Vanderbilt University (who else would order six months of *Variety* with a nod and a smile?), and from the Department of Archives and History, Jackson, Mississippi.

Thanks must also go out to the many people who consented to be bothered by questions, oral or written. I hope you know that your help is in this book—only in the good parts: William Maxwell, John Robinson, William Jovanovich, Timothy Seldes, P. L. Travers, Suzanne Marrs. Special gratitude to Pamela Russell and her husband, John Jessup, for their hospitality and interest, and for trusting me with Diarmuid Russell's letters.

Thanks hardly seem enough for those who have actually read the manuscript—especially in its terrible versions, which, I hope, have all been put behind us: Christine Kreyling, Reynolds Price, Harriet Wasserman.

Deepest thanks to Eudora Welty, who entrusted me with the precious material archive of her friendship with Diarmuid Russell. I hope this book makes partial amends for the small memorials in print.

Nashville, Tennessee M.K.
June 1990

ONE

The Benevolent Parasite

May 28, [1940]

Dear Miss Welty:

John Woodburn of Doubleday's has suggested that I write to you to see if you might need the services of an agent. I suppose you know the parasitic way an agent works taking 10% of the author's takings. He is rather a benevolent parasite because authors as a rule make more when they have an agent than they do without one. We ourselves are quite new but we have the good wishes of many of the publishers who have offered to send us all their authors without agents. Their feeling is that there are few good agents in New York and that these few are too large to be able to extend any editorial assistance; we hope to be able to do this.

I myself have been in literature for a long time being the son of an Irish Author (A.E.). I have been sub-editor on journals and worked in book stores and for a couple of years was editor in a New York publishing house.

If you should need the services of an agent we would be glad to help. If you are ever in New York I hope you will call to see us.

yours sincerely
Diarmuid Russell

*

It was not as if Eudora Welty, of Jackson, Mississippi, a thirty-one-year-old author of short stories (about a dozen of which had seen the light of publication by the spring of 1940), had received a letter from a perfect stranger. She knew there were such creatures as literary agents. She had been dealing with editors at literary journals and at New York publishing houses for at least five years. Moreover, in her own words, she had been "smitten" by poetry while in school at the University of Wisconsin. The poet was Yeats. From Yeats she had gone on to A.E.'s *The Candle of Vision*, an autobiography in essays that chronicles A.E.'s conversion from bland empiricism to belief in mysticism, intuition, the uncanny authority of coincidence, and the bankruptcy of purely materialist civilization. A letter from the son of A.E., offering help in her literary career, could only be trusted as more than mere coincidence. A year later Welty saw the "coincidence" in a larger perspective.

> I read The Candle of Vision and the books I have again. I don't know what I apprehended from them when I read them first—it was not what I understand now or what I may understand later—but I suppose it was what I needed. It was the first crisis of a certain kind in my life, and I was frightened—it was when I was sent to the Middle West to school. I was very timid and shy, younger than the rest and those people up there seemed to me like sticks of flint, that live in the icy world. I am afraid of flintiness—I had to penetrate that, but not through *their* hearts. I used to be in a kind of wandering daze, I would wander down to Chicago and through the stores, I could feel such a heavy heart inside me. It was more than the pangs of growing up, much more, I knew it then, it was some kind of desire to be shown that the human spirit was not like that shivery winter in Wisconsin, that the opposite to all this existed in full. It was just by chance, wandering in the stacks of the library, that I saw one of these books open on one of the little tables under a light. I can't tell you and it is not needed to, what it was like to me to read A.E. but it was a little like first waiting on a shore and then being enveloped in a sea, not being struck violently by a wave,

> never a shock—and it was the same every day, a tender and firm and passionate experience that I felt in all my ignorance but with a kind of understanding. I would read every afternoon, hurry to read, it was the thing the day led to, and at night what I had read would stay as my secret heart, for I did not let anybody there really know me. What you look for in the world is not simply for what you want to know, but for more than you want to know, and more than you can know, better than you had wished for, and sometimes something draws you to a discovery and there is no other happiness quite the same. [n.d.; reply to September 30, 1941]

What the university could not offer the writer, Russell's letter promised: a friend to whom she could, and immediately did, entrust the "secret heart" from which the writing came. There were no coincidences in these circumstances, only memory triggered and patterns completed: Yeats to A.E. to A.E.'s son. A.E. had helped in one crisis; his son would help in another.

Welty, well beyond those lonely years in Madison by 1940–41, had come to the clear realization that if she was to become anything more than a good writer with several respected stories in regional quarterlies and little magazines (most of which did not pay), she would need an agent on the site of the buying and selling. By the spring of 1940, the name of Eudora Welty was not totally unknown among readers of the short story, but her name had yet to appear in one of the nationally circulated magazines known for publishing the work of Katherine Anne Porter, Faulkner, Fitzgerald, and others who lived, more or less handsomely, on their "takings." For the previous five years Welty had been writing to editors of several New York publishing houses offering a collection of her short stories before any single one of them had appeared in a national magazine. She had even taken her stories and photographs, in person, to New York offices in search of a publisher. There had been admiration, but no contract to publish.

One of her earliest attempts, in the spring of 1935, involved sending her manuscript, titled "Black Saturday," to Harrison Smith, partner in the firm of Smith and Haas, Inc., publishers of William Faulkner's work in the early 1930s. "Black Saturday" included many of the stories later to be published in *A Curtain of Green and Other Stories*, as well as black-and-white photographs Welty had taken during her stint as a WPA publicist in Mississippi after school in Madison and at Columbia. Smith wrote back to the young author that he was "personally keen" on the manuscript, but felt that the prospective market for such a book—fiction and photographs with a Southern and black subject—had already been cornered by Julia Peterkin. Peterkin's *Roll, Jordan, Roll*, with "photographic studies" by Doris Ulmann, had been published by Bobbs-Merrill in 1933. Smith felt the popularity of Peterkin's book had already done what Welty's might hope to accomplish. Whether she knew it or not, the young author had had a lesson in the necessity of "the benevolent parasite"; to be published in the big time meant that one needed not only a worthy piece of work but also someone on the spot to anticipate market conflicts and clear them away.

Some good luck visited about a year later (March 1936) when John Rood, co-editor of *Manuscript*, a small, non-paying literary journal in Athens, Ohio, wrote to say that he and his wife had decided to publish "Death of a Travelling Salesman" and "Magic," two stories they admired much more than an earlier story from Welty they had rejected. Rood's two-page letter of good tidings also contains what, with hindsight, seems to be a mildly ominous inquiry. "We would like to know," he wrote, "what else you have written; whether you are working on a novel, or whether you have written many short stories which you consider to be as fine as these two. The reason we ask this is that we feel sure the various publishers will be interested as soon as we publish one of the stories" (March 19, 1936).

The apparently innocuous question of the novel would become the preamble to disappointment for the young writer. In the years before Welty met and agreed to accept the services of Diarmuid Russell, the question of the novel tolled with dirge-like monotony in letters declining to publish her collection of short stories and photographs. The question was posed in a wide range of tones, from mild to beseeching. However it was posed, it blocked acceptance of the stories.

The Roods were so impressed by "Death of a Travelling Salesman" that they set aside their customary publishing schedule and printed the story in the June 1936 issue of *Manuscript*, the first issue of the magazine to go to the printer after Welty's story landed in the mail. John Rood was not idly boasting of *Manuscript*'s power to draw the attention of New York publishing houses. In a letter dated just a few days after the appearance of the June *Manuscript*, May 13, 1936, Welty received praise from Harold Strauss, then an editor at Covici-Friede. He was full of enthusiasm for her strong characterizations and thought her powers of "dramatic development" could be stretched to greater lengths. Like too many in the literary business, however, Strauss concluded that success in the short story was only preliminary calisthenics for the novel. Welty wrote back offering to send her collection of stories; apologetically Strauss declined to consider them.

A relatively unknown author of short stories, from the South or anywhere else, coming into recognition in the middle of the Great Depression, faced a certain set of material checks and publishing prejudices that effectively barred the progress of her ambition. Few in the business objected to short stories in magazines and quarterlies, but books of short stories were very seldom welcomed by the publishers, and infrequently published solely for their intrinsic merit. One had to be "known"; there had to be a novel in the offing or in the recent, selling past. Scribner's, for example, had published a volume of Thomas Wolfe's short stories, *From Death to Morning*, in 1935, in order to keep the author's name before the public and to bridge the gap in the supply of Wolfe novels until *Of Time and the River* could be prepared for publication (Donald, 342). An unknown author, especially one who had yet to win the merit badge of the novel, stood practically no chance of acceptance if her manuscript was a collection of regionally published stories mixed with some new work. Welty was beginning to read and hear the familiar chant: "Do you have a novel we can read?"

Ironically, short stories enjoyed critical respect and were, as one commentator on the subject wrote in 1941, "the most widely consumed single item on the American literary menu" (Mirrielees, 714). But to the publishers they were snack food, not the entrée. A proliferation of magazine outlets for the short story—before paper rationing during World War II cut them back—and escalating prices in the 1930s made both supply and demand for short stories sharp. F. Scott Fitzgerald regularly made between $1,500 and $2,000 per story in *The Saturday Evening Post* and other "slicks." Thomas Wolfe collected $1,500 from *Redbook* for "The Lost Boy" in 1937, and $2,000 from *The Saturday Evening Post* for "The Child by Tiger" later the same year (Donald, 409–10). *Scribner's Magazine* (for the sake of comparison) had paid Wolfe $150 for "An Angel on the Porch" in 1929—his first published story. The range of payment an American short-story writer could expect, then, was quite wide. Depending on the reputation of the author and the circulation of the magazine, one could hope to "take" as much as $2,000 or as little as $150. In those years (the mid-1930s, the same years Welty was trying on her own to break into the New York circle) Thomas Wolfe could live in New York City for one year on the income from one story sold at the higher end of the range. Welty's habits were far more modest than Wolfe's; presumably the same amount would have gone further for her.

There was no way, however, for a writer on the outside of the circle to know the rituals by which literary business was conducted. Welty, for instance, had never been invited to lunch until she signed on with Russell. She knew the rules of the game only from the outside. There was, for example, the hierarchy in which payment was linked to literary rank and merit. There were the "little magazines," published monthly or quarterly—and not always as regularly as, for instance, the Roods' *Manuscript*. Some could and did pay their authors; *The Southern Review* paid by the page. Most could not; *Manuscript* paid only in prestige. Welty, by 1940, had published stories in several such magazines. One of her reasons for agreeing to accept Russell's offer of help was her ambition to step up from the little magazines to the national magazines, the "slicks," from which, with luck and work, she could make something approximating a living from writing.

Just above the "little magazines" in the unofficial hierarchy of American periodical publishing, the "slicks" were a relatively new phenomenon. Magazines like *The Saturday Evening Post, Collier's, The Atlantic Monthly*, and *Harper's Magazine* dominated the market for short fiction in the early and middle century. The latter two, with reputations originating in the Northeastern literary culture of Longfellow and Hawthorne in the mid-nineteenth century, carried a different and more lustrous reputation than most of the "slicks." Newcomers, such as *The Saturday Evening Post* and *Collier's*, could and did sometimes pay ten times what the older magazines offered for short fiction, but it was to be some time before they conferred equal literary prestige. Among the "slicks" were also the women's fashion magazines, *Vogue, Harper's Bazaar, Mademoiselle, Redbook*, and others. This new category encountered, not surprisingly, considerable condescending and suspicious criticism from the male-dominated publishing fraternity of editors and critics. Stephen Spender, surveying the publishing terrain in America later in the decade of the 1940s, was typically suspicious:

> But the fashion magazine, where poems and stories are buried under hundreds of pages of advertisements for underwear, are scarcely a medium in which a writer can be said to "appear." He is, rather, rewardingly lost, as in a drawer crammed with artificial silks. [Spender, 175]

Diarmuid Russell, it is reported, had been given the word as well in Maxwell Perkins's advice to open an agency as soon as possible before " 'the damned women take over the entire business' " (Berg, 333).

Another hardship Welty, as a new and ambitious writer, faced was the general condition of the writer in America. In the 1930s, a writer living in Mississippi was still on the far outskirts of the literary community. Jackson, Mississippi, afforded an astonishing number of literary colleagues, readers and writers of imagination, ambition, and intelligence, for a city its size, and Welty knew most of them well. But for stepping into the larger arena of national recognition and achievement, the young writer would need a different, but similarly known and trusted, jury and audience.

Stephen Spender is again a good diagnostician of the writer's problem, a sort of anemia of the literary community. His tour in the former colony positioned him to deliver an opinion that helps us to understand the felt and subconscious needs and forces that brought Welty and Russell together. "What is important, though," Spender wrote apropos of the scarcity of literary society in America, "is to emphasize that the American writer is confronted by a number of choices any one of which tends in the long run to isolate him, to dramatize his position within a society where there are writers, some good, some bad, some successful, some unsuccessful, but no literary life, no considerable public sustainedly and discriminatingly interested in seeking out the best, a kind of jury of middle-class middling readers to whom the European writer after all continually addresses his appeals, restates his case, and on whose judgement he is prepared to wait for twenty years if necessary" (Spender, 166). Russell was to become the keystone of such a group for Welty, the foreman of a jury of readers whose felt existence was a necessity for Welty, and still is for most writers.

An agent was to be materially and functionally important as well, for there was literary business besides the artistic service as first reader on the outside, first intelligence beyond the curtain of isolation behind which Welty and every writer works. Russell was to connect the nuts and bolts, to aim the manuscript at the appropriate editorial desk, then to negotiate the transformation of typescript into circulated, irrefutable printed page for which money (never enough, it seemed, to make anybody rich) and fame (that is, being read) would return. Whether the author or the agent ever phrased their working together in such mechanical terms, this is essentially how their partnership functioned. The man on the exchange, Russell, was indispensable, for there was a sort of business knowledge that he possessed and a certain practical judgment he exercised that the author could not supply alone. Even when he was not transacting business or reacting to a story in draft, Russell could simply keep the channel of communication to the literary outside open. Many of his letters devoted to the weather in the Northeast, the progress of the spring, the quality of his latest shipment of manure, did just that: maintained a human presence on the watch in that distant and much larger public world where Welty's writing sought acceptance. A snippet from a later letter will serve as an example:

> This is just gossip, not business. There is little mail this morning and the weather is beastly cold and annoys me because the feeling of spring is in the air. Graeme Lorimer of the Ladies' Home Journal wrote yesterday inquiring about you having seen the story in the Atlantic. I can't quite see you there but after some discussion we shipped off the Robber to him. . . .
>
> It looks as if John [Slocum] is going to be caught in the clutches of the draft. He has deferment till April. He goes off to Washington tonight to see if he can get some job down there. Being married so recently makes it rather a nuisance for him to have to go not to mention the nuisance to the firm. . . .
>
> It mightn't be a bad idea some time to have a picture taken of yourself. The Atlantic one wasn't very good and you ought to procure one that shows you tenderly bending down to caress a rose, or one that shows you in a room with black ceilings—but you get the idea—swimming the Mississippi would be good too or a picture of you clinging to the top of a church spire. [February 20, 1941]

Welty also faced the issue of her regional identity. In the latter 1930s, in the years of the popularity of Julia Peterkin, T. S. Stribling, William Faulkner, Margaret Mitchell, Erskine Caldwell, and others, Welty was identified and received as a Southern writer, a writer therefore responsible to a rapidly hardening literary identity and liable to receive a certain range of responses regardless of her chosen subject or style. Being rejected by Smith simply for following Peterkin was a sufficiently clear lesson that she was, whether she knew it or not, in the category of "Southern writer." The market would bear a lot of Southern writing, but not an unlimited amount. Southern literature was a crowded field in the 1930s; a little more than a year before

Russell and Welty joined forces, Faulkner had his portrait on the cover of *Time* (January 23, 1939).

Russell had never been to the South, and was actually not to visit his friend and client until the year of his death, 1973. Deeply schooled in the literature of the Irish renaissance, Russell was, nevertheless, an ideal candidate for counselor to the regional writer. He became the ideal counselor simply by never suggesting that "Southern" be a deliberate part of his client's writing. His ear was always attuned to the distinctive artistic voice of his client. From A.E. he had taken the belief that art rises above historical circumstances; journalism reports the names and dates. By his own mild obliviousness to the politics of writing as a Southerner, Russell helped Welty steer her own course through shoals of critics who expected a certain "Southernness."

Seemingly unperturbed by the calls for a novel, Welty continued to write short stories. Her early stories, according to the main currents of critical opinion and her own memory, seem to have come with happy ease into nearly flawless formal symmetry. Welty remembers them as almost "spontaneous" and "almost never revised." They were not necessarily published with the same ease. "Flowers for Marjorie" and "Petrified Man" were returned by *Literary America* (New York) in November 1936, and then again by *The Southern Review* in January 1937. Robert Penn Warren was nearly convinced to accept the pair, but "Flowers for Marjorie" seemed to him too similar to a story they had recently published. "Petrified Man," both Cleanth Brooks and Warren felt, did not seem to hold together as a story. Both were to have second and third thoughts about it. Discouraged by "almost every magazine in the country" rejecting it, Welty burned the manuscript of the first version of "Petrified Man." She had to rewrite it from memory when Warren wrote back that he and Brooks would like to see it again.

In May 1937, Warren wrote tersely that *The Southern Review* would publish "A Piece of News" and returned another, unnamed story. He asked to see additional work, for Welty was fast becoming a regular contributor. In August Brooks wrote, returning "In the Station" (probably an early version of "The Key") and "The Visit" (perhaps an early version of "Visit of Charity"), and added that he and Warren were not convinced by the ending of "In the Station." Although he would not, Brooks said, suggest that an able writer change a story too much, he would still be interested in reading "In the Station" with a different ending. Brooks seldom gave "editorial assistance" more particular; one of Russell's persuasive claims to Welty was that he would not hesitate to be more detailed.

New York continued to write. Typically, the great interest was sparked by a short story but directed at a potential novel. The longer work Welty was contemplating was still a collection of short stories accompanied by her own photographs, the original version of which she had sent to Harrison Smith in 1935. Two years later, a similar manuscript was at Covici-Friede, where Harold Strauss became an advocate. Although he liked the writing and the photographs, Strauss explained, he despaired of publication on account of marketing conditions. Strauss wrote that he and his colleagues had no doubts of Welty's talent as a writer. If it were not for the necessity to sell books, he continued, his house would publish Welty's work immediately. But, he asked, how could he market a book that was part short stories and part photography? Which sales table would be appropriate?

Welty's career did not exactly stall over the issue of the novel, but it was slowed down. Publishers consistently inquired about "longer work" as her stories continued to appear in little magazines and to draw admiring attention. "Lily Daw and the Three Ladies" was reprinted in Houghton Mifflin's *Best Short Stories* in 1938. *The Southern Review* continued to accept Welty's work. The volume of stories and photographs continued to accumulate rejections and postage charges. Whit Burnett of the Story Press (New York) declined on the grounds that, at a projected price of $3.50 a copy, the book would price itself out of the market. Book buyers were accustomed to lower prices, especially for new writers. They might spend $2.50 for Faulkner's *The Wild Palms* in 1939, or even $3.00 for Wolfe's *Of Time and the River* in 1935, but not $3.50 for an unknown.

In the spring of 1938 Welty decided to face the novel issue about halfway. At the suggestion of Warren (whose novel *Night Rider* was to be published by Houghton Mifflin in 1939), and buoyed up by the news that Katherine Anne Porter had agreed to recommend her, Welty decided to submit a manuscript to the Houghton Mifflin fiction competition. The "novel" Welty submitted to the competition in April was actually about ninety pages and a plan for the rest of a novel called "The Cheated," which, Welty later told Russell, was a version of "The Key," their mutual favorite among her early stories (March 21, 1941). Late in May the bad news came down from Boston: "The Cheated" was one of the few submissions to be given an "A" rating, but the final award for fiction "was given to a girl in Idaho for a novel dealing with the Mormon migration." Welty, however, was not unduly discouraged; she later told Russell that she had written the "novel" under "sudden pressure," had never thought it very good, and had thrown it away when it came back from Houghton Mifflin (March 21, 1941).

On top of the Mormon triumph came the news that "Keela, the Outcast Indian Maiden" was not acceptable to *Story*. The editor, Whit Burnett, instead inquired whether there was a novel he could consider. *The Southern Review* also sent "Keela" back, confessing that they could not see it as a story, but adding the good news that they were very impressed with "A Curtain of Green" and wanted to see "Petrified Man" again. In October, *Story* again disappointed Welty, returning "Why I Live at the P.O."; Burnett repeated his view that "a short novel might very well be your métier."

Late in the autumn of 1938, Welty's career briefly intersected that of Ford Madox Ford, then at the height of his reputation as a respected British man of letters with international connections. Ford had made many alliances with American literary figures, prominent among whom were Southern writers Allen Tate, Caroline Gordon, and Katherine Anne Porter. From Porter he had heard about the work of Eudora Welty. In November 1938, Ford proposed by letter to read Welty's stories and, never doubting that he would like them, send them on to his publishing contacts in New York and London. Ford, in effect, volunteered to become Welty's literary agent, but only for one collection of short stories. The young writer could hardly turn down the help of one of the most famous men of letters of the time: "Can you imagine," Welty later told an interviewer, "that he held a chair for Turgenev?" (Ascher, 32). He gave her instructions to mail copies of the stories to Stanley Unwin in London; with his own copy of the manuscript he would shop around New York.

By March 1939, Unwin had returned his copy to Welty with the bad news that in England as in America publishers were unwilling to risk collections of short stories. Allen & Unwin's market, Unwin explained, was "circulating libraries," and subscribers preferred novels when they borrowed books. Short stories were thought more appropriate to magazines. The novel refrain came with a transatlantic echo.

In late May, his health seriously failing, Ford wrote that he was sending the collection of her stories to Harold Strauss, now at Knopf, who had asked to see them once again. Ford, a month from his death in France, made his valediction to Welty with the familiar theme: he asked her why she had not written a novel. After Ford's death, Strauss wrote to Welty lamenting the loss, but he still could not recommend publication of the collection at Knopf. It was novel-or-nothing.

Welty's position was also what it had been before. Her stories were taken, once again, to New York in November 1939 by John Woodburn, a scout and editor at Doubleday, Doran. He had been visiting Baton Rouge, heard of Welty and her work, and had scooped up the stories in Jackson on his way north. He would work behind the lines in his firm to push for publication—guerrilla warfare for the cause of the short story: "Your stories are being read. I have perjured myself and said you were hard at work on a novel" (November 21, 1939).

As the secret maneuvering of Woodburn continued at Doubleday, additional letters of inquiry and advice came to Jackson. Stanley Young, an editor at Harcourt Brace, expressed sympathy for Welty's weathered skepticism on the novel-or-nothing issue, yet advised the striving author to set aside her experience of the flinty and hard-hearted publishing world. The only way to beat the other side was to join them.

By the spring of 1940, Welty's professional situation as a commodity in the world of American publishing was at an impasse. The expectation of a novel, long or short, was universal and inescapable, and with the death of Ford she had no one on the scene (New York) to argue her work with the ranks of publishers. John Woodburn worked within one house; he could not function as her agent should that house decline to publish the stories. Harold Strauss had been a sincere and constructive reader, but he too worked *inside* a publishing house. Welty needed someone on the outside to accept her on her own terms as an author of short stories, someone with an insider's knowledge of the business and a literary temperament she could understand and trust.

TWO

Inevitable

May 31, 1940

Dear Mr. Russell,

Thanks for your letter. Yes—be my agent. Just as the letter was given to me, I finished a story, and holding one in each hand, it seemed inevitable. Mr. Woodburn had told me to be careful, other people too, and so I have never done anything about agents, before. As a sign of the agreement, I enclose the story just written. How many do you like to have on hand? It will take some desk-clearing on the part of certain editors for me to get the stories back to send you. The Southern Review, a quarterly, which has helped me very much by being interested in and publishing my stories, likes to see them first, and I try to let them have their choice. This story I'm sending might sell there—or is this making it too easy for an agent? The fact is, they already have enough of my stuff on hand to read, without this. I am hoping that you can get my stories in other magazines. What you think of this one and its chances will interest me very much, and I hope to hear from you soon.

Sincerely yours,
Eudora Welty

June 3, [1940]

Dear Miss Welty:

Such promptness is not to be expected in this world. When one hangs out a shingle one has to sit down and wait—that is the tradition and business shouldn't come rushing to one. How do you know that we are honest or competent? We think we are but we never expected to be taken at our own word. I must say it gives us a warm feeling.

Now as to the story ["Clytie"]. I wouldn't dream of sending it to the Southern Review. That would be dishonest. Agents, as I told you, take 10% but why in the name of heaven should we take 10% for sending an article by you to the place where you could send it yourself. No, our job is to earn our money and not try to make money from you without work. What I would like you to do is to send me a few more stories when you can collect them; and I would like to keep this story until the others arrive. It sometimes works better to be able to send an editor several stories at the one time and give him a choice. At the same time, if it won't be too much trouble, would you send me a little potted biography of yourself and what work you have done. In this large and inhuman city editors like to know something about their contributors and every magazine carries little stories about their authors.

As regards this present story I like it but I don't think it is as good as others of yours that I have seen. There seems to me to be some obscurity about it that makes it difficult to understand. The face of love that you refer to is obviously some dream or imagination that has haunted Clytie as most of us have dreams we carry with us. But I think that that dream or imagination is hardly made clear enough to the reader to understand how the contrast between it and Clytie made Clytie commit suicide.

I hope you are going to excuse me making these comments. There is no use in having an agent unless you allow him to be as honest in comment as he must be in money matters. If the comment seems unjustified you dismiss it and write the agent a letter calling him an unliterate ass.

I hope you will agree with this view of the relations between agent and author

yours sincerely
Diarmuid Russell

Diarmuid Conor Russell was born in Dublin, Ireland, on November 17, 1902, the son of Violet North and George William Russell (1867–1935), self-christened A.E. upon his conversion to the visionary life. A.E. was an astonishingly versatile man: poet, journalist, dramatist, critic, painter, editor of *The Irish Homestead* (in which he published James Joyce) and later of *The Irish Statesman*, and consultant expert on the farm cooperative movement—a practical and philosophical expertise for which he was invited to the United States in 1935 by the Roosevelt Administration. A few years after his father's death, Diarmuid Russell remembered him as "a mixture of realistic hardheadedness and mysticism" ("AE," 51), a formula that partially defines the son: on the business side of the literary agency Diarmuid Russell was hardheaded and unsentimental; on the creative side he trusted his intuitive responses to works of literature and distrusted criticism. Once he had decided to represent an author, he never changed his mind. And once an author's financial interests were engaged, Russell turned hardheaded and practical. He saw limited benefit to his clients in the "honor" of being published. He preferred dollars.

For three years after graduating from the Royal College of Science, Dublin (1925), Diarmuid Russell worked in his father's editorial offices in Merrion Square as editorial assistant, or "sub-editor," on *The Irish Statesman*, gaining his first professional literary experience and creating a mild conflict between science (his formal education) and art (his lived experience) that he was to work out finally only after emigrating to the United States.

With so much literary and artistic culture in his parental circle, Diarmuid Russell chose an education in science. His parents' guests (a wide selection of the Dublin intelligentsia) provided, according to one memoirist,

> the finest talk on art and literature I have ever heard anywhere. One learned in a practical way how a poem was made, how a play was made, how a novel might be made, for the practitioners were there and delighted in expounding. [Colum, 170]

The Russell home competed favorably with any available university seminar in the arts. Art and talk about art went on more or less continuously as the background noise of individual life and social existence. Diarmuid Russell had, by virtue of his birth and rearing, one of the finest literary educations available at the time.

That literary education came to him, though, mixed with the example of his father's discipline and tireless steadiness. A.E. himself wrote large segments of the *Homestead* when, as was often the case, there was too little in the till to pay contributors. Joyce, whom he published, portrayed him, in *Ulysses*, as a "tall figure in bearded homespun" who excuses himself from a Daedalus dissertation with " 'I am afraid I am due at the *Homestead*' " (189).

Although to Joyce A.E. was a mildly comic figure, others remembered him as charismatic. Mary Colum, writing about Dublin before the First World War, remembered A.E. making entrances almost good enough for a movie set:

> The sudden entrance of this tall, broad-shouldered, bearded man into any assembly would give a thrill to the beholders, for he looked a prophet, a seer, a high priest of some divinity. [Colum, 172]

Among Americans, whom he liked and whose literature he knew as well or better than his Irish brethren, A.E. was always popular. When he visited the United States for the final time, invited by F.D.R. to talk on agrarianism in economy and philosophy, A.E. was hailed as "that collection of rich and varied personalities" (*NYT*, December 30, 1934, IV, 4) and was remembered at his death seven months later as the "genial big man with the patriarchal beard" (*NYT*, July 18, 1935, 19). Diarmuid Russell kept a portrait of his father on the wall behind his desk but eschewed the "larger-than-life." Throughout his career, he repeatedly insisted that his clients did the important work; he merely clerked for them.

A.E.'s rootedness in Irish culture and literature provided a lesson in the importance of place over renown. When others, Joyce and Yeats, for example, left Dublin to forge the conscience of their race in foreign parts, A.E. stayed at home. He fused into his life's work, through prodigious labor, the treasury of Irish legend and folklore (a material he had shared with Yeats when the two were young men and close friends in the 1890s); his own brand of mysticism; a practical knowledge of the science of rural economy; lyric poetry of his own and that of several of his fellow countrymen whom he sought out in rural papers and published in the *Homestead* and *Statesman*; painting in watercolor that was compared to Blake's; drama—A.E. wrote one play, *Deirdre*, and was a member of the Theatre Society and the Abbey Theatre until, in a dispute with Yeats over the nature and direction of Irish drama, he resigned. Diarmuid Russell paid homage to that career in his biographical reminiscence, "AE" (*The Atlantic Monthly*, February 1943) and in *The Portable Irish Reader* (1946), which he edited for Viking. Personally and culturally Diarmuid Russell was formed for a literary life.

Welty's sense of the inevitability of her agreement with the son of A.E. would not have puzzled the mystic in father or son. Just a few weeks after agreeing to be represented by Diarmuid Russell, Welty wrote:

> No, I shall never be bitter if you do not sell [the stories], but only struck with the weight of your influence if you do. I feel that I am fortunate to have you to criticize them. When I was going to school at the University of Wisconsin, in the winter afternoons when the snow kept falling, I used to sit in the stacks in the library in the Celtic

> division reading all the books they had of your father's and Mr. Yeats', and copying things into a notebook, not for use, but just to have, and I still have the things somewhere. [June 24, (1940)]

A.E., more overtly than his son, would have appreciated the symmetry in the relationship now (in 1940) completing its circle from father to reader, from reader to son. A.E. believed in the autonomy and unerring wisdom of the imagination; that his son would function as agent for a writer who admired him would have impressed A.E. as natural. In "Art and Literature" (1906), perhaps one of the essays Welty read in the Celtic division of the Wisconsin library, A.E. professes his faith in the inscrutable:

> With man and his work we must take either a spiritual or a material point of view. All half-way beliefs are temporary and illogical. I prefer the spiritual with its admission of incalculable mystery and romance in nature, where we feel how in the unconscious result and labour of man's hand the Eternal is working Its will. [*IR*, 52]

Like the undergraduate Welty, who shied away from the "icy . . . flintiness" of the world, A.E. counseled against too much materiality. Such despiritualized arts as psychology only thrust mankind deeper into an Iron Age where "we are met by the mighty devils of state and empire lurking in the abyss . . ." (*CV*, 20). A.E. saw such a crisis in 1918, with the horror of World War I fresh in his memory. "We need a power in ourselves," he wrote in *The Candle of Vision*, "that can confront these mighty powers [state and empire]" (20). Both Welty and Diarmuid Russell came to see the world as split by a similar dichotomy in the 1940s. The shared vision was one of the seals of their friendship.

After three years of apprenticeship in his father's editorial offices, Diarmuid Russell emigrated to America in 1929—not the best of years (after October) to be entering the American work force. He came with his engineering degree and took a job in Schenectady, New York. He also brought along an inbred distrust of cities that made his first few months as an immigrant deeply lonely and discouraging.

He adapted only slowly to the American urban character. His father, working for many years with Irish farmers in remote places and in primitive conditions, had developed a reverence for rural society that made him skeptical of cities. According to a lifelong friend, A.E. saw the modern city as a sort of purgatory to be endured so that nature might be enjoyed more fully (Gibbons, 197). At the close of his final visit to the United States, A.E. bade farewell with characteristic irony:

> Cities, you know, are an actual danger to life itself. Life becomes biologically sterile as a rule in three generations. There is only one living Londoner, that anyone knows of, of the fourth generation. [*NYT*, March 2, 1935, 32]

Jocular or serious, the theme of mistrust of cities passed on to the son. Diarmuid remembered, years later in a letter to Welty discussing their mutual love of flowers and gardens, that one of the most frequent visitors to the Russell home was horticulturalist Augustine Henry (1857–1930), who traveled the world in search of rare and undiscovered flora. By the time Diarmuid was in his teens, Henry had written his manifesto on the subject of cities and nature, *Forests, Woods, and Trees in Relation to Hygiene* (1919). One declaration might serve as Diarmuid's motto:

> The most important hygienic aspect of the forest is the purity of the air therein. Smoke, particles of dust, injurious gases, and bacteria, which are all found in the air of cities, are rare or completely absent in that of forests. [Henry, 16–17]

Russell carried the lesson of Henry with him throughout his life, for he was not only a dedicated gardener (his letters to Welty invariably carry news of the weather, the soil, rainfall) but also an amateur horticulturalist of significance. He was an expert on wildflowers and led fund-raising for the New York Botanical Garden that resulted in the publication of *Wildflowers of the United States* (Crown, 1953). Russell was as deeply, though less polemically, convinced of the correspondence between man and nature as his parents' visitor Augustine Henry. This transcendentalist streak in his character helped him respond to the temper of his new client, and added to the sense of inevitability in their partnership. Mrs. Larkin, the central character of "A Curtain of Green" (one of the stories Russell had read either in *The Southern Review* or among the collection Woodburn had left with him), enacts the mystical extremes of the human-earth attachment. Early in the story Mrs. Larkin is already so absorbed in the natural imperatives of germination and growth that she is "unable to conceive of any other place" than her garden, to which she is powerfully, almost obsessively, drawn. In the character of Mrs. Larkin, Welty pushes the agrarian instinct beyond rational control and probes the spiritual realms A.E. had glimpsed in his visions. Diarmuid Russell would have understood. When he had finally established a literary agency in Manhattan, he endured the noxious air of the city from nine to five and, like Antaeus and Mrs. Larkin, retreated to the earth and forest in his Westchester home and gardens when the city released him.

There was, however, and in legendary Irish fashion, some wandering before he finally planted self and business. Discouraged with industry and the Northeastern climate—personal and meteorological—Diarmuid Russell went west, to Chicago. Putting his engineering education into abeyance, he drew on his other education and took a job in Marshall Field's book department. In Chicago he met and married a Midwestern woman named after a flower: Rose Lauder. Not surprisingly, they chose to live in Lake Forest, about as far from the "injurious" city as they could afford.

In 1935, just before the death of his father, Russell moved back to New York, where he took a position in the editorial department of G. P. Putnam. He seems to have made his final farewell to engineering, turning in the direction of a career in literature. He enjoyed the work at Putnam until, according to a friend, he began to realize that book publishers were primarily in business to make money for themselves, not for their authors. This was a harsh lesson for the son of A.E., who had always put art far above business. Eventually, working *for* the publisher became, for Russell, working *against* the author. A few months after the initiation of the partnership, Russell told Welty his views, in a nutshell, of the relationship between writer and agent: ". . . I do honestly feel that an agent is a useful person to have even if his sole value is that he does all the commercial haggling for the authors and leaves only the higher thoughts to them" (December 13, [1940]). A few years inside a publishing house convinced him of the need to be outside. The story of his exit from the firm of G. P. Putnam was one he retold often. Discovering a contract that blatantly ignored an author's interests, Diarmuid bearded his boss in the editorial den and called him a damned fool for allowing such a contract to be drafted. There was a pause while Russell savored his punchline: "Then the damned fool fired me."

Being fired from Putnam was as good a reason as any to start a literary agency. A. Scott Berg, in his biography of Maxwell Perkins, reports that the sage of Scribner's had been urging Russell and Henry Volkening, a Pennsylvanian who had taught English at New York University with Perkins's protégé Thomas Wolfe, to open a literary agency as early as 1937. In the spring of 1940, Russell & Volkening, Inc., was formed, with Diarmuid Russell as president and Henry Volkening as treasurer. One of the first recruiting letters mailed went to Eudora Welty in Jackson, Mississippi.

THREE

The First Obstacle

What Russell thought about a story was just as important as his practical help in placing Welty's stories in magazines other than—and with larger and wider circulation lists than—the quarterlies. His first response to "Clytie" set the pattern for three decades of partnership between author and agent; before there were checks to cash, there was "editorial assistance." Russell's judgments of literature had been formed largely by the example of his father. The reactions Diarmuid communicated to Welty and the books of criticism he recommended (there were but a few; he tended to be skeptical of professional critics) had in common a moral-intuitive core. The writer was, to him, first, a sort of seer or philosopher with a vision that prompted the words. Literature came under the umbrella of aesthetics, and aesthetics (for the son of A.E.) transcended politics, psychoanalysis, and autobiography. Morality was a characteristic of thought as well as of action to Russell; and good writing followed and strove to recapture a visionary experience. A story or novel or poem was the visible product of a seamless vision, moment, or mood. Russell did not naïvely ignore political or economic circumstances as triggers to the literary expression; but a novel like Steinbeck's *The Grapes of Wrath* (1939) seemed to him journalism rather than literature. There was a world-out-there, and journalism reported its presence. Literature reported a different universe. Literary forms, thematic concepts, worldly intentions, personal states of mind were all secondary to the artistic vision. A reader served an author poorly if he brought his own circumstantial world to the writer's work and insisted upon a match. Spirit must intervene if reading was to do its healing work. A.E. had written as much when he insisted, in "Art and Literature," that the spiritual point of view was superior to the material for beholding the work of any artist. Diarmuid had his own version of that formula.

In his own essay on this subject, "An Experiment with the Imagination," Diarmuid does not depart from his father's beliefs; he only shifts the system from "*animus mundi*" (A.E.'s world spirit) into the realm of the mind and psychology. The son still believed, as did his father, that "the basis of a man's art is not to be found in his intellectual conceptions, which are light things, but in his character or rather his temperament" (*IR*, 58–59). It was this strong compatibility of character and temperament, stretching back from son to father, that manifested itself as the "inevitability" Welty felt in Russell's first letter.

Diarmuid Russell made decisions about people he would represent as literary agent based on his sense of their character and temperament. As years passed and the publishing business changed so that "business" eventually came to mean more than character, Russell began to feel a sort of estrangement. In 1940, however, he was at home in the business, and comfortable with his new client. He went directly to work in the first letter back to Welty by describing his reservations about "Clytie." "Obscurity" was not a new word to Welty (she had read it first, perhaps, in letters rejecting "Black Saturday"), but she felt encouraged reading it in Russell's letter because, inevitably, she trusted him.

Welty did not write by return mail dismissing the agent and calling him an "unliterate ass," as he had feared she might. Her actual reply shows that the sense of inevitability in the author-agent partnership was quickly growing into a relationship of implicit professional trust and continued communication. The new client bestowed on her agent a condensed history of her frustrations in the literary marketplace:

> Thanks for telling me what you think of the story. It is interesting to me to know what people think, though I seldom know how to go on from there. The face Clytie was seeking would have been more definite, except that Clytie could not ever concentrate. Perhaps the events were not strong enough to justify her sticking her head down the rain barrel, but I felt sorry for her. There is a real one, a little like her, who has never done it. Now I have something hard for you to do. I have a collection—a collection of short stories by an unknown writer who doesn't ever want to write a novel first. They are things I've written in the past year or so, and one trouble you will have is I don't know where they have been. They will throw you out and say "I've already seen these things once!" Ford Madox Ford, at the instigation of Katherine Anne Porter, had almost this same collection (I've changed it some) and was sending it around among his friends, but from his notes I could not ever be sure just who saw it. I know that Allen & Unwin in London read the stories, and Harold Strauss (extremely kind to me) of Knopf, both of whom wrote to me; and once Mr. Ford mentioned "Stokes." All of them said nothing doing unless a novel comes first. Mr. R. N. Linscott of Houghton Mifflin has been very nice to me—he read a long story I wrote, when I tried a novel, during the H-M Fellowship contest—I think it was a failure—and wants me to write a novel. (I don't think he read the stories in the collection.) Kennett L. Rawson of Putnam's has just sent the collection back to me saying they were "rapidly approaching a decision to make me an offer until the ominous developments of the last several weeks darkened the publishing outlook," etc. So far as I know, this is the history of my collection of short stories. Mr. Ford was a very kind person and for all I can be sure may have shown them to every publisher in New York and that will be the end of it.
>
> Please do not tell me that I will have to write a novel. I do not see why if you enjoy writing short stories and cannot even think in the form of a novel you should be driven away from it and made to slave at something you do not like and do badly. Of course I know nothing about publishing. One publisher wrote me that if he could just get me in a restaurant he could persuade me. What is this? [June 10, 1940]

Welty actually did know how to go on from Russell's critical advice; by the late summer of 1940 "Clytie" had been revised and the obscurity "all . . . cleared off." The story went for its first visit to *The Southern Review*. Russell declined his commission on the sale since the agreement to send the story to *The Southern Review* had been made before he was retained. He would not take money for work he had not done.

The client, grateful for the reading and comment, was still eager to test her publishing luck in the national magazines, and to place the wandering book of stories with a New York publishing house. Given the entrenched prejudice against publishing collections of short stories, even by well-known authors, Russell did indeed have a difficult task before him. In the early summer of 1940, the war in Europe made his work increasingly difficult. The "ominous developments" Putnam's Rawson had noted culminated, in June 1940, with the invasion and the fall of France. Images of the Wehrmacht on the Champs-Elysées had shaken more than just the publishing business. There was not much that Russell could do about the course of history—the abyss of empire and the state his father had dreaded in the First World War—so he set about a strategy for overcoming the publishing Maginot Line blocking collections of short stories. Several of Welty's stories published in the national magazines, he saw, would make the collection as a whole less resistible at the higher levels.

Russell was reassuring on the obstreperous prejudice against short stories in books. He believed that writers were to be taken at their own valuation, not redesigned to fabricate a different product, like a manufacturing machine. A writer was more akin to the flowers Russell tended scrupulously in his garden; an azalea could not be turned into a rose, nor be forced to bloom at an unnatural time.

> You needn't fear that I will attempt to persuade you to write a novel. I really have no desire to make a lot of money by trying to turn everyone into a writer for the S.E.P. [*The Saturday Evening Post*]. Not that I would mind having a few of these people but my interests don't lie there. You can write what you wish and all I will ever do will be to tell you what I think of the quality. If I was a suaver person I suppose I wouldn't even do this. But I was brought up by being criticised by my father

> when I worked on a paper in Ireland of which he was the editor. It was one year before he would even pass a 10 line review as being good enough to put in the paper. [June 21, (1940)]

When *The Saturday Evening Post* was paying as much as $2,000 for a single short story, these were brave words from an agent in a new and struggling business. Money was not the first thing Russell considered, though. And his client was to remember telling her father, when she announced that she wanted to be a writer, that she also did not expect to sell her stories to the *Post* (*OWB*, 81). Not right away at least.

The *Post* stood for a kind of literary retailing that both agent and client wanted to avoid. Russell had picked up his attitudes about money in the business of writing and publishing from his father. He remembered from childhood how A.E. had turned down a position at one thousand pounds per annum because he felt the work only worth two hundred ("AE," 55). Mary Colum wrote that A.E. confounded his friends because he would sell his watercolors, which might have fetched gallery prices, for sums that reflected the cost of materials and the artist's time: about five pounds for a small canvas, ten for a larger one (Colum, 170). On the other hand, the agent was not oblivious to money. When it came, he was scrupulous and aggressive; he squeezed every dollar he could out of each opportunity. Pleas from anthologists that the "honor" of being published was ample compensation fell on Russell's deaf ears.

Welty was reassured that she and the agent saw eye to eye on the issue of writing for a retail market, and quickly sent in an early and incomplete version of "a long awkward-length story . . . about bandits and romantic love" set near a place called Rodney's Landing on the Mississippi River near Natchez. The materials for the story had fascinated Welty for some time, and she hoped that Russell, with his background in Celtic folklore and fantasy, would like the story in spite of the marketing difficulty presented by its length. "The fantasy," as the story was informally named until it was published in 1942 as *The Robber Bridegroom*, became a favorite of both writer and agent.

Welty also sent along "The Key," which had been rejected by *The Southern Review, Story, American Prefaces*, and *Prairie Schooner*, and "The Visit," which had a similarly dismal record of rejection. A day or two later, Welty sent "Why I Live at the P.O.," rejected by *The Southern Review, Story*, and *Harper's Magazine*. On June 24, 1940, Welty bound up copies of her remaining stories and shipped the whole package to Russell. She felt no great expectations of immediate publication, but she did feel fortunate to have the son of A.E. as a reader.

Russell did not delay in responding:

> Giving all due respect to the editors of the various magazines to whom you sent The Key they must know little about writing. I claim no particular superiority in knowing the requirements of commercial writing, with its angles and wrinkles and slants. But for several years I selected the stories for a paper called the Irish Statesman and its general reputation in that line was the best in the British Isles. I would have taken The Key immediately and I would have been right. The Visit is good too but not as good as The Key. Both of them have gone out. The unfinished story I think is rather messy. Whatever feeling you have about Rodney's Landing has not yet become clear in your mind. The red truck seems a strange intrusion as also does the story of the old man. My own idea is that you should meditate on the old man's story for it has a wild kind of folk lore air about it and maybe in that little story alone you might find something valuable. Don't worry about being salable. The unfinished story isn't but the reason I am returning it to you is that I do not think it good. [June 25, 1940]

For the rest of the stories he had high hopes. "Powerhouse" he thought very good and was anxious to circulate it immediately; the copy with Brooks and Warren in Baton Rouge had to be retrieved first. The collection as a whole presented him with a versatile talent, and he was greatly encouraged to have all of Welty's unsold work available to him in one portfolio. It confirmed his judgment of the individual stories he had read. He was determined to pass his judgment on to editors and then to the reading public.

I hope we are going to be able to do something for you. We all like your work a great deal and we can't see why some of the editors up here shouldn't like it too. If our enthusiasm means anything then your work will be sold. [June 26, 1940]

That same day he started the process by sending "Why I Live at the P.O." to *The New Yorker*. It came back a few weeks later.

That became a melancholy pattern: hope followed by rejection. Two weeks after sending out the first story there had been no action on any of them. Russell's enthusiasm remained high.

If the Southern Review does not take Powerhouse they are just as crazy as the editor of the Atlantic Monthly who turned down The Key. I really get quite furious about editors. Here we are selling stuff to them for large sums of money and the authors of these pieces are not really good writers and when they refuse to take what is really a good story I feel they are incompetent. I hope when you come up here we will have some news for you. At the moment all have been refusals. Your mss. come into the office for an hour or so and then they are on their way again. I very badly want to be able to tell you when you come that something has been sold so that we can give you a cheque to make your trip here more fun. [July 11, 1940]

Three more weeks elapsed; early summer became the dog days of August. There was still no good news to report to Mississippi.

This is just a little note of woe to tell you we are having the damndest time trying to sell your stories. I had set myself the task of having some of them sold before you came here [en route to the writers' conference at Bread Loaf, Vermont] so that we could give you a little money to make easy your holiday. I think the editors are just about crazy and in my own mind I have determined that if all efforts fail I would like to keep your stories here, get some more stories from you, and then when your reputation has been established, make all the mad editors pay through the nose for the stories they had formerly turned down. My irritation with the editors is not only on your account but has now also become a personal matter with me. Either they are wrong or I am wrong and I am not accustomed to being wrong when it comes to judging literature.

I hope you will feel able to send us some more stories and will not think badly because we haven't sold anything as yet. When you come here we can show you the letters from the editors and all the places the stories have been to and I tink yu wil,—look how my fury overcomes my fingers—agree that we have been energetic in sending the stories around. [August 2, (1940)]

In mid-August Viking replied that they could not take a book of short stories "except in connection with a novel." Russell became genuinely anxious that he might lose his new client to languishing discouragement. But he was able to assuage that anxiety when the two finally met in New York in early August. Russell also invited Welty out to his Westchester home in Katonah, his retreat from the city. Both author and agent were delighted with the visit, and relieved to be able to move to first-name basis.

I can't tell you how pleased I was that you were able to come up and see us. Even more pleased that you turned out to be a human being. I was scared that you might have been otherwise. Now I am quite certain that we will be the best agents for you Not only is our seal of approval upon your writing but also on the person so that all the furious energy we have will be bent on making the miserable crew of editors around the country recognize your worth. Good luck and affection

Diarmuid
[September 6, 1940]

The renewed confidence was to be needed. Summer and fall, 1940, were not kind seasons for Welty's work. "Why I Live at the P.O." was rejected, in turn, by *The New Yorker, Collier's, Harper's Bazaar, Good Housekeeping, Mademoiselle,* and *Harper's Magazine.* "Powerhouse" was rejected by *The Southern Review* after an extended consideration; Brooks and Warren also returned "Acrobats in the Park," a story closely related to "A Memory," published in *The Southern Review* in 1937.

The doldrums in the publishing zone notwithstanding, the summer had been a good one for Welty. At Bread Loaf she had renewed acquaintance with Katherine Anne Porter, a recent friend and an ally in the cause of the short story. Porter had put Welty and James Laughlin, Pound's protégé and founder of New Directions, together. Laughlin was, Porter had revealed, considering a collection of Welty's stories for New Directions. Russell, just returned from a few weeks' vacation in Maine, was wary of the whole "scene" at Bread Loaf—sure that half-baked deals were made there.

> You must be having a fine time up there. It sounds to me like a species of madness. You will probably come back with fine ideas in your head of how writing is really done. Jackson will be amazed to see you being aroused by a trumpeter in a red uniform at 6 a.m. and then you will make a regal appearance, dressed in a flowing and artistic robe followed by a darkie carrying a gold typewriter. I don't know how fine the writing will be but you will make a reputation and I guess that is one way to start.
>
> To be honest I can't see how people can be taught to write. I suppose writing for slick magazines has some do's and don'ts but even there I suspect that the successful authors in that field write naturally in a way that appeals to the editors and the public. [August 26, 1940]

The Laughlin deal he would keep in the back of his mind, preferring "to see what could be done with the regular publishers first." James Laughlin had, in the early 1940s, the reputation of being an avant-garde publisher. In Russell's eyes that meant some prestige and very little money.

> Your suggestion about the New Directions Press will be kept in mind but I would hate to have your book published there if it could be published elsewhere. Laughlin is a nice fellow but his publishing house is a small affair and is not capable of doing as well for authors as the

> more orthodox publishers. The trouble with the latter is that they all keep wanting novels and God knows some of the novels they bring out could do no worse than the most miserable collection of short stories. [n.d.; mid-July 1940]

For Russell, publication had not yet become publication-at-any-cost; his strategy of breaking into the national magazines and thereby creating a demand for a book of Welty's short stories had not yet run its course. The recalcitrance of "nitwit editors" almost drove Russell, he swore, to "start writing nasty letters to the literary people who preside over the magazines." He would keep the New Directions possibility in the back of his mind, but stubbornly preferred an "orthodox" publisher with a fat bank account for his client. In the meantime, Russell could only offer hope:

> We have just had a couple of your stories come back from Virginia Quarterly—Key and the Visit. I think they will have to be put away for a while as they have been to all the possible places and many impossible ones. We sent them to the latter in the hope that a miracle might occur but such an event was not forthcoming. . . . I am sorry I can't send you money yet or give you good news but all I can say is don't worry for anyone who writes as well as you do is certain to be all right. Editors are kind of stupid people and it takes some time for merit to dawn on them for most of their time is concerned with what is openly commercial. So the thing to do is to write when you feel like it and send us the opus and let us try persistently to open the tired eyes of the literary folk here. [n.d.; early September 1940]

To soften the edges of his melancholy, Russell began to suggest topics and fields for new work—a "next" book before a first book had been published. It is clear to us now that the fiction they began to discuss would become the stories of the next collection, *The Wide Net*. Between the two of them, the Natchez Trace had surfaced from legend and history as the spur to new stories even as those already written came back to Russell's office with doleful regularity. They had both been reading Robert Coates's *The Outlaw Years* that summer. Russell was especially grateful for new knowledge of American folklore. Coates's book had, he wrote to Welty enthusiastically, a blend of fantasy and mythology that appealed to his Celtic imagination. It is not difficult to understand how and why the son of A.E. would be attracted to the lore of the Old Southwest. Coates's book, published in 1930, contains lively tales of the bloody Harpe brothers and of Murrell the visionary bandit. The "History" and "Poetry" sections of *The Portable Irish Reader*, which Russell was to edit several years later, are full of similar tales, episodes, and rough figures. Russell was prompted to imagine Johnny Appleseed as a figure ready for a written treatment in the Coates manner, and he suggested the subject to Welty. Johnny Appleseed, he wrote, seems to be "one of those innocent characters that existed when the earth was young and before wickedness and sin appeared to plague us all." "The fantasy," he added, had that prelapsarian halo about it for him (n.d.; July 1940).

Welty, whose time at Bread Loaf that summer did not permit much contemplation and meditation, did not begin to think about the artistic power of the Natchez Trace, its characters and spirit, until the long train journey back to Mississippi. Her first day home, she wrote a three-page letter percolating with ideas for a "Mississippi book":

> There are some things about a state that nobody could even know about who has not lived there a long time, and those things should determine the whole approach, don't you think? . . . and I believe I could find stories, old ones & new ones, and beliefs and songs and violent events all over the place to show what the life here is, to my belief. . . . Think of all the people who would be in my book—wonderful Indians to start with, and the Indian tales are beautiful and dramatic and very touching some of them—and Aaron Burr & Blennerhasset, and Lafayette, and Audubon, and Jefferson Davis, and the bandits (you keep "The Outlaw Years," there is one around Jackson), and Lafitte the pirate, and all kinds of remarkable people. You know, during the War between the States, there was a Free State of Jones, in Mississippi, and everybody up there thinks it existed because of sympathy with the North—but the truth seems to be that the boys down there didn't want to be in the War just because they were far too busy carrying on a

local feud to be distracted by anybody else's shooting problems— It is a wild county down there, Sullivan's Hollow, where they used to hitch up strangers to the plow to teach them to stay at home. There are some little towns down there, Hot Coffee is one, where it is downright dangerous to go. It is only a few miles from the town of Laurel, where millionaires in lumber live and a museum with paintings by Rousseau and statues by Epstein is haughtily opened a few hours each day. I do wish you could see Mississippi, because I think you might like the things I do about it, the folk quality to the little adventures and stories and the directness and simplicity, really the dignity, in the way they find and hold their beliefs, and the feeling of the legendary and the endurance of something rather wonderful in a way of life, that you get when you see some of the ruins and haunted houses. I don't think it's just in my imagination, I am sure there is a quality and a feeling that is inherent in these places, and I have tried to comprehend it. It would be so relatively raw and recent to you, with all that is in your country, that it might seem not so powerful and of course it is not in any way half so beautiful, but to make up for the sketchiness of what we know is all the long vast mysterious history of the Indians who lived here. Have you ever read or heard about the Natchez Indians, who were supposed to be the most intricately cultured of all the U.S. tribes—for all that is really known about them is that they were sun-worshippers, and at the last torturers to a very Asiatic degree, and were obliterated on the site of Natchez to the last man. I never have read the book Chateaubriand wrote about them, but I can imagine it is rather quaint, and maybe I will try it—The French never could stand the Indians, and the Spanish were always very good to them, I don't know why. Of course they both stamped them off the face of the earth. We have a few poor Indians now, up in a reservation, and let them marry Negroes, and ride their ponies in a little annual fair. [n.d.; early September 1940]

In the blaze of the new idea, current disappointment faded and the partnership with Russell stepped into a new phase, for Welty began to sense a link through the shared subject matter of folklore and a belief in the spirituality of places. She was not wrong to assume that Diarmuid shared some of the Celtic mysticism of his father. He was also the practical agent, and contacted Dodd, Mead, who were doing a series of books on the States.

Welty plunged into the Natchez stories so rapidly she was barely able to keep pace with the rush of ideas and images. Russell, by contrast, kept his temperature lukewarm so that he could handle the business end. Doubleday had declined the collection, and since no one else had signed it up, he was skeptical that the "Mississippi book," no matter how sprinkled with wonders, would be accepted from an author with little name recognition.

If the agent needed occasional cheering up, then the writer would do it; the pact between them worked in both directions. "Powerhouse" had finally been released by *The Southern Review* in mid-September 1940. Welty sent it up to Russell with a pledge of renewed faith in his "editorial assistance" and literary judgment.

> "Powerhouse" got in here today from THE SOUTHERN REVIEW and I'm sending it up, hoping you can place it in a good, rich magazine. Everybody told me how to change it, but it is the same as ever. I think people are different in their wisdom in as many ways as they can be—and wisdom is a strange thing—some people have wisdom for nobody and some for everybody (like poets, I guess) and some for only themselves and some for a few scattered people here and there. I don't know which yours is like but I think you have it for me, and I am going to do what you say about stories, as much as I can. At least, I can understand what you say. [n.d.; September 1940]

Through early fall, writing and encouragement both went north. Russell found "Powerhouse" reason for revived hope, and he showed it to another client, P. L. Travers, hoping she would recommend it, its author, and her orphaned collection to her publishers, Reynal & Hitchcock.

> The stories are in the hands of a publisher who is a friend and I have turned a close friend of his onto him with the instructions that she must read the stories and if she thinks they are as good as I do she is to pester the publisher. Don't worry about stories; they will come into your head when they want to and if they are not ready they will lurk

> in the mind for years if necessary. I remember father telling me he started a poem once and wrote two verses and then had to give up. Fifteen years later sitting on the sands in Donegal all the verses remaining surged up and he wrote them down as fast as he could write. [September 16, 1940]

As he waited for word, Russell drew upon the patience of the gardener.

> From the point of view of not arousing your hopes I should not be telling you how well I think you write but I have an incurable honesty and see no harm in saying what one feels and I feel sure you are going to make a reputation for yourself. [September 23, (1940)]

While Russell maneuvered and waited in the world of business, Welty was deeply locked into a project that required both fury and care.

> I've been writing like a demon, and you will soon get the result. How can I wait to know what you think of it—you will either like it, or throw it out the window. It is going to be necessary to be careful when I type the finished thing—as soon as I start writing on it, off it goes, with me holding on. Of course that's why I like it. Please don't worry because you can't make editors buy my stories now. I am sorry to think of you working so hard and diligently when you could never make any money from what I send you. It makes me mad too. Just don't send me the 6-day notice—I don't speak of the future much, but some day I swear I will write something, I don't know what, that is so furiously and so carefully done (both) that with the push from you it will simply leap over the boundary the publishers have set up to keep it out, and suddenly like magic turn into something both good and profit-making, and we will all be astonished and rich, and I couldn't say which the more— [n.d.; September 23, 1940]

By the first of October, the demon writing was over, and the rewritten Rodney story was on the way to New York. "I sit here and hope it seems wild and gay and scarey to you, the way it did to me when I was writing it," Welty wrote with the manuscript. The fantasia of Rodney and the legendary Mississippi was, she knew, no sure thing in the marketplace. But after a few months with Russell it was his estimate of her work, not his success at snaring the money, that Welty required. There was just a note of *faux* melancholy in the past tense of her note with the story: "I am glad you used to think I wrote well—it is a kind of security. Thanks for reading, and I care much what you have to say" (n.d.; early October 1940).

It took the office about a week to read the story. Russell knew immediately that the author had followed his advice about the version of the previous June by jettisoning the realistic and modern aspects of the framing story.

> I know I should have written to you earlier but I had to wait till Henry [Volkening] and John [Slocum, secretary of the firm] had read the book too. It is a curious and astonishing book and I don't really know what to say to you about it. John and Henry are both in high delight and I think John is going to write to you to say how pleased he is. Henry thinks it is going to be taken and will sell well. John thinks it is going to be taken but is not so sure of the sales.
>
> You will notice the cautious way Mr. Russell has been keeping himself to the end. I think you have extended the dream perfectly; it has that kind of chaotic and unreal reality that characterizes dreams. The mad blending of Bandits, Indians, the rich planter, the beautiful daughter is wonderful. It is as if you had spent many dreamy afternoons meditating on the romantic history of the South and on the fairy and folk tales of your youth.
>
> But Diarmuid, the old conservative, is doubtful about the commercial angle. Publishers, as a rule, are conservative, and anything that seems out of the way fills them with deep suspicion. They are as cautious as kittens approaching an unknown object. At the moment the general war hysteria has made them even more cautious; they seem dubious of everything that does not seem too familiar and shrink with panic from the original. [October 8, 1940]

Welty was undaunted by the old conservative's caution. She well knew that German military aggression in Europe was hardly a comfortable context for a folk fantasy of the Natchez Trace. She was encouraged, though, by the readings the story had received in the agency, sure that it had been welcomed in the very spirit of its creation.

> I was reassured that you seemed to think my story was what I thought it was, something that came out of dreamy afternoons. It didn't trouble me at all until after I had finished it, but maybe because it meant something more to me than the others, I worried about it.
>
> As for the commercial angle, I didn't know it had one. At least by itself—I was only hoping you could ease it into the collection by your persuasions, and it amazes me that even one or two of you think it will be bought and put out for sale. Let me know what Reynal & Hitchcock have to say, and I am patient through surprise. Practically hypnotized by it.
>
> . . .
>
> I forgot to say, here is another story—I had to do something while waiting for you all to read that. [n.d.; mid-October 1940]

What would the agent have felt had he known that, in "A Worn Path," the story written while Welty was waiting for the agent to read the Rodney story, he held the manuscript of an American short story that was to become about as well and widely known as "Young Goodman Brown" or "The Lottery"? Russell was melancholy, and candid about it, for on October 29, 1940, he did not know the future of any of his client's stories. All he knew was that he had yet to sell a single one. Some of the stories were "nearing their end" in the editorial rounds. In a resigned tone he asked whether the author wanted them back, or preferred to leave them in the agency files. One thinks of a friend writing to the distant next of kin about a death in the family. The collection had been rejected at Reynal & Hitchcock; the Travers intervention had come to nought. As usual, they wanted a novel.

> The collection of stories is in the office at the moment, R & H having turned them down with the usual request for a novel. John Woodburn is looking at the most recent offering because he said he would like

to see it and until he has finished I am keeping the collection here because they should all go out together. I wish daily that I could have some good news to report.

I have been doing some meditating on your stories and talking to some of the people who have read them to see if in general there was any comment worth while passing on to you. There is one and that is almost everyone says: "She's very good and at her best she is wonderful but many of the stories are obscure and the impression I get is that she hasn't got out all that is in her head." K.A.P. said this too but added that there was nothing to be done but to keep you writing and in the course of time everything would be all right. I give you these comments for what they are worth. I think there is some truth in them for when I don't like a story—e.g. the first Clytie and the Acrobats—it is for the reason that I find them confused and yet I never feel that you were wrong to write about them. Every time I have the feeling you saw or felt something and that inside yourself you had kept some of the essentials.

But as for any concrete suggestions I haven't got any. I am one with K.A.P. in thinking that all you have to do is to write and sooner or later some of the dumb editors will wake up. [October 29, 1940]

Russell's introspection and stock-taking were contagious, and Welty took the obligation of a reply to clear the air and to restate her commitment to the partnership:

Thanks for the letter and for the meditating you did on the stories, which is really of help. I have done a lot of wondering from this end, since I began to send stories out. The Southern Review people, while they were nice and friendly, and helped me greatly by starting me out and printing what I wrote, still never made any remarks or comments at all, and it was just like being kept in the dark. They stayed like that, after all they had done for me, up to the last story I sent, Powerhouse, which they returned without a word about it. Of course, their sending it back was a sort of sign—but were they bored, enraged, or what. They were a little sultanic, don't you think? An acceptance was equally baffling—they would just send me up a proof-sheet to correct. And I remember the day the Key came back, there was no letter at all attached,

> just the naked story—it may have been a mistake, but that was a blank feeling. Even with the good luck I had in finding them at the start, I wonder that I kept on writing. I would not say this elsewhere, and it does not mean that I'm not grateful for all they did. Anyway, in an isolation or not, I am one of those who believe that to communicate is the hope and purpose and the impulse and the result and the test & value of all that is written and done at all, and if that little spark does not come, and with a little sheltering, flash back & forth, then it's the same as being left confined within ourselves just when we wished most to reach out and touch the surrounding life that seemed so wonderful in some way. You can see that I have been burning to say this. If you keep telling me when what I write is clear and unobscured and when it is not, as it appears to you, then I will have something so new to me and of such value, a way to know a few bearings. Is this what was in our contract? I didn't understand it would be so much. [November 5, 1940]

The hopes and disappointments of the preceding five months had sobered both writer and agent. Welty was even pushed to question her obdurate stance against the novel. "It may be that I will try a novel some time soon," she continued, "since the lack seems to make such a difference. So Reynal & Hitchcock said those words too. . . . When I only think of a novel, it scares me. I never wanted to be contrary, but it is the natural thing for me to do what I can within a lesser space. I suspect that that comes from my being a female, and is permanent." It might well have seemed so in the late autumn of 1940.

Russell was quick to reply, for he seems to have sensed that his mood had seeped down to Mississippi and dimmed the spirits of the writer.

> Your letter sounds mildly discouraged but you mustn't imagine that there is really anything to get discouraged about. The way the Southern Review sends back stories to you is in a way a reflection of their opinion about you. When there is something wrong about your stories it is impossible to pin it on anything definite. What really happens with

> the rejected stories is that one sees them through a sort of mist. As I told you K.A.P. has much the same feeling and she thinks as I think myself that all that can be done is to go on writing and bit by bit your own mind will see things more clearly and then the stories will be good. It isn't a bit that you lack any expertness for when you know what is in your own mind you express it as delicately and precisely as it can be done. . . .
>
> You mustn't in the least think we are tired of the stories. We like them as much as ever; all we regret is that we haven't been able to sell them for you and it makes us feel vaguely inadequate. As regards writing a novel follow your own desires. If you really don't want to write a novel and start one it may likely turn out that it will not be good and all the effort will have been wasted. You do just as you feel like. Only by following your own path can you get anywhere. The only real value I can see in a novel for you is that a novel is an arduous piece of work that demands concentration and hard work and this is good for everybody. Short stories can be written while one is under an influence. Novels not and because of this more effort and more discipline is demanded. [November 7, 1940]

Russell had to be careful not to close options for his client; at the same time he knew that the imagination, once strapped in the harness of the conscious will, might never behave well again.

November 1940 continued to be a cruel month. "The Key" and "Visit" had both been returned by *Virginia Quarterly Review*, and there was no good news on the horizon in New York. Stories and ideas for stories continued to flow in Mississippi, mocking the snail's pace of the business. Welty was learning just how much patience was needed in the life of the writer.

> It was for your hard work I was feeling discouraged, and I couldn't help that, but for myself, that there are people like you and K.A.P. in the world fills me with the most opposite feeling to discouragement. A fine security, and I am all settled and writing in it. Soon I will have something new to send, and there is always the chance that this time this will turn out to be the one. Anyway, I can wait and wait, for time does not

> seem to press very closely down here. It is just in the city that it prods & presses and holds up delays to you and acts important. [November 12, 1940]

John Woodburn, from his post inside Doubleday, had read the Rodney story and was working on his superiors there, trying to generate interest. Agent and editor (Woodburn) had agreed that Russell's idea of "stringing a series of stories on the necklace of the Natchez Trace" was a provocative idea, something to present to the nabobs in the campaign to have Welty's stories and "the fantasy" taken in at Doubleday.

> John Woodburn has had the fantasy for some time and I talked to him today and he is evidently trying to fix up some plot to get the higher-ups interested in you and your career. Several people in his place have read the fantasy and rendered favorable opinions but I gather he thinks the more important editors will put the thumbs down on the book. But he thinks the opinions may make them interested in you to the extent that if they know what you are going to do in the future they might be willing to pay out money for an option on your next work. I talked with John on what kind of work you might be supposed to be working and he said something in the fiction line so I told him about my suggestion about stringing a series of stories on the necklace of the Natchez Trace. He thinks that would be a good idea. . . . [November 18, 1940]

Meanwhile, there were still two of the newer stories, "A Worn Path" and "Powerhouse," on the road at *The Atlantic Monthly*. Russell was keeping his fingers crossed, but knew that Edward Weeks and his editors always took more time than any other magazine staff to decide on what offerings to accept. Welty was, of course, happy just to know that *The Atlantic* was still a possibility. Her major enthusiasm and the better parts of her letters to Russell were devoted to the Natchez Trace idea. She had sent parts of a prospectus to Woodburn, and Russell had supplied more information. But Welty had just begun to explore the wonderful potential in the idea.

> The material is only dazzling and full of spangles to me as yet. I know a few stories though. Do you think I dare to have honest-to-God people walking around in the stories? The thing about this part of the country in the great days is that people like Aaron Burr, J. J. Audubon, Lorenzo Dow, and goodness knows who, were as thick as blackbirds in the pie, and once the pie is opened, they are going to begin to sing. [n.d.; mid-November 1940]

She had been priming her imagination with the *Journal* of Lorenzo Dow, and had begun a story centered in his consciousness. The miraculous occurrences of the winter of 1811—earthquake along the New Madrid fault, comet, the freezing of the Mississippi—had lodged in her imagination as the right stock for the stories she wanted to write. The actual Natchez Trace had become a place of dream, of release from time and the ordinary run of events: "I went down on the Trace the other day," she wrote to Russell, "and almost went to Baton Rouge."

To formalize the project for submission to Doubleday, Welty drafted a précis to be submitted by Russell. Dated November 23, 1940, it plumps up the flat spirit of the previous weeks. Confident that *The Robber Bridegroom* (as the fantasy was finally titled) and "the little story about the old negro woman on the trace" had already introduced the projected series from opposite extremes of fantasy and realism, the writer continued to describe the intervening stories. The series would rely heavily on the notion of the journey as the figure for the story. *One Writer's Beginnings* (1984), written more than forty years after the notes for *The Wide Net*, sheds light on the importance of the fact and figure of the journey in the working of Welty's imagination. The family's summer automobile trips, Welty recalled, were states of continuous revelation to the child: "Those trips were wholes unto themselves. They were stories" (*OWB*, 68). The Natchez Trace was an earlier "story" in potential, for in it was inscribed the reality and image of the journey.

> I believe that the Natchez Trace, like many another beautiful and time-worn place, casts a spell, because I have felt it, and many other people

> must have; and if I can show this spell, in a few of its dramatic or its modest aspects, that is what I hope to do. An old trail like that passes through so many times and enters so many lives, and stands for so many things, functioning heavily or lightly in the course it follows, that it could be a thing to hold a group of stories together as well as any other, and better than any other that I have heard of yet for me. [November 23, 1940]

While Welty's imagination was, like the phoenix, rising from the ashes of commercial disappointments, Russell had no good news to send back. The publication of the collection was apparently a lost cause that winter. Welty had shifted her energy and concern to the new, as-yet-unwritten stories of the Trace. They were calling upon reserves of creative stamina, and efforts of new growth, such as she had not felt before. But she was thankful, and gave the credit to Russell: "It was an inspiration with you."

December held a different mood. Russell sent a copy of a letter from *The Atlantic*:

> We decided yesterday [December 3, 1940] that we should like to buy both of them [Welty's stories under consideration]. "Powerhouse" we would plan to schedule at once and "A Worn Path" we shall have to keep for an interval because we are using an old man and an old lady within the next month or two.

Russell was relieved, ebullient, happy:

> The enclosed copy of a letter from the Atlantic Monthly is self-explanatory and very pleasing. Thank heaven for some perspicuity somewhere. . . . You might rush to me a potted biography of yourself, including age and so forth. I could have given them something myself but it might not have been accurate enough and I would not like to prejudice your future by saying Miss Welty was found floating down the Mississippi in a coracle with a sack of pearls beside her and a guardian fish swimming alongside.
>
> I really can't tell you how pleased I am. [December 4, 1940]

Whimsy and a degree of unsteadiness on the typewriter show that Russell was very happy indeed. Even the *Atlantic* editors' request that Fats Waller's "Hold Tight" be replaced at the end of "Powerhouse" did not trouble him. Welty was no less pleased.

> That is wonderful. To think you have done it. I am so delighted, I can't tell you. And not one, but two. And to think that THAT magazine is going to print THAT story. You ought to be congratulated twice as hard as I think—at Bread Loaf the unanimous opinion was that NOBODY would EVER buy "Powerhouse." [December 5, 1940]

One of the oldest and most prestigious magazines in the country had bought two of Welty's stories. One check would be in the agency by Christmas; Russell could actually fulfill one of his fond dreams—sending money to his client. *The Atlantic* paid $200 for "Powerhouse," about one-tenth what *The Saturday Evening Post* or *Redbook* might have paid for the story. But Russell was satisfied that, with its prestige, *The Atlantic* was the best possible national debut for his client. Moreover, he was confident that national literary attention in *The Atlantic* would trigger a greater demand for his client's work. The New Directions option could be put further back on the list of possibilities.

The "benevolent parasite," who had stood by his client since the previous June, who had read and talked and written to editors and tried to persuade them to buy his writer's work, who had fought off his own discouragement and his client's, deducted his agreed-upon parasitical commission: twenty dollars.

FOUR

Better and Better Stories

Twenty dollars, even at 1940 rates, was less than princely compensation for services rendered, but success and vindication at *The Atlantic Monthly* was cause for a bright new year. Russell's grouchy spirits made a modest rally. From his perspective as a commercial haggler, there was always a new obstacle, a new problem. Initial success had to cover a good deal of subsequent disappointment, for the story collection had been spurned yet again, this time by Harcourt Brace, who were, Russell reported, "nice but as usual asked for a novel" (December 27, 1940).

From the agent's point of view this was not an auspicious beginning to the year, but Welty was more hopeful. John Woodburn had the stories again at Doubleday and the weather in Mississippi was springlike.

> I'm glad John Woodburn has the stories now. He wrote me a nice note, and so did Ken McCormick, from there, about the Atlantic sale, and I do think of Doubleday's now as on our side, with two friends.
>
> I would like to take all that money now and go where there is a hot sun. Aren't you afraid that winter is absolutely non-magical? At its best, it is only a time for ingrowing—the acceptance of imprisonment—I

remember reading once in some art history how the long winter evenings must have set the German peoples to wood-carving—and that is how the intricate toilsome repetitive Gothic spirit (even in elation) got nurtured. Think how some early German engravings are nothing but accumulations, all vine-like—or little lost holy families in millions of veined leaves. Like puzzles. If it had been a little warmer and a little lighter, they might have thought of color. I never want anything in winter either, except spring. I think our feelings must keep closer than we imagine to the parabola of the seasons, and that as we have to wait for the spring we feel that much older (really ancient) in its opposite. O Persephone! some flowering quince and spirea and forsythia are blooming here, entirely at their own risk. Happy New Year. [December 30, 1940]

It was winter in New York as well, and Russell was in a sort of Gothic, wintry fit, embroidering plans for the collection should it be refused again at Doubleday.

We have nothing but the brown earth and the brown grass and dead leaves and the worst of winter yet to come. . . . If Doubleday don't take the collection I think we may have another and better bet. [Walter] Kerr of the Atlantic Monthly Press phoned me from Boston three days ago and I have a letter from him this morning in which he expresses the strongest desire to see the collection. He knows you are a short story writer and if he is not dismayed by short stories I don't see how he could fail to be impressed by the collection. His enthusiasm springs from the two the Atlantic took and as the collection has many as good he will not be let down. So things look reasonably bright. Of course one never can be sure but I would say you might feel optimistic about matters for the future. [January 2, 1941]

For author and agent, 1941 began on this reasonably optimistic note and continued to bring happy surprises. Welty was busy writing the "dazzling" stories of the Natchez Trace series. She mailed "First Love" for Russell's reading and opinion on January 9, 1941. She also reported a check for a grand total of nine dollars from James Laughlin, who had taken "Keela, the Outcast Indian Maiden" for a New Directions anthology. Russell's sense that "unorthodox" New Directions might not be too deep in the pockets was confirmed. Nobody was going to get rich at the rate of nine, or even of two hundred, dollars per story; but Welty's stories were reaching a wider audience.

Russell had been busy as well, finding time to write "An Experiment with the Imagination," which would not be published until September 1942 in *Harper's Magazine*. "An Experiment with the Imagination" illustrates, in anecdotal form, Russell's notion of creativity and gives us an oblique sense, at least, of the distinctions he saw between Welty's creative act of writing and his interpretive reading. The essay reports a series of dreams Russell recorded after struggling unsuccessfully to write a short story. In each dream episode a power or faculty Russell calls "the interior intelligence," a link between the human mind and the "*animus mundi*," or world spirit, supplies his dreaming consciousness with character and incident that his waking, struggling intelligence can neither discover nor invent. "These experiences," Russell concludes, "have made me believe that if a man is willing to bend his will toward the effort of awakening his interior genius he may succeed surprisingly and be delighted with swift visions" ("Experiment," 431). Welty had proven out this process in the demon writing that had resulted in *The Robber Bridegroom*; she had dreamed parts of the fantasy that, awake, she had only to transcribe. Writers in general, for Russell, were that tribe or order of mortals who shared the gift of linking interior genius or intelligence and exterior discipline and observation. The rest of mankind saw only the empirical process, the exterior, and often not enough of that. Welty found herself in agreement with Russell on the nature of creativity, for his synopsis in "An Experiment with the Imagination" tallied with her memory of writing "First Love."

> You know you have a standing warning to catch me if I fall, and so already I may have tried something too hard. Of course I don't think badly of you, your letter is a good thing and to me what you feel is a kind of advice. I did try terribly hard in this story ["First Love"], and

it may be the fault was not that it is not clear in my own head, but that I have not been able to do what I attempted. I think the only thing left to do is to give the story more time. You know when I wrote to you I said that maybe I should wait with this one. It has been in my head a long while, and I had thrown much away, and I thought it was as it should be, but after I had sent it off to you I found I was still writing away at it in my imagination, to a point where I knew it was not out of nervousness but from true corrective ideas, and I was sorry that I had been so quick to send it. I am really glad now that you did not think this story was what it should be, for now we feel the same way about it. At first I did think that I had done it, but that was only some kind of giddiness. You understand a great deal notwithstanding. But that is not the story's fault. Yes, I was using the extreme winter as a sign in the sky, and for contrast to the fiery meetings, and for the way it drove people to an inner intensity, and for its visual worth as a horizon & perspective, all the outward coldness. Maybe that was the trouble with the story, everything (for me) carried the burden of being so many things at once. But that trouble, and I hope you will think that I am right, I take as a sign that there is a good story possible, when there seem to be numbers of other stories being written in writing that, when every word that is put down will be carrying along with it all these things that are floating around it. Don't think I have delusions of grandeur about my little stories—that sounds so fancy. I agree with you that it is much a matter of balance—and I think too in the order and time intervals in which your story elements come, and in this story I think I can trust the feeling that the elements are right, but I was mistaken in the way I have let it take form. I don't know whether all people who write have this experience or whether it is a special lack of mine, but sometimes long after I consider a story finished I happen to see it with a fresh outlook, and find where some paragraph or sentence or even some word, that I knew did belong in the story, had been all the time in the most misleading & wrong place, or something had been said but by the opposite person to the one who should have said it—not a typographical error, but simply a product of an unfinished idea, and some simple but radically new arrangement would have to be made before I had the story that I thought all the time I had written. It was just something I had not known earlier, and I had put the story together in ignorance. I may never get this story right, but some day

> when I feel the whole thing again and after all the changes have been weighed, I will examine it with great care and maybe something will come of it then, and I will send it to you again, and you can see how it is. Here I have written so much about my story, and it probably all sounds wild. But what you tell me I think is good and you must remember that, because you may have to tell me many times again, and I hope you always will. Or what would I do?

Enough wild seriousness, though, and Welty closed her letter on the creative process in "First Love" by giving some literary advice to her adviser:

> I'm glad you wrote a story—it was always shocking that you didn't. I would like so to see it. But you know one should really not write short shorts, one should write novels. That is the only thing that will make publishers lay back their ears, a novel. Abandon short stories at once. [January 18, 1941]

The coincidence of Russell writing about interior and exterior intelligences and Welty sending him the first draft of "First Love" is fortuitous, for Russell had mapped the creative terrain Welty was actually exploring in her new stories. After a first reading of the story, Russell had not been totally convinced that Welty had achieved the best interior/exterior correspondence; he detected dangerous gaps in the "conversation" between the interior, Joel Mayes, and the exterior, Aaron Burr.

> This conception you are trying to work out here is a terribly difficult one. The idea of trying to make a deaf boy give an impression of Burr has an element of subtlety and nobility that I like very much. But what must have impressed Joel were things difficult to make come through in the writing—the expression of Burr's face, a sudden noble gesture, an aura of fate and personal magnetism. Henry was a little baffled by the emphasis on the winter scene but I suspect what you were trying to do was in some manner to link up the unusual winter with Burr,

much as the old Romans would link the appearance of a comet with unusual happenings.

But the whole concept, though magnificent, demands tightrope walking, and though you do this sort of writing superbly you sometimes fall off and I think you have taken a tumble here and as in the first "Clytie" there is too much obscurity and the full vision does not come through. . . .

Don't think badly of me and don't feel badly yourself. You are attempting something quite out of the range of the ordinary writer and that you shouldn't, in my opinion, have achieved it first go is not only not surprising but somewhat to be expected. [January 15, 1941]

Welty accepted the warning gratefully, but confessed that she was still so close to the complex heart of "First Love" that too little of it was out in the conscious area where she could revise and change. The story would have to go out "as is."

Writer and agent both understood, and both had stated in different ways, that the writing and revision they judged genuine was not a matter of tinkering with separate components (the "do's and don'ts" they both imagined as standard short-story procedure for "slick magazine" writers [August 26, 1940]) but, rather, a subtle process of reimagining the whole.

It's a relief to me that you are not breathing forth smoke and maledictions. I find it easy to criticize people who don't really write well and who have holes large enough in their methods to push an elephant through. But you don't do anything badly in the ordinary sense and because you deal with moods and emotions criticism must be to a large extent intuitive. I think if you meditate on this story you will bring it off and I think a useful point of reference to adopt would be to see if you as a reader reading about Burr's actions would react as you make Joel react. That is you are describing Burr's face, his expressions, his movements and all this is what affects Joel. Well in order for it to seem reasonable to the reader that Joel should be affected then he too must, in some degree, experience Joel's emotions. But don't, for heavens sake, give the idea up for it is good. [January 21, 1941]

The debate over technique and meaning in "First Love" brought agent and author into a new phase of their partnership, for both were becoming more self-conscious of their particular ways and means of writing and reading. There was, however, little time to explore the new phase of the relationship, for in one and the same letter Russell reported that Doubleday had made an offer for the collection that he had declined, and that a second offer, more to his liking, had come in while he was typing the letter.

> Doubleday's have made an offer for your book with which I have violently disagreed. I have made counter suggestions and I expect John [Woodburn] will this afternoon sometime give me their final offer. What they wanted to do was to bring out a limited, autographed edition of a thousand and send out a couple of hundred copies to the trade so that proper attention could be given to the book. I objected because it would limit your financial return to a couple of hundred dollars, would set you up as a mark for all the sneers of every critic who would ask "Who is this girl who starts off where other authors end?" . . . Here is a further flash from Doubleday's hot over the wire. They have dropped all the autograph business and limited editions and offer $250 advance, 10% to 2500, 12½% to 5000 and 15% thereafter. I have told them this is O.K. and as I will be seeing John this weekend I can settle the details of the terms. You had better tell me if you want the collection back to make changes. "Clytie" of course is new and ought to replace the old version. Will you write Southern Review and get permission to use any stories they have used and also get permission from the other places which have printed stories. You don't need to bother about the Atlantic. I will write them for I will have to make sure they will use Powerhouse before book publication—tentatively set for September. Do you want to have the Worn Path and the Robber Bride-groom in the collection or do you want to reserve these for the Natchez book? Dear Eudora, see how incoherent my sentences become when pleasure and delight overcome me. I will probably have to write again to make everything clear. [January 21, 1941]

Russell became coherent quickly, for the next major topic for consideration was the table of contents. Russell had on hand stories from different stages of Welty's young career, and one long story, *The Robber Bridegroom*, that seemed better suited for individual publication. Russell had never been pleased with "Acrobats," and Welty, in her first letter of reply to the good news of the sale, agreed that "Acrobats" should take a tumble.

The question of *The Robber Bridegroom* occupied author, agent, and editor more than any other single issue. On January 26, 1941, Welty wrote Russell that *The Robber Bridegroom* ought best be saved for the Natchez Trace collection. It had, after all, initiated that entire movement.

> For what my opinion is worth, and that is still questionable, I would say hold back the Robber Bridegroom to go in the Natchez stories, provided they are interested in bringing out a second collection of stories (can it be?), and unless they have a hunch that the addition of the long story might by one of those things that happen make the first collection go over. [January 26, 1941]

Both Russell and Woodburn agreed.

With more time to think, however, and sensing that Doubleday might not agree to publish a second collection but might, as had all previous publishers, insist upon a novel, Welty shifted her ground:

> You will shoot me for the way I do. Be forgiving for it comes out of elation. It may be too late now for a few calm assertions, but if it isn't, I would like only the best in this book and so I think the Robber Bridegroom ought to go in no matter where it leaves any second book. . . . For myself, I would like it in because I want the best to be presented from the first; and because after looking through the copies I have of some of the stories I definitely want some of them out. With the Bridegroom in, we could have a much better choice among the rest. I don't care if this leaves me bankrupt of material, I think that is only right, and I ought to have to write everything new and fresh afterwards. [January 30, 1941]

Russell wrote the same day, their telepathic waves at cross purposes. He preferred *The Robber Bridegroom* saved for another time. When Welty had time to consider, she reversed field once again and agreed. *Robber* would be saved for the Natchez Trace ensemble, but "A Worn Path," because of its place in *The Atlantic*, would be included in the first collection, even though it too had sprouted from the Natchez mood. The innovation that made this trade more acceptable to the author was Russell's suggestion that Katherine Anne Porter be invited to write an introduction to the collection. It was the first such introduction Porter had ever consented to write, but Russell, who had failed to persuade her to join his agency, had talked her into it. Welty thought the whole enterprise was "glittering" with miracles, but no one knew that waiting for Porter to deliver the introduction would keep both Russell and Doubleday on tenterhooks most of the summer and fall.

Once the table of contents was settled, a title had to be selected. Both Welty and Russell wanted "The Key and Other Stories," probably as symbolic vindication for their favorite among the early stories, as yet unsold. Doubleday was noncommittal. About a month later, John Woodburn, Welty's editor at Doubleday, proposed *A Curtain of Green and Other Stories*, a compromise acceptable to all parties. Selling "Why I Live at the P.O." to *The Atlantic* ensured its inclusion in the first collection, although the event did not help with the title. Perhaps the sale of that well-traveled story saved it altogether, for Welty was thinking of sending it the way of "Acrobats" (January 30, 1941).

"Clytie," "The Key," and "A Visit of Charity," a title Russell could never remember, possibly because he did not like the story and because it infallibly came home whenever it was sent out, were still orphans. They would go into the collection, but Russell preferred to have all the stories in the table of contents sold in advance of book publication. News of the sale to Doubleday brought some of the "nitwit" editors back to the office, and Russell was happy to report that magazines that had previously turned down Welty stories were beginning to see the light.

> The taking of the collection by a publisher has made them think they are missing something. They even asked that the stories they turned down before should be sent to them again—and this made me grin

> because it was what I promised myself they would do in my original fury at their having the ignorance to turn down so good stories. . . . I really feel so pleased I could jump and bambol (g, or is it better as bambol?). Nothing pleases the vanity of the literary mind more than to be proved right and we here were all so furious when one of your stories came back that it would have taken little to make us go out and horsewhip the offending editor for his insult to literature. As another by the way I think you will have to keep on writing better and better stories. The things I say about you would make you blush and to have me justified all you can do is to keep on getting better and better. I have set no limit on the things I say about you and it follows that you, in your turn, will just have to out reach yourself in what you do. [February 11, 1941]

"Outreaching" herself is what the writer had in mind. "First Love" was already proof of the first few steps beyond the earlier achievement in short stories, and the difficulty with that story hinted at just how strenuous becoming better and better would actually be.

The curious history of "Clytie" continued. *Harper's Bazaar* telephoned Russell on Valentine's Day, 1941, to say that they would take it for a price of $150. The sale left only two stories in the cupboard, "The Key" and "A Visit of Charity." Breaking into the pages of *Harper's Bazaar* was Russell's third coup in two months; it seemed almost easy after the sales to *The Atlantic* and to Doubleday. Appearing in the pages of *Harper's Bazaar* marked the beginning of a long association with the fiction editor of the magazine, Mary Louise Aswell, a second reader on the outside who saw much in Welty's stories that Russell, for all his perceptiveness, could not pick up. Aswell fought fiercely for Welty's stories when wartime paper rationing endangered them, and pointed out coherence in some of the more difficult stories when others saw mostly "obscurity."

More importantly, if less visibly, the author's fiction, in the process of outreaching itself, metamorphosed—grew to greater length, took on more fearlessly the challenge of its own obscurity by trying to make "every word that is put down [carry] along with it all these things that are floating around it," delved more deeply into combinations of myth, symbol, history, and psychology. The agent's promise of better and better stories came to mean more and more difficult stories for writer and for reader.

Inevitably the war in Europe and the Pacific closed in on Welty and on the publishing business. In thanking Russell for the news about "Clytie" being taken in at *Bazaar,* Welty reported that her friend, fellow writer, and high-school classmate Hubert Creekmore had been drafted. "All this business," she wrote, "makes a person feel so sad and angry as it comes to one after another that it seems a little flighty to be doing such rejoicing" (February 17, 1941). Creekmore was to become a client of Russell & Volkening.

In spite of the war, the unsold stories continued to circulate. Russell had sent "The Key" to *Bazaar* on the upturned heels of "Clytie." "Visit" went to *The Atlantic* and just as quickly returned. *The Robber Bridegroom* went to *Ladies' Home Journal,* along with the forlorn "Visit." Russell did not harbor great hopes for the fantasy or for the short story at the *Journal.*

> Graeme Lorimer of the Ladies' Home Journal wrote yesterday inquiring about you having seen the story in the Atlantic. I can't quite see you there but after some discussion we shipped off the Robber to him. We don't quite know what the effect will be but we thought it a good chance and one that ought to be taken despite our conclusion that we ought to hold it till the collection appears. [February 20, 1941]

The fate of *Robber* was still to be determined. Welty reported to Russell that, in a letter to Porter, she had mentioned *Robber* as "the one dearest to my heart," which news had prompted Porter to write back with the request to see the story (February 21, 1941). Welty was contrite, realizing that, should Porter like *Robber* and decide to mention it in the introduction to the collection, Russell, Woodburn, and Doubleday would be in a pretty fix. Porter, one of the most respected writers of the day, would have drummed up interest for a story that Welty's publishers had not made any contractual agreement to publish. Welty promised to defuse the situation if she could.

Russell was not too worried. In late February he was confident that Porter would concentrate on the introduction, and therefore on the stories actually in the collection, and leave future work to take care of itself. She had a couple of months, Russell figured, before the introduction was due. Publication was set for November. Surely something could be decided for *The Robber Bridegroom* in that span.

The Robber Bridegroom's future would not include *Ladies' Home Journal*; they had sent it back, Russell reported, "with expressions of mystification" (February 27, 1941). Welty had anticipated rejection with good humor.

> When I think of my Robber in the LHJ I laugh because I'm afraid he will have eaten all the desserts and menus, stripped all the fashion models, and all the men in the illustrations for the other stories will be tied up at least, and all the girls will be looking mussed and cross, by the time the magazine is on the stands. You can tell how modest I feel about his powers. [February 26, 1941]

So confident was Welty of the powers of *The Robber Bridegroom* that she had already chosen Katherine Anne Porter as dedicatee.

"The Key" found a home at *Harper's Bazaar* in early March. In fact, Russell traded "The Key," which Aswell liked more than "Clytie," for the latter story and twenty-five dollars—a sort of literary spring training deal. Poor "Clytie" was on the street again. Russell sent her down to *The Southern Review*, and she was published there shortly before the magazine folded in 1942.

As revision of the old stories proceeded to meet the deadline for the collection, new stories began to demand Welty's time and attention. The idea for a series of stories on the Natchez Trace was continuing to percolate. In early March, Welty sent up to Russell a version of a contemporary Trace story, "The Winds," a story that was to undergo as much cooperative discussion and revision, involving Welty, Russell, and Aswell as the new reader on the outside, as any story Welty has written. The three-sided discussion of the story illustrates how difficult Welty's "better and better" stories had become during the new period of outreaching, how Russell maintained his equilibrium as editorial consultant and first reader on the outside, and how Aswell contributed her editorial point of view as a woman reader attuned to a different pattern of communication.

"I am," Welty wrote in a cover note to the typescript of "The Winds," "a little anxious about how it will sound to you—it is so long for me to write—I'm tired too—maybe it will sound like an 'effusion' " (March 12, 1941). If it was difficult, Welty explained a few days later, Russell was the cause.

> This story was a bit of the out-reaching you mentioned for me—it may have failed. Those were little fragments out of my own life and what I sent you is the first story I've tried directly attempting to remember exact real sensations and the structure they might have built, and the structure may be all felt in myself and not communicated. Tell me how you feel about it. This is one of those stories about which I feel either elation or terrible discouragement afterwards, and wait anxiously. [March 15, 1941]

One of the benefits of Russell as an agent and reader was the rapid and dependable response he supplied to each letter and story. Welty had quickly come to depend on Russell's response to help her keep her "bearings." This was especially crucial navigational help when the new stories could be, and were, so strange even to the author. Before Russell became the first reader on the outside, several persons, some unmet, like the several editors of the magazines to which Welty sent her stories, had played that role. And because the players in the role were not full-time agents dedicated to a client, there was often a considerable delay of weeks or months between the mailing of a story and the response. For a writer deeply dedicated to writing as communication, this unsettled situation of the reader on the outside was awkward. When the responses did return, they were often curt and unforthcoming. Welty had mentioned as much to Russell when her stories had come back from *The Southern Review*; she did not know that Caroline Gordon had complained of the same cryptic communications from Baton Rouge (Waldron, 199). The presence of Russell created a dependable circuit of communication; writing did not necessarily become easier for Welty—in fact, it continued to become more difficult—but it did lose some of its isolation. When Aswell entered the circuit, especially in discussion of "The Winds," Welty had two excellent and perceptive readers; she was never to wait long for a response to any story.

Russell's first response to "The Winds" is dated five days after the author sent the story to him.

> We are in a kind of bewilderment about this new story and before I say anything about it I want to make our position quite clear. The first thing to say is that you are too good a writer to have to accept what anyone says about your stories unless you have some reason to feel very confident about some person's judgement; even with a person whom you trust it would be a bad thing to rely on them for ultimately any good writer has to rely upon himself and his own intuitive judgement about his work.
>
> Now to get to work about the story. We are all in some agreement as to the fact that it is not quite right. John Slocum finds the story obscure—which feeling is not shared by Henry and myself except for one or two little points. Henry finds the symbolism of the wind sounding like a batch of children on a hay wagon obscure and also he finds the note to Cornella at the end of the story obscure and this is obscure to me too. Both Henry and myself take it that the storm portending the end of summer also coincides with the child's intuitive knowledge that a change in her life is also due and that she is entering a new phase and that the snatches of memory about the past summer are looking back to something that seems fixed and permanent in comparison to the new aspect of life. Henry thinks and I too agree with him that the snatches of memory are too many and that the shortening of the story by the cutting down of the number of these memories would add. The real puzzle to me, probably stupidity on my part, is

the note that Cornella writes; I just can't fit this in even though I meditated on it. [March 17, 1941]

He followed his report of the agency seminar on "The Winds" by writing that, if Welty thought the story finished and ready, he would send it out as is. He realized that it was partially at his urging that Welty had undertaken to forge a narrative technique out of the obscurity that had always hovered about her fiction. Since Welty could imagine no immediate changes to the story, Russell started it in circulation. Its first stop was *The Southern Review*, where it was turned down. Eventually it went to *Harper's Bazaar*, and Aswell joined the round-robin discussion. Aswell, because of her keen interest in the points of contact between literature and psychoanalysis, was an ideal reader for "The Winds." Her approach to literature can be roughly outlined by the titles of two anthologies she subsequently edited, *It's a Woman's World: A Collection of Stories from "Harper's Bazaar"* (1944), in which she grouped "The Winds" under the heading "Women in Love," and *The World Within: Fiction Illuminating Neuroses of Our Time* (1947), co-edited with Dr. Frederic Wertham, a psychoanalyst perhaps most famous in literary circles as the doctor who treated Zelda Fitzgerald. Where others found powerful obscurity—but obscurity nonetheless—Aswell found coherent psychological patterns. In "The Winds," and in several later stories that she read and accepted for *Bazaar*, Aswell discerned a latent female psychology and inner experience that Russell sensed but could not identify. Months later, when "The Winds" was up for inclusion in *The Wide Net*, Welty acknowledged to Russell that Aswell, speaking for many female readers, had found something in that story "for the girls" that male readers had never detected.

"The Winds" was not published in *Bazaar* until August 1942, more than a year later. Discussion of it began immediately, and Welty began to see her own practice in ways never before illuminated to her.

With each story I know a little better what is required of me—but I don't believe I will ever reach or be sheltered by the illusion of thinking a story I have written very near to its pure & final & clear form—God help me if I do—though I think this ideal form exists truly in the mind, of writer & reader both, as a sort of allurement and as an explicit test of the work. All that I do is so sure to be always an attempt that I feel more than some others, maybe, that I must know how the story fares—does it come through or not—for all the way it has meant choice after choice. Being under some compulsion, I *am* sure, and yet how can I ever be? Yes I trust your judgment—and it is not that I have less confidence now but that I am going through darker places that I might seem to wish too much for your help. Just to show you how ignorant I am of how the stories appear to another person, I was astonished that the little bit in the last story about Cornella's letter blowing up to the child's house should bring bewilderment. I hardly know how to explain it, it was so plain to me. Maybe by its coming exactly at the end, it acquired a special obscurity. I wanted it to have that emphasis but as an object from without—it had to balance the whole story. You know how in a painting a required note of intensity or a certain unmixed color will be placed maybe on otherwise irrelevant material, as far as subject matter goes, for the sake of the whole composition—the final, compensating thing. Maybe the emphasis on the sign coming from without has lost its meaning (which concerned the commonplace & specified longing & grief to come) by being an actually worded letter, which might rightfully demand an explanation. This sounds involved for the simple thing I am trying to say. —It occurs to me that you write stories by one of two methods, just as you can think by one of the two, inductive or deductive—you sum up or conclude your story from all that you find and are able to relate of it, or you start out with a generality and it fills itself in—and this is the first time I have ever tried the inductive. Yet it should be the most honest and delicate and least "clever" approach— It might have been my scrupulousness of inclusion that kept the story from its proper resolution. But enough about this story—maybe next time I will have better success. In the meantime let me hear what an editor thinks of "Winds"—tell me the worst. [March 21, 1941]

As much as Russell himself believed in a largely intuitive art (he had accepted from A.E. some version of inspiration and mystery in the creative process), he knew that the majority of readers would need a waking logic in their stories or there would be few if any sales. He wanted more deductive process and less inductive. He disagreed with Welty that a detail could be both gratuitous and structurally meaningful. Welty's painting analogy triggered a reply from Russell, a painter himself:

> I see your analogy about painting but I doubt its true relevance to the making of a story. You see the painter does not put the bit of color in intuitively or by accident. He knows the laws of light and of color. In the real atmosphere light pervades everything but in a picture there is no light and it is part of the skill of the artist to try to create that atmosphere. He puts red to key up the green and yellow to key up the blue and violet to bring out the oranges and you will remember Monet when painting his haystacks separated the primary colors and put them side by side rather than mix them thinking by this method he would secure more effectively the impression of radiant light. But he has all the time a clear idea of what he wants to do and has a pretty fair understanding of the techniques by which he can carry out his idea. I have no objection to your working the same way but it would be a slur upon yourself and upon artists to suppose that a bit of color or an incident was put in intuitively. The reasons must be there even if they cannot be explained to some ignorant idiot like myself. [March 24, 1941]

Russell's strong argument for logic and controlled intention might have come from his father's deep and moral reaction to "modern" art as practiced by Picasso and Cézanne, whose work he had accused of reneging on the human promise to follow the logic of representation. More of this later. In March 1941, on the subject of fiction, Russell's resistance was sufficient to quell Welty's misgivings about "The Winds" and the means by which it had been envisioned and written. Gradually an order became visible in the story that, before Russell's intervention, she could not see and exploit.

> I did mean a feeling of cycles to move through the last story, and also an identification of some kind, of life & change with the revolving earth. It is a wonderful thing to find out, when you grow up and read,

> that the way you felt in the naïveté of childhood about yourself in the world is a literally true way—that every body exerts its influence & pull on every other body, no matter how far apart or how different they may be, stars on stars, or a falling flower on the motion of the universe—the pull is each upon the other, and it is only a difference in weight that keeps the rest of the universe from showing its disturbance and lets the flower float to the ground. [n.d.; reply to March 24, 1941]

By late April, Russell was pleased to write with the news that all the stories scheduled for the first collection had been sold. *The Southern Review* had taken the wandering "Clytie." *Decision*, a new magazine that had published its first issue the previous January in New York under the auspices of an editorial board that included such names as Thomas Mann, Somerset Maugham, Sherwood Anderson, and W. H. Auden, had taken "A Visit of Charity," the story that Welty called "that battered thing that's been so far" (April 6, 1941). Russell was mildly apprehensive lest *Decision* go the way of many little magazines, especially in time of war, and "lay The Visit on our lap at the last moment" (April 24, 1941). His worries were unfounded; the orphaned story had found a home finally. Not a palatial home, however, for the new magazine with the illustrious names was thin in the wallet. *Decision* paid only $30. "Blood from a stone," Russell grumbled (June 21, 1941).

Welty was less concerned with the commercial fates of stories already written than she was with exploring the various ways the Natchez Trace and its associations in history and the imagination were suggesting new fiction to her. "Asphodel," a Natchez story with "a little flute obbligato" (April 18, 1941), impressed Russell as pictorial rather than musical.

> I read ASPHODEL and thought it very good and very powerful in raising pictures in the mind. Is this going to be one of the Natchez Trace stories? A dozen as good would make an elegant book and an elegant

> reputation for you so that you would be able then to start writing introductions for other people's books. [April 24, 1941]

Easy to order a dozen elegant stories, but not so easy actually to write them. In an interview years later, Welty was to remember her first stories as "headlong" and usually completed with one impulse and little revision (Prenshaw, 84, 325). After *The Robber Bridegroom* and "A Worn Path," the stories of the Trace ensemble did not leap automatically from vision to print. "Asphodel" seemed an exception to the rule of the outreaching stories, reprising the temper of earlier work with the ease of the musical phrase. But the story coming next, generated by the figure and history of Lorenzo Dow, was stretching out to unfamiliar length, and yet "another one" (unnamed) had been long in the pondering stage of creation.

> I have been in a misery lately, for the desire to make a story do something it cannot do, or at least mine cannot, and the great care I felt simply laid a heavy burden on me, it weighted down my heart and I couldn't do anything, I wanted so to write these exact, perfect, magic stories I could just see. Have you ever seen in your mind all the steps of some impossible thing? It is like understanding how to juggle, just not being able to do it. Anyway, I am about to write away on the Natchez stories. There is one that is going to be a little adventure, in these days—a search, a man alone and he has a lonely walk, which is a vision and a dream sustained with him—I see whenever I think about the Trace now a kind of wanderer and all the gloom he walks in and the flicker of poor little uncertain lights about him that give him hope and the stubborn radiance he lets rise inside him and all that he passes by or imagines is there in a sort of panorama. I want to keep it very simple and very clear, almost abstract, the way you see things when you are lonely and on a journey. But I will send it to you. [n.d.; mid-May 1941]

Welty had come to the point with the Natchez stories that the motif of the journey expressed her own engagement with the material. Form gave her fewer troubles than content.

Never before in her career had the future seemed so full of challenge, of mystery that needed study before she could pass to the next clear stage. Before leaving New York City, where she had stopped on the way to Yaddo, Welty went to the top of Radio City for a look at the sunset. It was near the anniversary of her first year with Russell & Volkening, and she wrote Russell with thanks for the change in her life brought about by his friendship and careful help. She was taking story notes to Yaddo, and hopes for a new kind of fiction that as yet seemed all but impossible.

> I came to the top of the building in Radio City and looked down on the sunset before leaving New York—so beautiful—the grand purple mountains in the distance showing—river shining— I think it is about a year ago now that you first happened to write me and it made a change in my life so I had a tender place in my heart for the day when it came around again. It has seemed like a magical year and whatever is ahead, that will keep. Today I've been studying over story notes, and I read all I could on Johnny Appleseed—then I'll go float on the Finger Lakes hoping that in that nice calm way they will come to something I can do—I must have seemed flighty on this trip—it is all because of a kind of tantalization (is that a word?) over one thing and I am trying to get it straight in my head— Don't worry for fear the product will be impossible and wild, until you see it. Thanks for the good times— It was fine to see you and to get to Katonah and see everything coming up and looking that bright new-green— It made two springs. I must have been in a dream awhile ago, I thought a taxi had "Dostoevsky" on it, and it was only "DeSoto Sky View"—[n.d.; late May 1941]

The writer clearly felt herself on the threshold of giving up daylight logic altogether. Russell responded as the hardheaded, benevolent "intermediary," a label he had conferred on himself when "parasite" began to sound too harsh. He assumed as certain that the artist in Welty would achieve what she had envisioned; nothing would be impossible. And he added an injection of hard-edged practical reality:

> Now as to Natchez Trace. I think the stories you have outlined together with the Robber will be on the short side for a book. The Robber is between 25 and 30 thousand words and four stories added to it of

5,000 words each would make it 65,000 [sic] which is a lot of words but about the shortest a book could be—in publishers' eyes. Don't let the next book keep nagging you. Just write what you please and in the course of time there will be a book. But if the Natchez Trace is besetting you then I think that about eight stories more will be needed to make it an acceptable size to the publisher and to make it seem filled with enough variety.

But as I am always quoting [from A.E.], "Let the joy be in doing and not in the end." In other words write what you want and when you feel like it and in this way you will be doing better work than if you get rigidly fixed in your mind the idea of another book or indeed anything very definite in the future. There are some writers who have nothing but a technical facility to them and these people can keep on turning out two books a year and so on and can do things on commission. But I think it would be bad if you ever got anything of this kind fixed in your head. [June 2, 1941]

Russell's advice and his confidence in her and in her writing were reassuring for the writer in a difficult time. Welty, still on the way to Yaddo, wrote back with thanks and the promise of a new story soon, one that, she hoped, might carry her out of the confusion.

Thanks for the letter. The joy is in the doing. I believe that, but the joy has to be kept alive like any other, by letting it grow with the work growing. I know how good and patient you are not to press me. But when I send you the next story, which I hope will be soon, tell me all you can—you couldn't tell me enough or too definitely after it is written what you think. I need and hope for that. [June 7, 1941]

Much of the darkness in circumstances, of course, was caused by the threat of war. There was, even in the secluded world of Yaddo, where Welty spent most of June and July, the intrusive and unwanted presence of war politics. Working close to Katherine Anne Porter, who was struggling with "No Safe Harbor," the working title for *Ship of Fools*, and with the introduction to *A Curtain of Green and Other Stories*, was both invigorating and tense. Porter, both Welty and Russell hoped, would have the introduction finished by June 1; by June 17 she had only notes, which nevertheless impressed Welty, who had seen them, as "elegant" (June 17, 1941). Elegant notes could not be sent to the printer, and Russell continued to fret.

Close to Porter and the novel she was working on, Welty could not eradicate the unwelcome closeness of "events." Revising "First Love" was not the joy she had hoped; she feared that many readers, in the politicized climate of 1941, would interpret her story as pro-Fascist.

> I'm working on "First Love" but even though it is better now it would not do for you to send out— Do you realize that it might be interpreted as pro-fascist, poor Aaron Burr's unexplained little dream, that I meant to be only a symbol of what everyone has—some marvelous sway and magnetism that it can give— It is stupid and wild, but that is the way people seem to be thinking, everything is dynamite, suspicious. Even KAP, who wants us to enter the war instantly, sees fascism in everything she doesn't like, and while it may be a very intricate insight into deep relationships, I still hate that fever to creep into what we think of books or music, because eventually it will leave nothing to be itself. . . . It seems that nothing is to be left clean or abstract or safe in its old places of the mind or the heart or the wild impossible dream. I keep saying to myself that it is because I was born feeling it and I always will feel it, so I think that all people must really feel it too, but they talk so bloodthirsty. [June 26, 1941]

To force her attention away from the "bloodthirsty," Welty reported to Russell on the foibles of her fellow Yaddovians. But he was less than diverted. He had the Porter introduction on his mind; delay jeopardized the new publication date: September 5. Everyone but Porter seemed to be mesmerized by the deadline.

While Porter lingered over the introduction, Welty finally completed a revision of "First Love" early in July. She thought she had fixed the "diffusion" of the early version (July 8, 1941), and Russell agreed:

> I like the new version of FIRST LOVE. It seems to be all of one piece now, the same mood prevails. It seems to me that you have an aston-

ishing perception of what is wrong with your stories when they are wrong—which is not often. This benighted office which is supposed to help authors could only vaguely say it wasn't quite right and you translate that nebulous criticism into fact. We have sent it off to the Atlantic. Slow as they are they like your stories and both Harper's and Harper's Bazaar have some of your stories now. [July 11, 1941]

Weeks and his staff returned "First Love." They also sent back a trio of other stories: "The Winds," "Asphodel," and "The Wide Net," which they thought not as fine as the two they had taken in December. One of these, "A Worn Path," was chosen for inclusion in the O. Henry volume of 1941. The "honor" caused a minor flurry of controversy that summer, for Russell, hearing from Martha Foley and from Herschel Brickell, editors of the volume, that authors of selected stories received no payment, threatened to withhold "A Worn Path" unless his client was paid at the very least a permissions fee. The editors replied that in the history of the O. Henry volumes no fee had ever been paid. Russell was not cowed. He was placated only when he learned that Welty's story had won first prize and, therefore, the cash that went with it.

Toward the end of July, heat and horse-racing fans collected in Saratoga. Porter was finishing the introduction, too late for the September publication date, and still wrestling with her own novel. Welty felt that she had done all the work she could on the foreign soil of upstate New York and wanted to get back to Mississippi. The sight of so many strange and apparently grotesque visitors to the spa and the track depressed her. She felt as though she were in a haunted museum, and turned the experience into a sort of self-examination. She was beginning to be as tough and analytic about herself as a writer as some later critics would be.

It's hot here and I feel depressed and ready to go. The most incredible looking people have come to town, whose lives couldn't be anything but awful—the streets hold one long procession that is sometimes Daumier, sometimes Hieronymous Bosch, or Goya nightmare creatures all swathed and draped—I stand hypnotized and wonder why I am

> here too—I don't really know anything about their lives but there is a moment as they go by when it *seems* I do. Why all this is concentrated at Saratoga is very strange—there's absolutely nothing to do, the general races haven't started, and it's a tiny, expensive little place, but here everybody is, walking up and down the street, some painfully, taking the waters I guess but it's all evidently a holiday and meant in their minds to be pleasure. I don't know what it means when the sight of people on the street can put me into a state of shock, but now and then it can, and for somebody who undertakes to write I feel far too easily battered & bruised, and the sight of pain makes me inarticulate, and real distortion & monstrosity, of the flesh and the spirit, makes me want to run away. So there you see why I can never be very good. The time comes when I can't bear things on their immediate, ugly, unexplained level but have to look back at them through some vision or reason. I am very late and retarded in understanding, and sometimes not being able to wait I trust to instinct. Maybe it's my dreamlike life in Mississippi where things are long ago or far ahead but never now. [July 26, 1941]

By early the following month Welty was back in Mississippi, working in the garden beds where, like Mrs. Larkin in "A Curtain of Green," she found a kind of rejuvenation. "I got home about dark Thursday," she wrote to Russell on August 11, 1941, "and went out with a flashlight and lo the big pink insects were cutting away at my little camellias, and the closer I held the light and the more I said 'ouch' the better they worked, just like surgeons. It was time I came back to them." In deep and mysterious ways Mississippi was home, and the garden an intensification of home.

> Every evening when the sun is going down and it is cool enough to water the garden, and it is all quiet except for the locusts in great waves of sound, and I stand still in one place for a long time putting water on the plants, I feel something new—that is all I can say—as if my will went out of me, as if I had a stubbornness and it was melting. I had not meant to shut out any feeling that wanted to enter. —It is a real shock, because I had no idea that there had been in my life any

rigidity or refusal of anything so profound, but the sensation is one of letting in for the first time what I believed I had already felt—in fact suffered from—a sensitivity to all that was near or around. But this is different and frightening—no, not really frightening—because for instance when I feel without ceasing every change in the garden itself, the changes of light as the atmosphere grows darker, and the springing up of a wind, and the rhythm of the locusts, and the colors of certain flowers that become very moving—they all seem to be a part of some happiness or unhappiness, an unhappiness that something is lost or left unknown or undone perhaps—and no longer simple in their own beautiful but *outward* way. And the identity of the garden itself is lost. This probably sounds confused, and I am, but *it* is not. [August 28, 1941]

Russell was a fellow believer in the mystical attractions of place.

I think I understand the feeling you speak about. It is really a curious melting of the personality into nature and I think every now and again it happens to all people who like the outdoors even if they are the grossest of human beings. Emerson in his essay on the OVERSOUL tried to speak about it and I think Wordsworth when he wrote the poem about "A being whose dwelling of the light and setting suns Etc." also had experienced the same curious sensation. I have had it myself on several occasions but the feeling comes and goes so quickly that no memory can ever recapture it though I find the memory can recall the surroundings in which the experience came with the most minute detail. [August 29, 1941]

Events, however, swept aside such moments of transcendence. The remainder of the late summer and fall of 1941 was consumed with the publication and reviews of *A Curtain of Green and Other Stories* and the ongoing work of writing and trying to get published. Porter finally got the introduction to Doubleday late in August, and sighs of relief could be heard from Manhattan to Mississippi. "First Love" and "The Purple Hat," both turned down at *The Atlantic*, were sold to *Bazaar* in August. "The Wide Net" had gone to *The Saturday Evening Post* rather than to *Bazaar*: "more masculine than feminine," Russell thought (September 11, 1941). Guggenheim fellowship papers went back and forth, with reminders of the October 15 deadline. But above all ordinary business, Russell was "anxiously awaiting" advance copies of the book. "There is a finality of fact about the appearance of a book that is always pleasing," and Russell was a connoisseur of such pleasures (October 16, 1941). But he was agent first and connoisseur second: when the first advance copy did arrive in the agency office, he hustled it off to England, hoping to line up a British publisher as soon as possible.

Reviewers of *A Curtain of Green and Other Stories* were supportive, even if a few seemed to have read Porter's introduction rather than the stories. This was the gist of Russell's complaint about the review in *Time* (November 24, 1941). *Time* called the publication of the collection "a literary event." But the event did not, in the reviewer's opinion, break free from the straitjacket of Southern gothic, a descriptive convenience already, in the early 1940s, hardening the arteries of book reviewers. Russell fumed that the anonymous *Time* reviewer had read a category rather than the stories. Such sentences as this set him off: "But like many Southern writers, she [Welty] has a strong taste for melodrama, and is preoccupied with the demented, the deformed . . . the highly spiced" (111). Perhaps he could have laughed off his ire had he noticed the comically out-of-context caption to the picture of Welty carried along with the review: EUDORA WELTY *A Spinster Drowned in a Rain Barrel.*

This was precisely *not* the critical line Russell had hoped for in reviews of the collection, and the hint that his client was derivative and unoriginal brought him to the simmer. He was especially upset at a review by Rose Feld in New York *Herald Tribune Books* (November 16, 1941). "As a whole," Feld wrote, " 'A Curtain of Green' shows too great a preoccupation with the abnormal and grotesque. Some day someone might explore this tendency of Southern writers" (10, 12). Russell disliked all the attention thrown to "bitterness and frustration," "twisted" and "dreadful" characters and situations (Feld, 10); the agent thought the entire review stupid and misdirected.

Russell brooded over the reviews very little: one thunderous oath and he went on to the next duty. There was, in fact, not much he could do. Welty's first book got reviews tailored to fit Southern writers as diverse as Faulkner, Erskine Caldwell, Porter, and a dozen lesser-known. Reviewers in Southern newspapers hailed the universality of the stories; Northeastern reviewers tended to use the one-size-fits-all review. The pattern changed slowly for reviews of Welty's future books. The vindication of his literary judgment and the finality of the fact of the published book carried Russell over the disappointments of reviews. He could not pass up a little crowing over the editors who had doubted his recommendations. He followed sales figures closely, and even for non-readers had a sales pitch: A first edition of *A Curtain of Green* would make a fine investment for the future, given the inevitable appreciation in the reputation of the author. He was right; currently, first editions of the collection, with a dust jacket, sell for $600 and more.

There was less than a month, however, to enjoy the success and to brood over the imbecility of reviewers. December 7, 1941, changed the atmosphere practically and spiritually. Welty and Russell exchanged Christmas greetings darkened by the melancholy reality of global war. The art of writing and the work of marketing had to continue, but in a world they saw as spiritually violated by a failure of leadership and conscience.

> I think myself [Russell wrote] all this great war has come about because people and governments all over the world have refused to see and have even denied the existence of a world spirit. [December 26, 1941]

And Welty was just as downcast.

> What the war has done to the people this time I believe will be more powerful than what the people can do in making the war, if that could be a physical fact. But it is true, it must be, that it is the outrage to the world spirit you mention that we feel above the viciousness of each single thing, and all seems to be in the solemn shadow of this violation—no, in the shadow of this spirit to which the violation is done, which is still as powerful as ever and in being denied is the more irrevocably defined. All this must take place in each heart—how strong our heart must be that nothing has ever been too much. [n.d.; late December 1941]

FIVE

New Stories/New Logic

On the outside, in 1942–45, the world war raged. Welty's brothers and several friends were drafted; their fates in Europe and the Pacific wore upon her concentration. Welty herself was asked to "be in charge of the volunteer publicity to 'popularize' and 'sell' all local war doings," but she declined. The spirit of the enterprise of popularizing violence seemed, at the outset of the war, false to her (February 4, 1942). Russell, as always, backed her up in the promptings of her conscience. He served in the Civil Defense in his local community.

On the inside, the writer's stories demanded greater effort, ran to more pages, concerned themselves less with action and more with the private heart confronted by action and its consequences in the world. The new stories of the Natchez Trace sequence, beginning with "A Still Moment" and the revisions of "The Winds," demanded a new logic that Welty herself only barely knew. Russell had pulled her up short on her sense of the intuitive logic of the gratuitous fact in "The Winds," and Welty was reluctant to challenge his authority. And yet her stories seemed to require rebellion: a new technique of narration, a new configuration of gesture and meaning attuned to the heart, not to the logic of events-in-the-world (plot). Plot, as a symbol of enlistment into conventional understandings of the world, was more expendable than ever before now that the world presented war as its logic. For several years "plot" had been synonymous with novel, and novel represented a direction that took Welty away from the center of her vision. She had determined to resist it. Until work on her own novel demanded a new technique, Welty had not consciously worked out a style to carry her resistance.

Mary Louise Aswell's critical appreciation of Welty's "difficult" stories was a crucial catalyst in the forging of the new technique. Welty told an interviewer many years later that Aswell "fought for her writers" (Prenshaw, 186) against the Hearst advertising department, which looked through the handle of its scissors, aiming to cut *Bazaar*'s fiction and replace it with advertising revenue. Aswell, in fact, did much more for Welty than defend her fiction against the legions of profit and loss. She bore witness that the strange new "logic" developing in the fiction, rather than corrupting communication, did successfully tell a story, circumventing conventional plot in ways the author wished. As a woman and an acute editor, Aswell found codes in Welty's so-called obscure stories that male readers, in spite of good intentions, could not see. Aswell voiced a strong, insightful point of view that encouraged Welty to believe that her new, strange, sometimes baffling and tiring stories did, in ways as powerful as they were indirect, communicate. *Delta Wedding* was an important consolidation of this process of discovery.

By early January 1942, Russell reported that "The Winds" had been all over—*The Southern Review, The Atlantic Monthly, Harper's, Virginia Quarterly Review*, and *The Yale Review*—with no takers. As of the fourteenth it was at *Bazaar* with Aswell, who decided, only a few days later, to take it, provided some minor revisions were made (January 16, 1942). She did not know that an earlier version of the story was still at Russell & Volkening. Russell sent that one to Aswell's office, hoping Version I would answer editorial questions and reservations about Version II. Aswell, Russell reported, was high on a story that had had such a disappointing itinerary.

> I sent Version II of THE WINDS to H.B. and a few days later they asked me to send along Version I, which I did. I gather Mary Lou Aswell is rather excited over the story, thinks it may be the best you ever wrote

> and wants to see if there were any particular bits she liked in V. I that you left out of V. II. And that is how matters are there. The Atlantic, to our horror, returned THE WIDE NET, saying that they didn't think it up to your level. We think they're nuts and have sent it to Harper's Magazine, who have so far remained sternly obdurate to your appeal. If it comes back from there we are going to hold it in our files for a decorous period and then send it to H.B. We don't want to deluge them and we don't want to send it to lesser paying places until they have seen it. A STILL MOMENT also came back from the Atlantic, with the note that it wasn't clear to them what precisely you were trying to say. We're more or less in agreement with this and so are going to hold it. [February 4, 1942]

As more Welty stories made their way into editorial circulation, more and more "Weltys" seemed to pop up. Sometimes Russell found the navigating difficult.

Aswell and the author, however, very early reached agreement that, as Welty put it in a letter to her agent, "The Winds" "is a girls' story so H Bz will be a good place for it to rest" (n.d.; reply to January 16, 1942). Welty was satisfied that, whatever else Aswell had written about "The Winds," the "logic" of the story was not obscure to her.

> I looked and looked but I never could find Mary Lou's letter in the envelope unless it had changed into that cardboard that came around the story. But the MS is marked plainly so I can tell what she wants even if the reasons are missing. It is nice to have her so interested and I probably am not cooperating very well. None of the changes seem to me important enough to contest except in the case of the long cut, and if you think neutrally there, that is something—but to me the last few paragraphs of that seem important to the story for being transitional, turning the storm into the summer. And I would rather save the image of the turning wheel of light or that of the boat being stepped into, in those passages, than any casual one like the dressing-gown pattern stamped on the room, for they have the function of giving the impetus to start the child's reverie—at least it was so in my head. I marked the copy to show what I thought ought to be retained for the

> story's sake, but in fairness to Mary Lou I'm holding the MS until the next time you write, in case you think her letter might make me do more, or rewrite anything. [February 9, 1942]

A year later, when contents for *The Wide Net* were under discussion, Welty was willing to exile "The Winds"; but, she added in a note to Russell at the time, "it is a funny thing, men without exception say it is not good, girls say it is—of course I haven't heard many opinions in all, but that holds, and in what strangers wrote in to say too. It might stay in, for the girls" (January 9, 1943).

Aswell's female perspective was not her only contribution. She indirectly coaxed the author to articulate her literary procedures. The cuts to the story Aswell suggested prompted Welty toward a fuller awareness of the logic of her newer fiction.

This is the paragraph that Welty wished to stand as written:

> They looked at one another, parents and children, as if through a turning wheel of light, while they waited in their various attitudes against the wicker arabesques and the flowered cloth. When the wind rose still higher, both mother and father went all at once silent, Will's eyes lifted open, and all their gazes confronted one another. Then in a single flickering, Will's face was lost in sleep. The house moved softly like a boat that has been stepped into. ["The Winds," *The Wide Net*, 120]

The instant of family balance dissolving just as it is felt triggers Josie's ("the child's") reverie. Several times the narrative rounds back to the storm and the symmetrical, strong, balanced figure of the family of four (two adults, two children, two males, two females; two willfully manful in strategies for confronting the change, the other two curious and resigned to having to absorb it). There are details in the story that are casual and therefore expendable, and there are details that function as signals of the progression of the "reverie." Welty was learning through enforced attention to her own story the meaning of that distinction. She was beginning to deal, consistently story by story, with the world-out-there as a porous phenomenon permeated by the feeling self. Conventional narration of event-to-event, with its conventional logic and conventional assumptions about the self and history, could not serve this vision. Nor could the vision make its own way without a certain degree of conscious direction. The balancing act that Russell had mentioned was difficult indeed.

Other stories built upon the same logic, the dissolution and reformation of self and world in the moment of beholding, had less happy fates initially. "A Still Moment" had been returned by Weeks of *The Atlantic*, and as Russell had reported, he was going to hold on to it. Welty acquiesced in the decision, but defended the logic of the story:

> No, the story is not symbolical, but I can see how it would give that impression and of course not be clear. I wanted it to state literal facts, but since the facts were about character & experience in themselves the terms I used sounded as if they were symbols. And it was a method that condensed the story until it lacked motion, and all that I stated so without hesitation took its warmth away, and so I lost the feeling of life that I most wanted to give. I guess that's why it depressed me so afterwards. Do you understand what somebody better could have written—these real men with these real convictions & beliefs were all traveling the Trace at the same time, and the truth was that the road and wilderness did actually take part in their inner lives—there, visual sights were taken directly as personal signs, all that is true. I wanted to show that they were all using the same thing, and that this thing, whose spirit was the little white heron here, has its own life. In this case the literal seemed to me more wonderful than the symbolic. I think often it is more wonderful, for it takes its place in a higher organization of knowledge than most symbolism. All these men acted directly, literally, but unconsciously—that is what I felt. But this is too much about an unsuccessful story, and don't worry too much about selling it and I will try to improve it at this end. [January 16, 1942]

"A Still Moment" was subsequently accepted by Paul Engle, editor of *American Prefaces* at Iowa State University. Perhaps not surprisingly,

Engle, a poet accustomed to the ways in which the lyric voice makes an unconventional logic in the phenomenal world, found elements in "A Still Moment" that the more conventional Weeks did not. In any case, Welty decided to let *American Prefaces* have the story as it was.

> Paul Engle of AMERICAN PREFACES, State University of Iowa, Iowa City, Iowa, which is enough of Iowa, wrote and asked me for a story and I thought if you liked you could let him see the new one, Still Moment, just to see what he would say. They don't pay, but I think they are a good little magazine—at least they used to be—they rejected everything I sent them. I wrote him that I would ask you this and thought you would not mind, since chances for a sale on that story are slight. But I read it again, having taken it off with me to work on, and felt a hope stirring that it might not fail so desperately as it seemed to at first—and still I could see no way to write it differently, for if it fails it fails in its fundamentals. [March 6, 1942]

"The Wide Net" had also bounced back from Boston with the comment that it was not "up to your level" (February 4, 1942). But *Harper's Magazine* ("so far obdurate to your appeal," Russell archly reminded her [February 4, 1942]) bought the story eagerly; the editor, Frederick Lewis Allen, considered it "a work of genius and one of the funniest stories they have ever had," Russell was happy to report (February 6, 1942).

Welty was confronted by conflicting signs of the appeal of her stories: on some readers the new logic worked, on others it was powerless or too oblique. Even Russell was divided; he had not felt at all clear about "A Still Moment" and was much more confident about "The Wide Net." Weeks, who had liked some of Welty's stories, was just as adamant in not recognizing others. Was the inconsistency real or apparent, in the readers or in the fiction?

Before "The Winds" made it into print another story surfaced, giving additional signs that the "easy" and "headlong" stories of the earlier phase might not all be exhausted. "Livvie," like Athena, sprang almost flawlessly into print during a passage of trancelike happiness. In March

1942, Welty learned that the John Simon Guggenheim Memorial Foundation had awarded her a tax-free fellowship ($1,200) to continue her writing. Around Jackson, Welty wrote to Russell, "Guggenheim" was not a household word: when she told a friend's aunt that she had received a Guggenheim, the lady seemed pleased for her good luck, but had to ask " 'A Guggenheim what?' I think she thought it was a hat" (n.d.; reply to March 23, 1942).

The lift of the Guggenheim conspired with the season. On Easter Sunday, driving through the black section of town, Welty saw several black men in zoot suits, "a style all their own," she wrote to Russell: satin shirts, pegged trousers, bright socks, long coats with split tails, wide-brimmed hats with turkey feathers—all in pastels (Easter, 1942). The vision was the catalyst to the spring story. By the thirteenth of April, Welty's thirty-third birthday, "Livvie" was complete and in the mail to Russell's office. Now and then a story seemed to come in the old way—apparently inseparable from an instant's vision, like a photograph, but with more work in the developing. "Livvie" was immediately sent to Weeks at *The Atlantic*. Russell liked "Livvie" and, even though he could not say why, did not feel cheated for lack of reasons.

> I rather like the new story. I don't know what magazine editors will think of it. I never do know what they will think but I foresee that in this case they may raise the objection of it being static. Americans are creatures of movement and they expect characters in stories to be moving around all the time, beating people on the back, chewing gum, jumping over trees and so on.
>
> But it all seems to me to be in the one mood, which I think important, for when your stories are not as good as they might be it nearly always is because the mood isn't held. It goes off to the Atlantic today with our hopes. Weeks was in a few days ago complaining of the scarcity of good material. We hope this will look like an answer from Heaven. [April 17, 1942]

"Livvie" had not, however, left the author in such a celestial mood. After finishing the story, she wrote to Russell, she felt "worn out and depressed" and curious about the workings of her imagination. More than simple logic seemed to be at work.

> I am glad you thought the new story all of a piece. It was a supreme effort, really, that I made to have it so, but I thought the odds were against me, and felt worn out and depressed afterwards. If there was any way to get the envelope back out of the slot in the post-office after mailing, like with a long hook and a string—you would never get a story, though I will race down in the middle of the night, I'm so anxious to put it in. [April 23, 1942]

"Livvie" embodies the two logics, realistic and intuitive, Welty felt vying for her imagination. Solomon, in the story, lives by a strict geometry, the clarity of total disclosure coupled with the stasis of orderly arrangement. This is immediately apparent in the description of his interior space. Cash represents impulse, life on its own spontaneous terms, the organic "logic" of the garden, sufficient for its own existence and imposing itself on no other—"a style of its own," as Welty observed of the black men she saw on that Easter day. Livvie, like the author, is crucially placed in the middle, challenged to choose between what can be seen and guaranteed (Solomon's logic, entailing a vow) and what must be taken in the instant of possibility. Livvie might desire both, but she cannot possess both. A story might be told by Solomon's logic, every event known, the sequence necessary and inviolable; it might be told by Cash's unpremeditated associations. What troubled Welty after "Livvie" was that the unpremeditated logic seemed to be operating in powerful ways she became aware of only *after* completion of the story.

> I suppose the subconscious mind as well as the conscious can take a great liking to some time and place in history and see it in everything—but why? Isn't it mysterious? I have never known much about the thirteenth century in France, though I like it very well—enough to have cut out and framed some of the "Très Riches Heures" a few years back to hang over my bookcase, and on penetrating through the superciliousness of Henry Adams in this book [*Mont Saint-Michel and*

> *Chartres*] I find the things I do most greatly admire, in the directness, simplicity of belief, gaiety, strength, aspiration, purity, exuberancy, etc. of that time reflected in all he relates, but I have not got this *passion* for it that lies underneath. I feel depressed, though not scared to go to sleep at night or anything. Maybe you noticed that in my new story ["Livvie"] the Natchez Trace turned into a moat for a minute. I was writing fast, in the center of my concentration, and put that down, and just left it in. How can I speak of this to anyone—they would think I am crazy, and maybe you do, and maybe I am. It all may be just spring fever. Then longen folk to goon on pilgrimages. There may be somebody in the world now thinking so hard on the 13th century that in my openness of dream and vacancy of mind I caught it. I guess it will pass—although now I am determined to read and ponder all I am able on the time, and force the connection through and see what is so marvelous to me. I have to, when I can't doubt it— I had to say this to someone. [April 23, 1942]

"Livvie" connects these two logics, the one run by the conscious mind, the other by the subconscious. Welty goes on to tell Russell that she had been looking particularly at the scene for April, her birth month, in the *Très Riches Heures*. In its highly stylized International Gothic peace and symmetry, it seemed so far away from narrative as to be its opposite. The author was worried that the "marvelous connection" was much too close to "effusion" and babble. "Livvie," the author knew, was a much more complex story than it appeared to be on its surface. It seemed to have outreached its author, not to mention its audience, and Welty was a little concerned that the best of her vision was beyond the control of her narrative skill.

Weeks expressed no misgivings; he snapped up the story almost immediately. By the end of April 1942, he had notified Russell, and the agent relayed the good news:

> Atlantic writes today they are taking LIVVIE. Weeks says it "has that singular blend of color, pathos, and other worldliness which we have come to look for in her best work. We shall publish it in the July Atlantic with a feeling of pride." They say nothing about price but I

imagine it will be $200 and will inquire about that matter when I have to write them next. I think old Weeksy is typing you—I don't quite know in what pigeon hole but I suspect the phrase about "other worldliness." [April 30, 1942]

In practical commercial terms the editor's approval and his check were more immediately important than "old Weeksy's" tendency to typecast Welty and her anxieties about the creative process. Russell was not entirely sure that Weeks's praise was wholly benign; there was the echo of a mind going shut. Edward Weeks was a personage of wide literary influence, and his support so far had been a godsend to Welty. If he were to begin to expect a certain type of fiction, however, his expectation could become a problem. Author and agent, however, had little time to do more than pause momentarily over the editor's remarks. "Livvie" bore out Weeks's good faith. Although his schedule changed and the story was held for the November 1942 issue of *The Atlantic*, it won the O. Henry first prize for 1942, the author's second consecutive first prize and her third O. Henry award in three years.

After "Livvie," the next story Welty sent up to Russell was "At the Landing." Like "Livvie," "At the Landing" positions a vulnerable young woman between two logics represented by different men: the grandfather and his code of responsibility and house-centered life, and Billy Floyd's impulsive, risky, renegade life on the borders of the unpremeditated. Unlike "Livvie," "At the Landing" had no quick success with editors. All the major magazines returned it. For Russell, the story had the same impenetrable quality that had made "The Winds" mystifying to him. "At the Landing" actually makes a more crucial step on the way to the novel than does "Livvie," for all its popular success.

The logic that had produced "The Winds" also accounted for "At the Landing," making its narrative apparently non-logical and oblique. Russell was puzzled by it, put off his puzzlement as summer woolgathering, and casually remarked that *Harper's Bazaar* (Mary Lou Aswell) might be the proper place for the new story: as if, once again, a story different in its psychological underpinnings had come up to him. Welty herself remained loyal to "At the Landing"; in retrospect it is easier for us to see that the logic of this story was important to her developing sense of how to tell the longer stories of the "outreaching" phase.

"At the Landing" worked its way out of Welty's imagination in the midsummer of 1942, and seemed to have come from much farther away than "Livvie."

> I feel like trying to find some old silent niche this morning, that I must have had somewhere around, just to be still, for that's all I can be about my own evolving ideas, if I ever have any. There was something starting off in my head that I wanted to try in N.Y. if I can come away. Everybody is different, but for me ideas must go far off into excursions of their own, once they start, like somebody that walks along a little road in some country and samples the various berries and breaks off a stick to climb over the wild places with and drinks out of the brooks that come, and on & on, and you have to wait till they come back before you know what they found, but you had better be there when they get home. I think you might whistle to them, but not talk about them. [July 13(?), 1942]

Returning signed contracts for the English edition of *A Curtain of Green* was the occasion for sending the new story to Russell on August 8, 1942. "The story has been something of a trouble to me and may be bad. Maybe it should be thrown away." Russell read it quickly, as if to save valuable cargo about to be tossed overboard.

> I've read the new story and like it. I think it's good but in some vague way I think it might have been better. I can't put a finger on my mental question mark but must just leave it as an intuition. It's not like some stories of yours where I can say the mood is not sustained and so doesn't come off. The mood is sustained here and the only thought that came to me is that with greater length a certain shadowiness might have disappeared. However that's just a thought and the Russells in summer aren't much for thinking but for sleeping in the sun and whiling away

> time dreamily. It has gone off to the Atlantic though I think it more in the line of Harper's Bazaar. [August 11, 1942]

Welty herself had not finished with the story when it went off to Weeks; the sense that the text, as it left her, had not yet reached the condition of embodying what she really felt about an experience continued to call for change and reshaping. On August 13 she wrote back to Russell thanking him for his prompt reading and comments. She had felt "some lack or slack too" and had added "one or two little things" to the new version she enclosed.

Russell's prediction about *The Atlantic* was correct; they deliberated until October but eventually returned "At the Landing." It went promptly to *Harper's Bazaar*. Welty was less than confident in the new story after three months and two versions. "I have a feeling that nobody is going to take the new story—have you?—unless it *is* HB—they always surprise me. I don't know when I will have another to send you" (November 7, 1942). Aswell had rescued "The Winds," finding meaning where Russell had seen confusion and question marks. Both writer and agent seemed to hope that "At the Landing" might be rescued in the same way.

By Thanksgiving "At the Landing" was back in Russell's office.

> We're not having any luck as yet with the new story. Atlantic turned it down and so did Harper's Bazaar with an anguished note from Mary Lou Aswell which said that it seemed to her as if the story wasn't long enough, that it looked like a condensation of a larger work—didn't I say something like this, too? It's now at Harper's and if it comes back from there will be sent to that Tomorrow magazine.. . . . [November 25, 1942]

"At the Landing" did come back from Allen at *Harper's*, and since it was too long for *Mademoiselle*, which was planning a Southern issue for February 1943 and had asked Russell for some of Welty's work, it went to *Tomorrow*. *Tomorrow* eventually paid $200 for the story, about twice what Russell expected to get. The money effectively ended discussion of revision and expansion. The moment was not yet right for Welty to listen to and to act upon the two hints that "greater length" (Russell) might improve a story that "looked like a condensation of a larger work" (Aswell). She was not yet ready to think of "At the Landing" as a longer story, much less a novel. "I think of what you said, and Mary Lou Aswell, and remember at the time of writing throwing large parts of it away, but far too late now, to recall them or know about them, but the chances are I would still throw them away—maybe I should have thrown more" (December 16, 1942).

SIX

The Novel

Eudora Welty has always given Diarmuid Russell credit for spotting her first novel, *Delta Wedding*, in a short story called "The Delta Cousins," a story she had sent to him in November 1943 after several months of work. She suspected that, like all the "outreaching" stories, "The Delta Cousins" was probably too long for an easy or quick sale. The story grew out of and extended the challenge Welty faced first in "The Winds" and then in "At the Landing." With these three stories Welty was stretching her short-story technique close to the snapping point.

She had always justified her career as a short-story writer in large measure in the belief that the short story was a legitimate literary genre in its own right, and her genre by natural skill and inclination. Russell was first drawn into her work with the promise never to urge the novel. She had resisted all the opinions that the novel was intrinsically a greater achievement. From 1942 to 1946, writer and agent negotiated—sometimes consciously and sometimes not—a complex set of conditions that produced a novel, *Delta Wedding*, out of a commitment to short fiction and a rejection of the novel as a genre with privilege. Aswell's recent inclusion in the epistolary discussions of the new stories was of particular help in the protracted and often anguished movement toward the novel; her support for Welty's increasingly lengthy, "obscure," and "plotless" fiction helped the author to maintain her faith in a mode of storytelling she could not abandon for the more traditional, linear, realistic narrative of plot. With two books of her short stories in print (*The Wide Net and Other Stories* was published by Doubleday in September 1943) a certain plateau of success had been reached. Neither Welty nor Russell had actually plotted the next stage of writing—at least not as consciously as they had "plotted" the Natchez Trace stories.

Gradually and surreptitiously "novel" was beginning to be the answer to a question no one, including the author, actually asked, until Russell himself brought it up indirectly on December 29, 1942. After "At the Landing" had been sold, Russell showed it to John Woodburn, who was a holiday guest at his home.

> I brought home for Christmas AT THE LANDING so that John [Woodburn] could read it. He said it sounded incomplete. I read it over again myself for there is something tantalizing about the piece. Don't think it is bad for you could write nothing bad like some slovens of writers do, but the fact that Mary Lou Aswell, myself, and now John more or less feel it wasn't long enough, added to your note that you threw away a lot of material, seems to me an indication that a story which started to be about one character outgrew that theme and, in fact, too many things crop up in the story that need more expansion. The people in the story, the three old ladies, the albino, the fisherman himself have all a condensed feel. The title itself, AT THE LANDING, carries a sort of intimation of a community, while the story has been contracted to one about a character and even though this has been done one still feels the emphasis has been misplaced. Maybe somewhere here is the theme of that novel about which publishers have been—and will—plague you. [December 29, 1942]

This was quite a New Year's greeting, and Welty played for time to deal with it. "I'll think about 'At the Landing' some more," she wrote, "but I am afraid it is something that I can never organize. I don't think it would take a novel—just a better story" (January 8, 1943). The habit of resistance to the novel died hard.

Circumstances helped prolong its death. *The Robber Bridegroom* had been sold to Doubleday, Doran in June 1942, and the writer suffered mild anxiety attacks over its possible reception by the critics and by Katherine Anne Porter, to whom it had been dedicated. There were some clues that it might find a rough course ahead. David Cohn, a fellow Mississippian, one of the William Alexander Percy circle in Greenville, was editing a special "Deep South" issue of *Saturday Review of Literature* (September 19, 1942) and had asked Welty if she would submit a short story or sketch of 2,000–2,500 words. His two-week deadline was too close for any new work; Russell sent him *The Robber Bridegroom* with the suggestion that he excerpt a part that suited him. Cohn declined, saying only that *The Robber Bridegroom* was not quite what he had in mind for the Deep South issue (July 15, 1942).

Cohn's editorial itinerary of the South ran through the territories of politics and sociology; it is easy to understand why he found nothing to his purpose in Welty's "fantasy." "Deep South writing," Cohn wrote in his editorial preface to the issue, "proceeds from a strange environment. It is, first of all, the poorest, most illiterate, most violent, and emotional section of the country. It has had, in general, no literary background such as distinguishes New England." Because "there has never been a free white man in the Deep South" [the presence of a large and sometimes overwhelming population of blacks negating freedom], the white Deep South writer is a scarred individual. He deals with deformed human beings as his everyday subject matter, "distorted whites suffering from more or less severe psychological aberrations" (*SR*, 3). Cohn had made an investment in Southern gothic; Russell (especially) and Welty had regretted the sideshow aspect of Southern gothic in the reviews of *A Curtain of Green*. Welty satisfied her regional obligation, however, by supplying one of the several book reviews Cohn included in the Deep South issue. First serial rights to *The Robber Bridegroom* were eventually sold to the *Philadelphia Inquirer* in November 1942, far north of Cohn's steamy rhetoric and aberrant psychology.

Welty's editor at Doubleday, Doran, John Woodburn, moved to Harcourt Brace in December 1942, forcing the author to decide whether or not she wished to move with him. There was little question she would: Woodburn enjoyed Welty's confidence. He had been the one to give her name to Diarmuid Russell in 1940. Russell explained that professionally he could give no advice on the move, for he did not want to risk any client's fortunes by seeming to impugn any publisher. He was, however, pleased when Welty informed him that she had opted for the move to Harcourt Brace. Dealing with the new publisher gave the agent renewed, and expanded, bargaining room. Doubleday was one of the oldest and strongest houses in American publishing, but careful with the promotional dollar. Doubleday's "big" book the same year as *A Curtain of Green* was Edna Ferber's *Saratoga Trunk*, for which the publisher announced an ad budget of $20,000. Russell was miffed that his client's book got almost nothing.

He announced on January 6, 1943, by way of New Year's greetings, that he had negotiated a contract with Harcourt Brace for a new book of short stories—the Natchez Trace collection, presented to Doubleday but never accepted—with an advance of $750 and a flat royalty of 15 percent. Immediately Welty began to assemble a tentative list of contents: under the heading "For Sure" were "First Love," "The Wide Net," "Livvie," "A Still Moment," and "Asphodel"; under the heading of "?" were the three stories about which Welty still harbored deep misgivings, "The Purple Hat," "The Winds," and "At the Landing."

Russell campaigned mildly for "At the Landing." He had never really liked the story, but it did seem to him to be mysteriously crucial in Welty's development and the agent did not want to stifle any growth. Besides, it had been sold. He continued to hint obliquely that more might have been done with it, and that the "more" might require expansion into a novel.

> The thing that hovers at the back of my mind is that the Landing has cropped up in more than one story and more than once in conversation—if I am not making mistakes or having hallucinations—and so it seemed to me that if this was the case maybe there was more to be said. [January 11, 1943]

If there was more, the author preferred to save it for the new work of the future. "At the Landing," in the early weeks of 1943, had ceased to draw substantially upon her imagination. It was, for better or worse, beyond the "line" that divided the quick stories from the dead. The truth was that, except for collecting, arranging, and touching up the stories for *The Wide Net*—work in which the author was engaged for most of the early part of the year (doubly engaged, since the corrected manuscript was lost by the express company on its way to New York)—the author's story-writing mind lay fallow. She began to review frequently for Robert Van Gelder at *The New York Times Book Review* in February 1943. Welty enjoyed the work and kept at it steadily for more than a year. She even reversed her attitude toward war work in general and considered inquiring about a job in the Office of War Information (February 15, 1943). "It is nice of you not to ask me why in the devil I don't send in a new story—I just can't—or I would," she wrote to Russell that month (February 8, 1943). Thus began a long and apparently fallow period.

By June 1943 more than a year had passed and Russell had all but abandoned silence on the subject of Welty's "sabbatical" from stories. Reviews and revisions to the stories for *The Wide Net* and a commissioned essay on Rodney, Mississippi ("Some Notes on River Country," *Harper's Bazaar*, February 1944), were fine in their own way, but Russell was concerned that Welty was not busy in "the center of her concentration." By the middle of the month Russell had stepped up his polite pressure, asking why no new stories appeared when they were in such demand.

Summer 1943 progressed; writing did not, except for "The Purple Hat," a story neither writer nor agent mistook for important.

> Don't worry about that story for for what it is it succeeds—it has been sold in England. I think your objection to it in your mind is that it is trivial, that it expresses no deep mood of the mind or nature. And this may be true but don't forget, I think I have said this before, that a kitten playing with its tail is delightful in spite of the fact that the action has no deep meaning for the universe. The light, the inconsequential is just as real as anything else and in that scheme the PURPLE

> HAT fits and is the reason it is liked by us, England and Harper's Bazaar. [June 10, 1943]

Jackson baked under a relentless heat; there was no relief at night or in the early morning. "I haven't been able to do a thing with the story I was telling you about. For a while I had good ideas but this seems to be just a bad time. The weather has been hot, about 102—so that just the act of typing seems erratic. You will want to fire me for a client," Welty wrote from the inferno (August 6, 1943).

An additional reason for the stall, on top of the reviewing work, might have been anxiety over the reception of her new book. Welty's second collection of short stories was published on September 23, 1943. As John Woodburn wrote, in a well-tempered letter about a month later:

> Some of the reviewers were apparently lying in wait for you with, if not a cudgel, at least a peach switch. That, alas, is the price of fame. I don't know whether Diarmuid has been sending you reviews or not, but if he has, if you will tell me what ones you have I'll try to supplement them with others from here. [October 30, 1943]

Fame, as the jocular Woodburn termed Welty's recognition, was not an unmixed blessing; when the reviews came out, Welty and Russell found themselves confronted with a reviewing cadre almost as difficult to anticipate as editors, and more ideologically determined to find fault with the Southern subject matter than those who had written about *A Curtain of Green*.

Most reviewers acknowledged Welty as a literary stylist in the tradition headed by Porter, but many cut their praise with reservations. *Time*'s anonymous reviewer could not quite make up his/her mind about the fiction: "These eight stories about the South present as perplexing and exasperating a mixture of good and bad as U.S. writing can show" (*Time*, September 27, 1943, 100). The sentence with the sting followed:

> At her best, 34-year-old Miss Welty runs a photofinish with the finest prose artists of her time and displays a delicateness of sensibility which borders at once on genius and indecency.

Time was no more specific than this on the meaning of "indecency." Russell was angry at the hit-and-run review, but Welty had developed a thick skin for a new writer: "They say those things just because I happen to live in the South . . ." (September 27, 1943).

In *The Nation* Diana Trilling leveled more substantial charges, and signed her name to them. Russell did not see the review immediately, but passed along John Woodburn's displeasure. Trilling granted that Welty had a legitimate claim to "technical virtuosity," but judged that the writer's art, in the case of *The Wide Net*, "outweighs the uses to which it is put," culminating only in "stylism," "a heart for decay and an eye for the Gothic in detail." Performance, Trilling decided, had outrun communication (*The Nation*, October 2, 1943, 386). The flaw as Trilling saw it was that the author had allowed obscurity to drift into the fiction and muffle "rational content," heightening only the emotional impact. The stories of *The Wide Net* were more ballet than prose, and *danse macabre* at that, creating only confusion between the logic of reason and the logic—Trilling would have debated the use of the term in this parallelism—of vision. Trilling was close to the heart of the matter; her prejudice in favor of reason prevented her from appreciating the dilemma the stories actually enacted.

Such criticism on the spot of publication seems not to have concerned Welty or Russell too seriously. "Yes, I read the Nation review," Welty responded to Russell (October 18, 1943), "and she says all the things about me I always say about Carson McCullers! So I get slapped right back." Welty's prolonged struggle to complete her own new fiction worried author and agent more than the reviews of what was, to them, the work of the past. Russell was careful to ask:

> Is the story-telling mind still in a state of withdrawnness—is that a right word? I ask because when I was going through our book in which we note receipt of stories I saw that LIVVIE, the last story, came in over

> eighteen months ago—which is a long time. Of course there's nothing to be done about it for if stories and the internal compulsion don't naturally arise there is no use trying to force things. One is either internally compelled to write or externally by a bank balance and the latter method doesn't produce good literature. [October 14, 1943]

The "center of the concentration" was still distant territory: "I don't know what has been holding my brain in such a clamp for so long—I've *wanted* to write things" (October 18, 1943).

The writer's "clamp" was real, and was attributable to many causes coming together in concert: weather, rough sledding in a couple of reviews, the demands of the new material, anxiety over friends and brothers in harm's way. The Delta material, out of which the long story and eventually the novel were to come, was, like the Mississippi Delta itself, fertile and prone to inundation. Welty had become accustomed to stories arriving in satisfying aesthetic wholes so concentrated and accomplished that, as she told Russell, each word virtually accounted for every other word. Other readers had detected some straining for such internal coherence and accountability in "At the Landing" and had suggested greater length as the cure. Not until Welty was deeply and personally committed to the Delta story did she begin to see the same necessity.

By November the hot summer had passed, the skirmishes over *The Wide Net* had subsided, and the "story-telling mind" had become reactivated. "I have about finished the story I was telling you about, but be prepared for a bad length—about 30 pages, it looks like—and I'm not sure it's good either" (November 1, 1943). Welty was using a typewriter with a very small font; one typed page carried about 350 words. Thirty pages meant roughly nine or ten thousand words in the new story, about double the customary length of her stories. Russell, however, was worried only about practical matters.

> The story we look forward to without qualms for we know that whatever you send out has passed your own scrutiny as being the best you can

> do—and that's what most authors fail to do, to send out their best. It is long though and will be a sore worry to magazines on account paper is short these days and by all accounts is going to be shorter by another 15% (on top of the 10% cut they've taken) beginning in the new year. But these are commercial considerations and should not be thought of in writing. [November 2, 1943]

After reading the new story, "The Delta Cousins," Russell was in a quandary still, but decided to bow to "commercial considerations." Paper shortages would certainly work against the new story until the war was over; yet it was desirable, if not urgent, that Welty reappear in periodicals with new short fiction. One way out of the fix, he suggested, was to make the story "shorter" by eliminating a few of the incidents and scenes.

> Both Henry and I have read the story, have talked about it and are more or less in agreement—every individual section seems good and yet as a whole it doesn't quite have the effect it ought to have. I wish we could say why this is but this is the feeling we have and so we mention it to you. I mention it because the subsidiary thought I have as to why this might be—a sort of speculation on my part—would, if it made any sense to you, make the story from a purely commercial point of view better—that is, shorter. [November 10, 1943]

Since the editor of *Ladies' Home Journal* had dropped into the office while Russell was reading and pondering the story, he packed it off before Welty could change it.

For the author, however, the problem with "The Delta Cousins" was not the commercial or practical aspect but the same problem of the fusion of two seemingly antithetical logics into one narrative logic that would support the burden of storytelling, a method of reconciling individual parts to one another and to the vision of the story complete. Welty knew that no story succeeds without a sense of something happening. She also knew that the "something" and the mode of telling were not simple life.

> I think you are probably right about the story, and it's true that putting incidents together this way assumes a logic, when a logic is not enough, I feel very certain too. The only defense the story does make (for me) against that is the ending, with the child asleep and not really reached by the incidents' culmination. If I could show that there is a logic, but that only flashes of it appear and fade for the child, it would be what I intended—but it's still too new for me to think how to work further on it. I will think about this but you do as you think best about sending it out, now or if changed later. It will be interesting to hear what Ladies' Home Journal thinks, though I don't guess this counts as a real sending out of the story—more like betting for a race on a 200 to 1 horse. (Mr. Weeks wrote me this fall and asked me to "unbend" in that direction, so maybe some time or other in this story's case history on your little card you can let him scrutinize it.) I was sorry about its getting so long, but I couldn't stop it—like one of those jinxed pots that cooks more & more pudding. [November 13, 1943]

When the story returned from *Ladies' Home Journal*, where it failed for "lack of plot," Russell sent it immediately to *Harper's Bazaar* (November 22, 1943).

The only obstacle to publication at *Harper's Bazaar* was the story's length. Paper shortages had hit Aswell's magazine particularly hard, Russell noted; so hard, in fact, that *Bazaar* no longer sent authors complimentary copies of issues carrying their work. Aswell explained her situation forthrightly, and repeated the agent's suggestion that eliminating a few scenes might improve the story rather than cripple it. The only way she, Aswell, could see all the present episodes retained was in a novel.

> If it can possibly be cut to proportions that can hope to fit into the Bazaar even during the first period *after* the war. We have desperately little space for fiction now, so that I must warn you we may not be able to run the story until our paper allowance is increased. . . . That means, dear Eudora, will you cut every word you feel you can eliminate. . . . Here are some suggestions: perhaps Laura could (and should) get to Innisola a little earlier in the story; perhaps there needn't be *quite* so

> many cousins (it's rather confusing); perhaps some of the digressive interludes could be omitted—not Partheny, but the bee man episode, definitely, because it's not an integral part of the story. The part about the store is wonderful (of course it all is), but it doesn't have to be in a short story about the Delta cousins. It would have to be in a novel, but not in this more compact, intensified form. [Aswell to EW, December 16, 1943]

Here was a situation the writer had not faced before: On the one hand, trusted readers were suggesting that what had originated as a short story could bear the burden of the novel—that is, "The Delta Cousins" could, perhaps more ably than "At the Landing," carry itself off as a novel; on the other hand, commercial circumstances seemed to dictate that the story be shortened. The writer's dilemma was complicated even more when Russell reported that *Harper's Bazaar* would pay five hundred dollars for "The Delta Cousins" *if* it were "shortened a good deal."

> After this day the nights grow shorter—even if only imperceptibly so for a while—and so we may assume that spring is on its way. But this letter isn't about that. As you see I enclose a letter to you from Mary Lou about the story. You mustn't think we have been opening your mail but Mary Lou asked me to open it to see that it represented fairly conversations we had about the story. Well it does and it doesn't. What is omitted is the fact that they promised a price of $500 if you wanted to do work on it to shorten it—and as you can see they would want it shortened a good deal. So the matter is up to you to decide. The story has not yet been to either the Atlantic or Harper's but I feel quite sure they haven't the space (this morning's paper announces another paper cut starting Jan. 1, 1944, for all books, newspapers and magazines) and that if shortening doesn't seem possible to you then it is likely the story will remain unsold for the duration of the war. We will, of course, try it around as it is if you decide that you can't do more work on it but the most probable fate is that it will be too long for the other magazines and that we will have to set it by for the duration. So now we dump the matter on your hands and hope that it will not disturb

> your sleep and we will sit here and await your word before doing more with THE DELTA COUSINS. [December 21, 1943]

Five hundred dollars was more money than the writer had yet earned from a single short story. The dilemma was serious.

By New Year's Eve, Welty had decided to pass up the *Harper's Bazaar* offer. The cuts to "The Winds" had not seemed as vital to her as those requested in "The Delta Cousins." Rather than cut the story to *Bazaar*'s requirements, Welty wanted the story sent to Weeks. His comments in the January 1944 "Atlantic Bookshelf," in circulation by late December, had spurred the request. Weeks had found little in the field of new fiction he surveyed at the close of 1943: "We have had nothing from Hemingway for reasons which he has explained, and next to nothing from Eudora Welty." She wrote to Russell that the story might get her off Weeks's list of writers "with unexcused absence" (January 13, 1944).

Russell fixed a high price on the story when he sent it to *The Atlantic*. If *Bazaar* was willing to go to five hundred, *The Atlantic* could be asked for seven. His sense of the market, he wrote to his client, told him that the asking price was not too high.

> I do think magazines are stinkers the way they expect the author to keep on taking the same old prices while the magazines themselves are rolling in money. It was that moral indignation that made me write asking for more. [February 28, 1944]

Weeks did not respond quickly (he seldom did), and by early March both author and agent were mildly curious. Welty half-seriously feared that the high asking price had unnerved the frugal Bostonians. "Maybe Mr. Weeks is not going to get in touch with you at all but send an armed man to meet you by the old stump and catch you in the act of blackmail or extortion—so be careful. The story hasn't been shortened any further, but any day I may get it down on the floor, which is the best way, and cut it with scissors and pin it this way and that and squint at it" (March 6, 1944). Any intention to shorten "The Delta

Cousins" seemed fated to fail; all of Welty's work on the story only made it longer and disclosed close connections to other "Delta stuff."

> . . . it's sort of like a jigsaw puzzle the way it gradually gets in my head, and proves I should just be able to think harder and not have to sort of catch on, the way I've done about it. Do you want to see the new part, as finished now, or wait and get a look at the whole? [February 23, 1944]

But the stumbling block at *The Atlantic* was not the price; it was the length. Like all publications, Weeks's magazine had been pinched by wartime paper rationing. The editor had publicly noted in his "Bookshelf" column that, in 1943, "approximately two hundred fewer novels [had been] published," and as a consequence publishers were forced to choose which books to publish and which to keep in print. In the particular case of "The Delta Cousins," he told Russell, he was ready to discuss price if and only if the author was willing to agree to cut between three and four thousand words (March 8, 1944). The issue of cutting the story was suddenly rendered moot, however, when *The Atlantic* selected Van Wyck Brooks's new book, *The World of Washington Irving*, for serialization. The run of five months, from June through October 1944, would put Welty's story back six months at least. Weeks was necessarily vague about a commitment, but was still more definite than *Bazaar*. The delay meant that whatever cutting and reassembling took place could be done with a more careful eye. Welty was glad of the "reprieve" and confident enough to expect that another story would be finished before the six-month delay had expired (probably "A Sketching Trip"). She would feel easier, "with so much money at stake," giving Weeks his choice between "The Delta Cousins" and the new story (March 18, 1944). The Delta material, however, continued to expand, like the contents of the "jinxed pot."

After Weeks's tentative agreement to publish "The Delta Cousins" as a short story, with cuts amounting possibly to one-third its length, Welty did other piecework. "Literature and the Lens" for *Vogue* and several more book reviews for *The New York Times Book Review*. Among all the reviews, one stands out in the present context as indicating the private process by which the author's imagination covertly reconciled itself to the idea of the novel. Welty's review of Virginia Woolf's posthumous *A Haunted House and Other Stories* (*NYTBR*, April 16, 1944, 3) seemed even to Welty special among all the reviews she wrote in that season. "I had to review Virginia Woolf's last book of stories," she wrote to Russell (April 11, 1944), "and if they print my review as written (they never do) I would be interested to see if you agree."

Welty has frequently and freely expressed her admiration for Woolf's work, acknowledging a sort of influence by the older writer, who had committed suicide in March 1941. Welty's review of the posthumous work is significant for its timing; just in the hiatus between the completion of a long story that seemed to require either serious cutting or recasting as a novel, Welty was brought back to a writer whose fiction had "opened the door" (Prenshaw, 25). When "The Delta Cousins" next appears, it is already in the process of becoming a particular kind of novel, one connected coincidentally as well as substantially to Welty's rereading of Woolf in the spring of 1944.

Woolf's work, "the unperfected work of a perfectionist," struck Welty the reviewer as primarily visual, positioning the reader as observer of a reality "too intense for us not to watch it through a remove of some kind" ("Woolf," 3). The obscurity that Welty had been exploring and exploiting in her own work seemed to find its counterpart in Woolf's successful use of the "remove," the technical means by which she achieved the essential relationship between reader and author in her fiction.

> Obliquity gives its own dimension to objects in view, and elongation, foreshortening, superimposing are all instruments of the complicated vision which wants to look at the truth.

To all those reviewers who had devalued her work because of what they deemed obscurity or amateurism or "stylism," Welty had an indirect answer, sponsored by the achievement of Virginia Woolf. The instruments of vision are many and complicated; there is no iron rule regarding what can be beheld and how.

Welty singled out Woolf's "An Unwritten Novel" for special attention in the review. It is tempting to superimpose *Delta Wedding*, by no means finished, upon these comments:

> In the experience of observing, the observer is herself observed, her deft plunges into another's obscure background become reachings into her own hidden future, error makes and cancels error, until identification between the characters examined and the writer examining seems fluid, electric, passing back and forth.

Not only does Welty's sentence faithfully predict the character of Ellen Fairchild in her own impending novel, it also enunciates, albeit obliquely, a sort of novelistic policy on the crucial issues of mimesis or representation, point of view, and plot. Forster's *Aspects of the Novel* was another work of criticism Welty was to acknowledge as guiding her instincts on the novel, but Woolf's fiction seems to have been more suitable as a model for the fiction Welty could "see" herself writing. By the precedent of Woolf's fiction, Welty felt permitted to play with the otherwise strict discipline of representation that a critic with the outlook of Diana Trilling, for example, held to be inflexibly rational. Critics would not cease faulting Welty's fiction for its apparent failure to present the world in a shadowless, rationalistic light. Obliquity, however, the long, slanting shadow, was the light Welty preferred. If that "remove" presented objects and experience in unfamiliar contours, it was no less legitimate and "true." Point of view, the element of fiction that disciplinarian critics were promoting to a privileged status from which it might order the entire house of fiction, became for Welty a sort of oscillating condition of attention, a dance rather than a stance. And plot—assuming first a discrete entity in time and place denoted "event" and then a logical, Aristotelian order of such events—would be for her a "journey of unspecified purposes, in a moving vehicle with panoramas flying and fading without, the changing and merging features of persons, landscapes, character, color, motion in place and time, hope and despair [seeming] to seek at the very source the attraction and the repulsion in each moment of being" ("Woolf"). The opening of *Delta Wedding*, Laura's journey on a train into the fluidly changing Delta landscape, is an indication, in this context, of how Welty's meditation on Woolf found expression in her own fiction. The child Laura not only enters a time and a place in that opening scene; the novel ushers the reader into a condition in which conventional representation of action and phenomena is suspended. Not a line, but a field; not a progression in which event after event is encountered in logical lockstep, then lost in the wake of the single line of forward motion, but complementaries in rhythm transforming a line of time into a single moment, and the beholder into the object of attention.

Almost immediately after completing the review of Woolf, Welty wrote to Russell that she was working on a new story, not revising "The Delta Cousins." "A Sketching Trip" has not been preserved in Welty's collected stories; in a later letter to Russell she confessed that she was forgetting it rather quickly. It comes out of this fertile passage in her career, taking on resonances in the context of the Woolf review and Welty's apparent interior resolve to do the novel in a certain way regardless of conventional assumptions. One of the photographs Welty had sent to *Vogue* for "Literature and the Lens" was a picture of an old haunted house in the Delta—a haunted house to match the one in Woolf's posthumous collection. That haunted house "happens to be in the new story I am working on" (April 25, 1944): "A Sketching Trip."

Weeks admired "A Sketching Trip" and bought it for *The Atlantic* when Welty finished it after a summer (1944) of living in New York City and reviewing for the *Times*. It carried, Weeks wrote to the author, "the Chekhov secret" of reverie and timelessness (December 13, 1944). He was confident enough to call Welty "one of the indispensable contributors to the Atlantic" and looked forward to publishing the "enchanting story of the Delta cousins" in part or whole when the author had finished revisions.

Revisions did indeed seem to be going very well that winter, even though Welty's mother had trouble with cataracts and had to consult an eye specialist in New Orleans. The rereading of Woolf and the work on "A Sketching Trip" seem to have shown Welty the way to finish "The Delta Cousins." Three days before Christmas Russell wrote with his approval of the latest version of the story.

> The story came safely, has been read—and greatly liked. I think it just confirms me that somehow or other you must get your mind in the right kind of mood and expectation to work on the DELTA COUSINS for here as there is the same kind of wonderful atmosphere—the South just as I imagine it must have been, may still be for all I know. Henry has not yet read it and won't be able to do so till next week—it is now 2 p.m. and the faint weakness about more work is beginning to come on us. But when he has read it we can determine whether we ought to spare the time to try for the big money or to settle for H. Bazaar. [December 22, 1944]

On New Year's Day, 1945, Welty wrote back with thanks and relief. "I am glad it does seem all right to you—. What all this Delta stuff will turn into I don't know." Two weeks later: "You would never say 'novel' to me, I know, and would be my support in what happens to the [Delta] material—I can't tell what, though. Spring is going to make me wonder and ponder" (January 14, 1945). Less covertly, now, the novel seemed to be entering the circle of possibility.

Although the literary problems of the novel as a form she could not subdue were considerable, they were not the sole complicating factors impeding the progress of *Delta Wedding*. Almost all the Delta material came by way of Welty's relationship with John Fraiser Robinson, the man to whom the novel was eventually dedicated, and with his family, who had lived in the Mississippi Delta from antebellum times.

Welty had met Robinson a year or two earlier, and their relationship had become serious by the time he was drafted into military service. Robinson's Scots ancestors had cleared and settled several plantations in the Delta. While John Robinson was overseas, and frequently incommunicado, since he worked in Intelligence, Welty drove over to the Delta for visits to the family. During these visits she read through the diaries and journal of one of John Robinson's female ancestors. This "Delta stuff" (oral and written) not only burgeoned into a long story and then a novel; it flowed later into another short story, "Kin."

Worry over John Robinson's safety contributed several emotional pounds to the "clamp" that had seized Welty's writing concentration in these months during 1943 and 1944. Eventually word came from Robinson that he was safe, in Italy. War concern, however, continued to press. Welty's brothers were posted to minesweepers in the Pacific, and communication was irregular. With a struggle, she kept the story going. Working close to the end of what had become, for all intents and purposes, the draft of a novel to present to Edward Weeks in lieu of the long story he had tentatively accepted, Welty heard the news of the first atomic bomb dropped on Japan. The ending of the war seemed to her as ominous as the declaration had been.

> I'm typing on page 164, and hope to finish it this week. I'm very anxious for you to see it as a whole—I can't see it by a good long-sight yet, or correct the proportions. . . . I hope this [war] ends before we have to do any more—before we drop another one. I am one of those that tremble about the universe—only you can't really tremble for a whole universe. In an H. G. Wells story, the scientists could have the bombs accidentally fall on their own heads and somebody would say, better that their secret died with them. [August 13, 1945]

Weeks serialized *Delta Wedding* in *The Atlantic* in four installments (at $1,000 per installment) beginning in January 1946. Harcourt Brace published the novel at the end of its *Atlantic* run in April 1946, with a first printing of 10,000 copies. Russell's preference for Harcourt's greater inclination to take risks on a first-time novelist had paid off. There was a second printing of 10,000 in April, and a third of 5,000 in May. The novel sold well enough in the first month to earn back the publisher's advance of $5,000 by mid-May. Out of trials came remarkable success where Welty had least expected it: in a novel. *Delta Wedding* drew more critical attention than any of Welty's previous books, proving that a novel was in fact considered intrinsically more significant than a book of stories. Diana Trilling, who had disapproved of some of the prose of *The Wide Net* because of what she judged excessive "stylism," found the same tendency carried to "narcissistic" extremes in the novel. She could not swallow "the narcissistic Southern fantasy" of the Fairchild clan (*The Nation*, May 11, 1946). Isaac Rosenfeld, in *The New Republic* (April 29, 1946), confessed that he could read no more than about one hundred pages of *Delta Wedding*, finding it too "dull." Rosenfeld claimed not to be put off by the Southern material in itself. He could read about Southern society, he claimed, but Welty's novel conveyed only the "sensations" of a society, not the real, credible heft of one.

One did not have to be the author of another *Gone with the Wind* to attract negative attention. Welty, a Southern writer who had never made a special cause of being Southern, found herself pushed into a corner. Her answer, in private to Russell, not to the reviewers, shows that, although she had not crusaded as a Southerner, she knew the territory over which literary sectional war was fought.

> When Herschel [Brickell] read my book he said he was not in the least surprised at the lack of understanding of the book in the reviews and that I should have expected only respect for the writing's being satisfactory, and take that for what it is worth, because I was dealing with a quality that never was and never will be understood by the North and that will always be met with suspicion and resentment up there—which I sort of subconsciously knew, and do know in people themselves—the North simply does not comprehend the South and for that reason will always cherish a kind of fury at it, it doesn't understand our delights and pleasures or even anything abstract about our ways. You aren't any more a Yankee than we are down here so there was nothing incomprehensible in my book to hang between you and it like a curtain to conceal its aim and idea. Herschel said his only regret was that he was not asked to write a review—he told me he thought it was really right and the real thing, which pleased me not only because he

> is a good critic but because he came right out of the Miss. Delta himself and knows every small thing firsthand about it. He also said he wished Stark Young [Mississippian, author of the novel *So Red the Rose*, and theater critic for *The New York Times*] had been asked to review it somewhere. And I wish you could have, so that makes three dream critics that might have changed the course of the book. In my heart I am contented because the people whose opinions matter to me are all, I believe, satisfied with the work, and I don't feel anxious on any level but the one, the one Harcourt operates on, and that mostly because they oppress you which I hope they are not doing now, with success. [April 23, 1946]

Once she had the time to read Rosenfeld and Trilling, Welty had further answers for them:

> Yes, I was pleased to see the good review in the New Yorker today [May 11, 1946]—glad Edmund Wilson turned it over to the sympathetic Mr. Basso.* He was nice to Hubert's also. Did you see the bad reviews of mine by I. Rosenfeld and Diana Trilling in the New Republic and Nation? They fussed because I didn't stay in my place as a Southern writer, and Mr. Rosenfeld's logical steps were (a) all Southern books are regional, (b) this book deals with people as if they were like any other people, therefore (c) it fails and (d) it is escape from reality, and as a kind of extra point he adds that he doesn't see how any southerner can write anyway living in such a place. The worst thing he said though was the first, that he only read 100 pages and couldn't get through any more—too dull. Mrs. Trilling said ever since my stories stopped dealing with poor white trash I have been guilty of xenophobia and narcissism. I hear there is another bad review by Sterling North (do you know in what?) but nobody has sent me that one. [May 11, 1946]

Some homegrown critics like Harnett Kane, a prolific journalist and author who specialized in New Orleans and Louisiana material,

* Basso's review of *Delta Wedding* actually is a review of three "Southern" novels: Erskine Caldwell's *A House in the Uplands* ("the most disastrous piece of feeble pretentiousness I have ever read by an author of presumably serious intentions" [89]), Hubert Creekmore's *The Fingers of Night* (a work of "complete honesty and sincerity" [94]), and *Delta Wedding*, accorded the privilege of appearing first in the review. *The New Yorker*, "Books," May 11, 1946, 89–90, 93–94.

wanted more political realism, more one-dimensional representation and straightforward doctrinal exposition on the woes of Southern politics (New York *Herald Tribune Books*, April 14, 1946). The curmudgeonly Sterling North, who wrote a nationally syndicated book review column, objected to a prose technique he considered amateurish, flowery, and obscure. North, like Kane, preferred "the larger background of political and economic feudalism" (his understanding of the way Southern society was constituted) for viewing the character and action of the novel. Orville Prescott, in the daily *New York Times*, disapproved of "private experiments with form and cryptic, elusive vaguities of style too tenuous for communication" (April 17, 1946, p. 23). Charles Poore, in *The New York Times Book Review* of April 11, gave the novel a good reception on page 1; without actually mentioning Virginia Woolf or Welty's review of her, Poore repeated some of the language of Welty's earlier review when he observed that "the light comes obliquely in Welty's writing." Hamilton Basso, whose review Welty welcomed, not only because he was a Southerner, but also because she was sure Edmund Wilson, a notorious scold of Southern writers, had been scheduled to write it, proclaimed *Delta Wedding* "as fine a novel as any contemporary American author has turned up with in recent years." And Paul Engle, who had published Welty's "A Still Moment" in *American Prefaces*, reviewing the novel for the *Chicago Tribune* (April 14, 1946), noted the subtle rhythm of world time and psychological time, of event and perception, that made the novel like a poem.

Aware and not aware, Welty continued to write. Before the reviews receded from memory she had a new story under way, but was reluctant to say much to Russell for fear of jinxing it. The novel, once finished, did not prove to be addictive as a genre. With the financial success of novel and serialization, Welty could afford to think of new directions in life and work. William Maxwell, fiction editor at *The New Yorker*, had been in to see Russell about Welty's work. Russell had been trying to make Welty's way into Harold Ross's magazine since 1940, when he had sent them "Why I Live at the P.O." After the success of *Delta Wedding* the omens seemed right for a new try.

SEVEN

Into Literary Criticism—Beyond the Novel

Completing *Delta Wedding*—the arduous work of composition followed by the reworking and retyping of the manuscript for serialization in *The Atlantic* as atomic bombs fell on Japan; reviewing galleys for the book and adding still more changes—clarified certain elements in Welty's literary practice and creed. The writer felt more confident than before that her artistic gyroscope was right, and the agent worried less than before about getting Welty "well-published." One of Russell's first moves with the novel was to argue Harcourt, at Welty's urging, out of a campaign of "prestige advertising" for *Delta Wedding* (April 8, 1946). She was not yet ready to become a celebrity or to call in blurbs from friends and writers she admired—writers like E. M. Forster, for instance, whose letter to Welty had come to the attention of Harcourt, their mutual publisher. Besides, Harcourt had charged her $165 (April 6, 1946) for changes to the galleys of the novel, and Welty was not entirely sure she liked the way the bill had come: no explanations, no apologies.

For the period of these four and a half years, from 1946 to 1950, Welty felt confident "to go where fancy takes me," not only in her writing, but also in her traveling. Russell's strong anchorage at the agency was at least as important to the wandering writer as the family home in Mississippi. She made two extended visits to San Francisco, one long vacation to New York City, the usual weekend trips, and capped the decade of the 1940s with plans for her first trip to Europe on the strength of a $5,000 advance on *The Golden Apples* and a second Guggenheim fellowship. In the midst of these peregrinations, work proved Welty's stabilizing force, and Russell kept up the gentle urging.

The signs that this writer was continuing to change and grow were the essay "The Reading and Writing of Short Stories" and the collection *The Golden Apples*: "the lecture thing and a kind of a novel (or something)." Both works are products of a new mood of confident familiarity with her "taproot" in technique, of the zest for wandering from place to place, of the development of a critical voice beginning to venture beyond the scope of the review to state the author's case. More clearly than before Welty knew where she fit, knew what her writing was to do, how it was to be produced, and at what cost. Russell too adjusted to the new conditions.

The relationship between author and agent that had begun with the decade had become, by 1950, an almost telepathic communication in which matters of business and art were transacted swiftly and surely. Welty came to rely more deeply on Russell's opinion of the stories, as she was traveling away from home and had few local readers to express opinions. As usual, each new story seemed to the author too long and unmarketable. The agent, as usual, found a way to reconcile Welty's writing and the expectations of the market. He kept telling her to keep writing, while she repeatedly apologized to him that her stories were not earning the agency any money. As Welty fretted over stories that grew longer and seemed to emerge from her typewriter only after more and more hours of unpleasant toil, Russell counseled patience. He kept emotional tabs on his peripatetic client, defused her anxiety about the stories, came through with deals that sustained the writer financially and psychologically, learned to handle business with a new tribe who had taken an interest in Welty's work (adapters for the New York stage and Hollywood screen), and simply kept the channel of communication open when the author felt so distant from the familiar.

By September 1946, after *Delta Wedding* had been published and greeted with mixed critical reviews, Welty had two stories in the works simultaneously. Russell questioned the earlier of the two to arrive on his desk. It required the meshing of two types of "reality" and he was not sure shifts from one to the other always occurred smoothly. Welty was more confident of her command of the ambiguity in "The Whole World Knows," and decided that the changes he had suggested were not really necessary.

> I don't think I know the answer to the transition question—I think I had better leave it ambiguous, because I felt it like that—I think part in the mind and part real. As you say, it doesn't matter so much, except I hate to have puzzlement creep in unnecessarily. Does it really bother you? When I was coming down in the train [from one of the many visits to New York] I felt I could hear voices like that all sad and intense, coming out from all those little places in the night, that's why it's in the first person—and I felt open to them or something. In the first person it *could* be ambiguous and get by couldn't it? [n.d.; early September 1946]

Welty's confidence in her own voice(s) overrode Russell's trusted hardheadedness. There had been a time in the not-too-distant past when Welty might have been less confident in her technique. A lesson Welty had learned in writing *Delta Wedding*: ambiguity might be the proper mode for certain experiences, obscurity might be more powerful than clarity in the right circumstances. And the lesson was materially backed up by the three printings of *Delta Wedding* to that date.

"The Whole World Knows" could survive its own technical ambiguity, its own envelope of sad intensity and creeping despair. The second of the two new stories, "Golden Apples," later to be retitled "June Recital," was still in the early stages of drafting; there were as yet no connections between the stories except the coincidence of being written consecutively. It is intriguing to see in hindsight that the darkest point in *The Golden Apples* came first. The story fraught with images of disintegration, of descent, of forlorn human hopes preceded the overarching integrative force of the work as a whole; the several voices of "The Whole World Knows" preceded the single integrating voice and vision of Virgie Rainey in "The Wanderers."

Russell sent "The Whole World Knows" to *Good Housekeeping*, with whom he had had some dealings himself. They had taken three brief pieces of his: one on conversation ("The Art of Conversation," May 1944); a second putting forward a parental reading policy for children ("Let the Children Read What They Want," March 1944); and his argument for planting memorial trees for the deceased rather than cluttering up the landscape with stone and marble markers ("The Memorial Tree," March 1945). He knew that *GH* paid well. He hoped, he wrote to Welty, for a "slab of big money for you—if it can be got" (September 11, 1946). Russell was more aware than anyone else that Welty could still not live solely on the income from her writing, and he was eager to move her up to the level where that was possible. Welty was ready for the move too, and let Russell know by way of encouragement that she had had a note from William Maxwell at *The New Yorker* asking for a story (September 6, 1946). The next stop, for Russell planned for all contingencies, was not to be *The New Yorker* but *Harper's Bazaar*, for Mary Lou Aswell had not had "a Welty for a long time"—for four years, since "The Winds" in August 1942. Russell's plans were, of course, all right with the author. She relied on Russell's professional judgment, but knew her story, and the market, by now and cultivated no hopes for a "miracle" at *Good Housekeeping*: ". . . it's fine with me whatever you want to do with the story—send it anywhere you take a notion, but it will be an overwhelming miracle if any of the rich folks take a fancy to it—" (September 30, 1946).

The second new story, Welty reported, proceeded slowly and might, when finished, give Russell yet more practical difficulties: it was going to be a long one. She was still glad to be working on "Golden Apples," for it was rooted by the allusion in its title to their shared admiration for Yeats's poetry, an admiration that had been renewed in Russell's recent work on *The Portable Irish Reader*. Finishing

"Golden Apples" stretched out a few weeks beyond Welty's original estimate.

> I'm late sending in my story—but now hope to get it in this week. Afraid it's going to run between 45 and 50 pages—will that be a difficult item? This is larger type, though, so it's not as long as I think it is. [October 7, 1946]

It was an additional ten days before the manuscript, "entirely too long for the contents" (October 17, 1946) and "messy" with last-minute changes, for Welty had decided to give the characters new names, was sent up to Russell. Russell wrote back that he liked it; scheduled for some minor surgery, he had little time to be more detailed. Welty wished him well in the hands of the doctors, was thankful for even a brief note, and fretted—as usual—about the length of the story. She had recently read and admired a story by Caroline Gordon, "The Captive," "41 pages long and every one *compelling*" (September 16, 1946).* The problem of length was on her mind frequently that fall.

> I'm glad you liked the story. Do you think the title too fine? [At this stage the title had been expanded to "The Golden Apples of the Sun."] I thought maybe I should call it "The Window and the Door," but yielded in the end to the more beautiful one. I expect it needs more work—did you feel it? I knew the form, length, would be the devil for you, and am sorry for such untoward length—but it kept getting longer the more I worked to get it shorter. [October 28, 1946]

After "Golden Apples" went off to New York, Welty's writing schedule made room for the first of two long visits to San Francisco, where her friend John Fraiser Robinson was studying languages and working at writing himself. Robinson's own story "Room in Algiers" had been published in *The New Yorker* that fall (October 19, 1946) and Welty

* Probably as reprinted in *American Harvest*, eds. Allen Tate and John Peale Bishop (New York: L. B. Fischer, 1942), pp. 445–88. Tate and Bishop had also selected "Petrified Man" for the anthology.

Doubleday's party at the Murray Hill Hotel to celebrate the publication of *A Curtain Green and Other Stories*: from the left, John Woodburn, Welty's editor; Welty; Ken cCormick, chief associate editor at Doubleday; Eugene Armfield of *Publishers Weekly*, ere the photo appeared in the November 22, 1941, issue; Robert Simon, president of rnegie Hall; Diarmuid Russell (standing); and Henry Volkening

"Flowers are getting more and more in my thoughts these days. But I can't speak about them in th office because the others don't know much about them. Henry, who is a remarkably fine and intelligen person, didn't know what a pink was when I mentioned the name to him today and it filled me wit horror that a human being and a good human being should not know this. I am going to get him ou in the country to dig and plant flowers so that he can really know what the earth is like. Besides will make him a better critic of the one acre and a cow sort of literature. I am already relishing th thought of seeing him lift his face to the declining sun while he wipes the sweat off it with an earth stained hand while I recline in a comfortable chair watching his labors. Having done this many time myself I feel noble and generous enough to share these pleasures with those I like. And of course a Tor Collins tastes better after one has worked a little" [DR to EW, March 20, 1941]

Russell (left) and Henry Volkening, dressed for work on the soil, at the Russells' home early 1940s

Russell the weekend painter sketching near his Katonah home, early 1940s

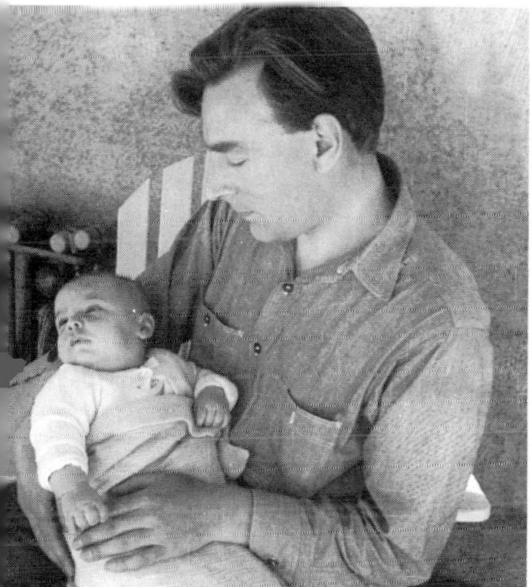

The benevolent parasite and his family in the early 1940s: (from top to bottom) wife, Rose Lauder Russell; Diarmuid and son, William; with daughter, Pamela

John Woodburn, Welty's first editor, at Doubleday and then at Harcourt

John Robinson, dedicatee of *Delta Wedding*, in about 1948

Edward Weeks, editor of *The Atlantic Month[ly]* from 1938 to 1966

ary Louise Aswell, fiction editor at *Harper's Bazaar*, in Paris, 1949–50

William Maxwell, editor at *The New Yorker*, who had been after Welty's fiction for that magazine as early as 1942

Herschel Brickell, fellow Mississi pian, who edited the O. Hen Memorial Award *Prize Stories* vo umes in which several of Welty short stories appeared

Kenneth Millar, author of detective novels under the name Ross Macdonald and a longtime friend of Welty's

Elizabeth Bowen, in County Cork, Ireland, in 1951. *The Bride of the Innisfallen and Othe* *Stories* is dedicated to her

decided to visit him for "a few weeks" to test her writing luck away from Mississippi and to test a relationship that had survived one long crisis—the war—and was faced with a second: two writers sharing the same career.

Welty left for San Francisco in November 1946. By New Year's, Robinson, new friends, and the Northern California climate had succeeded in keeping her in San Francisco longer than she had planned, first in small hotels, then in a sublet apartment. The closest of the new friends were Art and Antonette Foff, a writing couple and clients of Russell's, whom Welty liked immediately. Antonette Fereva Foff was trying her hand at detective novels, a minor obsession of both Welty and Russell, but she did not have any luck at publishing until 1955, when *The Year of August* appeared under the pseudonym Anton Fereva. Her husband, Arthur Foff, had published one novel with Harcourt in 1945, a collection of stories with Little, Brown in 1946, and was in the last stages of a second novel when Welty met him. Foff's second novel, *Glorious in Another Day* (Lippincott, 1947), caused Welty no little worry; local bookstores in San Francisco, and local reviewers, knew nothing of the book as publication day approached, and the reviews themselves, when the book finally appeared, varied from negative to noncommittal. Welty wanted to help, but could only watch, knowing that she, as a writer, would probably not have been comfortable with the sort of help she contemplated arranging for Foff. San Francisco provided an unforeseen lesson: watching another writer suffer the anxieties of trying to live by writing made her more aware of her own progress and prospects. She wrote to Russell often with cautious requests—not so much for help for their friends, but for guidance on what sort and degree of help might, in his opinion, be appropriate. Russell was sympathetic but hardheaded; he did not "cosset" his flowers, he could not see how writers were well served by similar "kindness."

The two writing couples would have enthusiastic literary discussions, Welty wrote to Russell, usually beginning on the pretext of dinner and sometimes lasting late into the night. On New Year's Eve, 1946, the evening started with a spaghetti supper, escalated to a discussion of Faulkner's *As I Lay Dying*, and was memorialized in a postcard to Russell mailed at three the next morning, festooned with stamps of various denominations (one upside down) and carrying cheery greetings for the new year in the styles of Faulkner's Vardaman Bundren (from Robinson) and Hemingway (from Art Foff). Welty, the steadiest head among the four, addressed the card. She followed up the postcard, which must have arrived in New York to some puzzlement, with an explanatory letter promising to send Russell the Modern Library editions of *As I Lay Dying* and *The Sound and the Fury*. "You can read them some sweet day," she hoped (January 2, 1947).

Welty liked everything about San Francisco—the company she had found in John Robinson's friends, the sunsets, the fog, the ocean, even the batty landladies she encountered in her quest for a cheap apartment or furnished room. She planned to stay longer than originally planned, found an apartment to sublet, and asked Russell to send her income tax figures (a meager sum) out to San Francisco for filing by January 15. The ultimate test of San Francisco, however, was how well she and Robinson could write out there. "I hope to write a story in such a nice quiet place [the sublet]—it will be a lot better than the room in the boarding house—those women that ran it were really weird though" (January 4, 1947).

The nice quiet place for writing was only $14.50 a week, but even at that rate Welty could not think of staying indefinitely. Welty enjoyed the "room of one's own" she had established almost as much as she did the beautiful city. "It's hard to stay inside at all," she wrote to Russell (January 10, 1947). "The weather is beautiful—sunny every day, and not so cold—what you'd call between mild and fresh, I think. I go out to the ocean a lot. Yesterday walked over [to] Land's End, do you remember that wild path hanging over the sea?" The news that Harold Ross had turned thumbs down on "Golden Apples" did not discourage the writer in such surroundings. She asked wryly if the quirky Ross himself had spoken to Russell or had used a surrogate; the odd ways of the editor were well known beyond the offices of *The New Yorker*.

Welty was more deeply concerned for John Robinson's success, for he was depressed, needed money, and had set for himself a "good long list of things [to be] written" that, without the buoy of more critical and financial recognition, might sap his stamina for writing in general. Welty had learned from experience how necessary a little recognition could be; every check, even the "snippets" of fees and royalties payable only in postage stamps that Russell forwarded, confirmed her claim to being a writer. Russell did his best for Robinson, and probed gently about Welty's own plans by inviting her to return to Mississippi by way of New York (January 23, 1947). The cost, Welty replied, would be too high. She had decided to stay in San Francisco a little longer. The sunsets were beautiful—she took the streetcar to see them every afternoon—and as yet there was no pressure to surrender the apartment. "I write on a story in a 'composition book' and cook—you should taste my biscuits" (January 29, 1947).

The story she was writing would eventually carry the title "Music from Spain" in its second version. In February 1947, it was called "Dowdie's Guilt" or "Guilt," tentative titles that both author and agent found a bit pretentious. The story itself had given Welty trouble; in this case, length seemed not to be the central complication, she just did not know whether it was good or not. Since "Guilt" was the first story she had tried on "foreign soil," Welty had no automatic sensor to indicate its authority. In early March, Welty wrote that she hoped to finish it before returning to Mississippi; she had begun to feel guilt of her own that a planned two-week visit had stretched out to five months (March 11, 1947). A bogus story about a killer tornado that had wiped Jackson off the map—told by a stranger Welty had met in the San Francisco post office—had added to her anxiety about being away from home (February 9, 1947). Her story stretched out too, like the visit itself, to thirty typed pages, but still seemed manageable.

By March 13, Welty still had not started for home, although she was fully prepared; she had been seeing things and places and friends for the "last" time since the first of the month. Edward Weeks at *The Atlantic* wanted cuts in "Golden Apples" before he would consider it, Russell reported, but Welty hesitated to add that worry to her intellectual and emotional inventory. The story had been written long ago, and she was not enthusiastic about looking it over once again.

> I got your letter with Weeks' letter, and it's not much of a surprise, is it? My own feeling, without reading the story over, as I haven't it, is that regardless of its awkward length for magazine purposes, it still ought to stay long. Maybe I'd make changes in it, but I doubt if I'd whack on it much, so the same condition would still prevail for sales. It's obviously no good for sending around, so why don't you maybe let Lambert Davis [former editor of the *Virginia Quarterly Review* and now her editor at Harcourt] see it? Would his opinion on it be worth having as the story is now, maybe to ask him if he'd like it as is for use in a book of other stories? Meantime I guess I could go over it—but I'm pretty sure without looking at it how I feel about length being necessary. This doesn't make me feel I want to do a *novel* about those people though. All I want to be sure of is that the length it is is valid for the story's sake, if the story stands up all right the way it's written.
>
> My new one ["Guilt"]—I just don't know about it. It's nearly all typed now, but I feel it may be something to put a reader off. I don't know whether to send it to you as is, or wait a while and see before I let you see it. I'll probably send it. [March 13, 1947]

Sending it would have to wait at least another ten days, for farewells to San Francisco and unsuccessful attempts to set up a visit with Katherine Anne Porter, who had moved to Los Angeles to work for the movies, kept her from her typewriter. Russell, the diplomatic agent who still cherished hopes of recruiting Porter to his agency, had more or less suggested a visit. He also feared a rift between the two writers over the novel *Delta Wedding*. The "pupil" had finished a novel before the teacher.

> I think KAP is a little miffed. Her own novel has been talked about so much and there you are, in a sense her protégé she feels probably, who has had the impudence to bring out a novel first, almost going behind her back. I don't know where she got the idea she has, probably her own subtle way of slighting the work. If you want to miff her more in your next letter you can say that the Modern Library wants the

> book—which is true because I had lunch with Bennett Cerf and he asked me could he have it. But it won't work out because the type page of DELTA won't fit the Modern Library page. [January 31, 1947]

There was more joy, though, at seeing Danny Kaye perform on stage or Pierre Monteux conduct the San Francisco Symphony. By contrast the San Francisco story seemed "depressing," to write and to contemplate. John Robinson had read a version and had found it so.

> My story will probably get to you in the week. John's read a version of it, I've done it over a few times, and thinks it's depressing, so I warn you. It is, too, but I hadn't realized anything but the work part of it, until I got to typing it up and can hardly drag through it—sounds worse every minute, doesn't it? I'll be anxious to know what you think of it, for I did a lot of hard work on this baby. [March 23, 1947]

Three days later, on the eve of her departure for home, Welty sent the story off to Russell. Begun in San Francisco and sent on its way just hours before she herself left, "Music from Spain" is a sort of oblique diary of her stay.

Russell found the new story "all right," and dispatched it to *The New Yorker*, a new volley aimed at the citadel of Ross. Welty herself had moderate expectations; anticipating rejection, she had already prepared a new copy, with significant changes, on the train home from California. The changes, "mostly cutting," she wrote to Russell, were for "the long visit with Mr. Weeks" that she was sure was to come (n.d.; March/April 1947). By the seventeenth of April the new version, under the title "Music from Spain," was through the typewriter, shorter (!), and on the way to Russell. The train ride home had provided the occasion for another story, one she had barely begun, a story that needed the seasoning of a trip "down into deep country." "Deep country" usually meant a visit to the Delta; the story Welty was contemplating was "Moon Lake."

Weeks took the author and the agent by surprise; he bought "Hello and Goodbye," a "little story" Welty told Russell she had forgotten (April 21, 1947). She was, in fact, just a little embarrassed by her good fortune. So low was "Hello and Goodbye" in the author's ranking that she omitted it from *Collected Stories*. When the galleys arrived from Boston, Welty requested a more modest layout. The design *The Atlantic* had drawn up, she wrote to Russell, "just looked too fine, like a grand hat on a little unpretentious body. I guess they don't have a heading saying 'An Atlantic Little Do' or the like. They shouldn't have bought this—they should buy John's [Robinson's] story, 'Rite of Spring' " (April 26, 1947). But Weeks's "typecasting" of Welty still held sway over his editorial opinion; he liked the palpably Southern stories (like "Hello and Goodbye") Russell sent in and was ready to champion those rather than publish the longer, more complex work set outside the South. As strong and sincere as his support was, it was also inflexible. "Hello and Goodbye," about a local reporter who interviews a small-town beauty pageant contestant, has the feel of much earlier Welty—as if, for instance, she had written it immediately after "Petrified Man."

Revisions of "Golden Apples," provisionally taken by *Harper's Bazaar*, its third stop, occupied most of Welty's time during the spring. She labored to make the story shorter and more compact, but as the work went on, she gradually lost confidence that she could succeed in revision: "[Hope] to be sending 'Golden Apples' up next week—I believe it's better but God knows if it is *shorter*" [n.d.; late April 1947]. About the only part she could be sure was getting shorter was the title; "The Golden Apples of the Sun" had become simply "Golden Apples."

> The long story is not going to sell to anybody—it's just as long as ever, though I hope it's *better*. Maybe it will be a few pages shorter, but nothing to make it usable to a magazine. I ought to tell Mary Lou that too—it wasn't till I started copying the revised MS that I saw the pages running neck and neck. You'll think it improved though, I believe, and hope. Will be anxious to know. [May 15, 1947]

When the retyping was finally finished, by the end of May because of several interruptions, the story was eighty-one typed pages rather than the original seventy-three, its length when it had come back from Aswell. Welty was tempted to think of it as a novella, and proposed to Russell that "Golden Apples," "Music from Spain," and the story she had under way ("Moon Lake") be considered a book. She knew that "Golden Apples" as revised "will be no use to a magazine though it's a better story now, I hope" (n.d.; late May 1947). And she wrote Russell to let Mary Lou Aswell know that she no longer expected the commitment of the *Bazaar* to be binding on either party. In fact, she repeated to Russell several times that she could see no way the story could be cut now—in her own way she was warning him not to put it out to an editor who might have to ask for cutting. Russell agreed. The problem of a confrontation over cutting was mooted when Aswell, again carrying on the battle for fiction, got *Bazaar* to accept the story as it was.

> You're a wonder-agent and I'm collapsed at the thought of a magazine parting with that much cash [$750] for a story.—Quit apologizing! it lends a further note of unreality. It's good that Mary Lou wants the story—I'm pleased about it—and am so glad it's rewritten and not cut both. [June 25, 1947]

Just as revisions of "Golden Apples" were nearing completion, Welty accepted an invitation to participate in the Northwest Pacific Writers' Conference, to be held in Seattle at the University of Washington in August. Her duties included attendance at the sessions and one address to the conferees. The fee was to be eight hundred dollars, a sum that could finance a second visit to San Francisco. What she did not foresee was that "the lecture thing" would give her more trouble than most of her fiction. The night before she left for Seattle, the speech was not complete.

> Leaving tomorrow night on my trip, but still have to put my little talk together—it's done in little pieces but not pinned together yet or shortened. How I wish you could look it over first. . . . This speech

has demoralized me, it is worse than getting a book review done by a deadline. I'm talking about The Bear by Faulkner and The Fox by D. H. Lawrence, and some by K. Mansfield, Chekhov, Stephen Crane, H. James, etc.—just telling them in the main to write out of passion not calculation, to learn sensitivity and perception and not worry. Rather simple. [n.d.; late July 1947]

Simple to talk about in a letter, but not so simple to write, especially when "Music from Spain" had finally come back from Weeks—a disappointment to Welty because she had really wanted Weeks to like the story—and the new story ("Moon Lake") had to be left literally in "patches and bits" (n.d.; late July 1947). Welty toiled over the "little talk" up to the final moment, and even threw out expendable pages on the podium in Seattle, "like largess as I read." Reading it was no simpler or more enjoyable than writing it. Russell got some of the details:

When I gave my lecture I read it, having worked so hard on it, and there was a big auditorium and a faulty microphone—they say it is notorious for not working right, so you can imagine I had a hard time and so did the audience. [August 8, 1947]

Her debut as a critic was not as inauspicious as she might have imagined from her side of the microphone. The *Seattle Post-Intelligencer* had been following the conference in a spirit of local pride for the entire week. Welty spoke on a Wednesday afternoon, the third day of the conference, to an audience of nearly three thousand. "Gathering intellectual steam with every successive speech," according to the *Post-Intelligencer* reporter, the conference hit a high plateau with Welty's address.

Russell and Welty shared a wary distrust of literary criticism in the academic way, and Welty wanted Russell to review the speech and assure her that it was indeed "rather simple" communication that preserved the passion she had advocated for the writer. She wanted her address to be more akin to making jelly than to the "ingrown and tedious" palaver that criticism could often be. The model of clarity and moderation she had implicitly in mind was E. M. Forster, whose work she greatly admired. She had had a note from Forster in the spring, which she shared with Russell:

> You'll be pleased to know I'm the recipient of a wonderful letter from Mr. E. M. Forster. Could you think of anything that would please me more, here it is, delighted to copy out every word for you to see. Dear Miss Welty, Finding myself in your country, I feel I should like to give myself the pleasure of writing you a line and telling you how much I enjoy your work. The Wide Net, with the wild and lovely things it brings up, have often been with me and delighted me. I am afraid that I am unlikely to have the good fortune of meeting you while I am over here, since my itinerary keeps to the North and the West. Still, there are meetings which are not precisely personal, and I have had the advantage of one of these through reading you, and I would like to thank you for it. With kind regards and good wishes. Yours sincerely, E. M. Forster. [May 15, 1947]

"The Reading and Writing of Short Stories" owes much to Forster's *Aspects of the Novel*, and did much to shift Welty into the role of critic.

Its fate, however, has been to be pared down from the moment of first public reading. At every stage, "the lecture thing" has been hacked at and shortened. Now it seems only respectful, and revealing, to remember it as it was originally: the statement of an author just entering a kind of maturity, intent to go on with her own writing "as fancy takes me," secure in a modest fame and sure of critical coordinates for locating herself in the ongoing enterprise of reading and writing the short story. She had found her bearings among a cosmopolitan group of writers—Chekhov, Woolf, Forster, Yeats, Lawrence, Crane, and others—and she meant to state her position in that company.

As a general rule, Welty preferred to draw a line between the analytical (critical) and the synthetic (creative) faculties of the imagination. She did not, in her speech, "deny the powers and achievements of good criticism" (*SS*, 8), primarily because the living audience was largely composed of English professors ("Lit. not 'creative writing,'" she told Russell), but also because she herself, by virtue of a stint as a staff reviewer for *The New York Times* in 1944, was a card-carrying critic. The distinction she strove for, then, lay between "blind . . . ingrown and tedious" story criticism and the kind that illuminated and revealed "large wholes and . . . subtle relationships" (*SS*, 8). That much conceded, the author still would not grant that criticism, "or more strictly analysis," could reveal how a story was written, or recover the "passion" in the imagination in which and because of which the story originated. "The arrow of creation" flies only once and only in one direction, she wrote (*SS*, 9). Moreover, "analysis," a word she preferred to "criticism," was fraught with scientific resonance and characterized the critic as poised to kill and dissect the "passion" at the heart of the story.

Even so, a writer of Welty's subtlety could suggest the arrow's flight by reading her favorite authors' stories with the attention of an accomplished and passionate critic. Lawrence's "The Fox," Hemingway's "Indian Camp," Crane's "The Bride Comes to Yellow Sky," Mansfield's "Miss Brill," and others received the separate tributes of well-honed attention, just enough to illuminate the hearts of the stories, but not so much as to shrivel them. The only critic she felt comfortable quoting was Forster.

"The lecture thing" also provides insights into the workings of Welty's creative imagination, for in one section, later excised, she discusses rival "validities" in art, a rivalry that bears crucially on the issues in creative imagination she had to resolve in order to write *Delta Wedding*. The artist, she explains, has to negotiate between different ways of seeing, logic and reverie.

> Which brings us to the interesting disparity between integrity—which emerges in a story as truth or validity—and plausibility. The validity of everyday life is notoriously dependent on certain things. The validity of a story—not quite so notoriously—depends on things of an entirely different order. There's no need to hedge about—the two validities

> conflict. That is, there was never any question of their tallying. [*SS*, 48]

The point she is trying to make is not so simple as the one the local reporter carried away from the auditorium: "Plausibility doesn't matter . . ." (*Seattle Post-Intelligencer*, August 7, 1947, p. 14). The two validities do not negate each other, as Welty herself once seemed to fear as she wrote "Livvie." Five years earlier, "the validity of a story" had seemed not only different from "the validity of everyday life" but subversively hostile to it. The two logics Welty sought to reconcile in the writing of *Delta Wedding* embedded themselves in the lecture as deep lessons not yet fully learned about the complex mutuality of the divided human imagination. She was trying to demonstrate how difficult it actually could be to live with both, draw from both. The months of thinking and working, the rereading of Woolf, then writing the novel herself were remote prologue to "The Reading and Writing of Short Stories," and the essay in turn the justification of that experience. Once it was said out loud—that the plausibility of life and the plausibility of story need not tally—Welty seemed free to continue with the present stage of her own work, as yet veiled behind some promise of unity and coherence.

She was anxious to hear from Russell about the speech, but the response would have to wait for retyping. Her text was in such a state that it was not fit to be read by anyone but the author herself.

> The lecture thing wouldn't make a Harcourt job, I think—not so pretentious to be published alone. [Harcourt did just that, using the essay for their Christmas greeting to the trade in 1949.] But I would like you to read it for your comments. I did work so damned hard on that thing, harder than a story. I'm no critic—even your pressure-from-firecrackers plan wouldn't turn me into one. [August 17, 1947]

From Seattle, Welty went down to San Francisco for another visit with John Robinson, who was then living in Berkeley and attempting to earn a living by writing. She also planned to try writing away from home again; one of her first purchases after settling into a "clean and cheap" hotel right around the corner from Chinatown was a new "Royal with good type." "Am real pleased," she informed Russell (August 22, 1947). Pleased and deliberate too, for her plans also called for establishing the free and independent writing enclave she had recommended to the Seattle audience: "When we are in the act of writing we are alone and on our own, in a kind of absolute state of Do Not Disturb" (*SS*, 3). She summarized the plan for Russell, figuratively submitting it to him for approval.

> I thought of renting a little place (if I can get it) for a few months—settling in with my typewriter—if I can, I really wish you and R. [Rose, Russell's wife] could take off and visit me—think of how nice it would be. —As to the next story collection—I'm not sure I want the book to come out yet. Do you understand, for I think the stories in it are all of a certain kind, or of a long, ruminative, etc. turn of thought—and it would be nice to have one or two other kinds in a book—do you agree? The longish story I started in Jackson ["Moon Lake"] doesn't look so good to me now—I worked on it yesterday—it may or may not turn out—but I want to send you a few others before a book is put together. Let me know your feelings on it. [August 22, 1947]

The ensemble of the future *The Golden Apples* is adumbrated in this letter to Russell; in her mind's eye it resembles a gallery exhibiting works in various styles by the same artist. Perhaps the "other kinds" she distantly imagined turned out to be "Shower of Gold" and "Sir Rabbit," not long by the standards of the others in the book, nor of "a ruminative turn of thought." Welty also spent a part of each day typing and repairing the speech (a sort of catalogue for the exhibition), only five or six pages at a stretch, since a back problem made sitting at the new Royal an ordeal. The rest of the day was devoted to fiction—"Moon Lake"—or the "rumination" that seemed to her the key to the meaning and arrangement of the new stories that were presenting themselves to be written.

At around page 30 in the lecture, she wrote to Russell, the thought occurred to her that *The Atlantic* might be interested even if it turned out to be longish. Then again, the "ash can" might be "the best destination" for the whole thing. "I feel less and less amiable toward its being printed, and you may feel downright opposed. Well, we'll see" (September 2, 1947). It had also occurred to her to offer it a second time as a lecture to the class in writing at the University of California Extension just around the corner from her hotel; she could use the cash for the rent. She went no further with the plan than mentioning it to Russell (August 27, 1947). The more time the speech demanded, the less joyful the time became. Like a tiresome relative, the text called forth obligation, not pleasure.

If Welty had tried to find a quiet sanctuary in San Francisco, an "absolute . . . Do Not Disturb," the literary crew was not about to oblige. She was famous enough to be missed, to be talked about in her absence. Browsing in a bookstore she picked up *Prize Stories of 1947: The O. Henry Awards* ("to see if I took any of the cash but I didn't"). Not only had she not won any of the prize money ("The Whole World Knows" had been given an Honorable Mention), her failure to do so was remarked by the editor, friend Herschel Brickell. Echoing Weeks's baleful comment of a few years earlier, Brickell issued an all-points bulletin for Eudora Welty:

> The editor would hesitate to rank the present Welty story with her prize winners, but he found it admirable in its complete realization of setting and atmosphere, and also touching in its portrayal of the pathetic—not tragic—plight of its betrayed husband still in love with his wandering wife. . . . It is interesting to note that Miss Welty has published only the two short stories ["The Whole World Knows" and "A Sketching Trip"] in the past two years. [xv]

"What does he mean, do you think?" Welty inquired of Russell. "Does he think that signifies I'm on the downward path, as he says this story is not as noteworthy (or something) as the earlier stories that have won prizes. I just wasn't sure if he was shaking his head over me or not? I shall ask him next I see him" (September 2, 1947). Success had, after all, its minor trials, one of which was being asked, "What have you done for us lately?"

The apparent retreat was not as significant as Brickell had guessed, for the author was on the outskirts of the realization that her next book would be an innovation, something as yet dimly understood but promising to express her evolving artistic ideal more fully than previous work. Patience was in order; rumination would produce the answer. The competing ideas of novel and collection played like mirages in her thinking.

> About the book next year—I also had a letter from Lambert [Davis]—one thing I don't know about is my long story Golden Apples [later "June Recital"]. I've had ideas about *that*—maybe fruitless ones—that it might be really a novel, in which case I wouldn't want it coming out as a short story, prematurely. And it would make up the bulk of a short story collection. The ideas haven't been solid enough to speak about yet, but it's one reason why I don't want to do anything definite just at the moment about a collection. In the same way it seemed to me perhaps the short story I've been working on just lately ["Moon Lake"] may be a part of a novel too—hadn't realized that, till yesterday on a cable car. I got the idea and they clanged the bell like mad. [n.d.; early September 1947]

The plan of *The Golden Apples* had not revealed itself fully yet, but with each letter to Russell the writer seemed closer to a vision of the book.

"Moon Lake" "intruded gently" into the drudgery of typing the speech (September 17, 1947) and Welty just went ahead and wrote it out. Too long, about fifty pages, she wrote to Russell, but she was not alarmed that at that length Russell would not be able to sell it. The slow pace of the new stories, as they made the editorial rounds, did not worry the author as much as the yet unresolved question of just what ultimate vision of completion and wholeness drew her onward.

> Why do I write such long things, what happens? What gives? as they say around Times Square. And what? Nobody has yet bought the S.F.

> story ["Music from Spain"], have they? That really makes me think less of editors (said the author)—I do think that a good story. Probably nobody thinks I have any business writing outside the precincts of Miss. Pure nuts to them. [September 17, 1947]

When she finally mailed the manuscript of "Moon Lake" to Russell from San Francisco (September 21, 1947), she confessed that she was still not sure what it was or how it fit, if at all, into a larger work.

> Sure, I'm confused too, but you see from the story that it looks like a sector from a kind of novel (or something) all about Battle Hill [later, Morgana] people, for Loch Howard [later, Morrison] from Apples is the boy scout, and Jinny grows up to be the wife in Whole World Knows—doesn't she? It does sound suspiciously like that conglomeration you threatened, holding everything under the sun. Anyway, as a story I think this will stand, and I finished in it what I began—so let me know what you think. I hope you like this story. It looks bad for length, doesn't it? Maybe there will be the end of a cycle, ending the way it began, with you working like hell to sell my stories but nobody buying a one. [September 21, 1947]

With the conglomeration or novel, or something apparently headed toward several possible finished shapes, the author worried more about individual stories and their own internal dynamics. The genuinely arresting thing at this point is the sense Welty has, and voices to Russell, that her writing career might actually have flattened out after four books, only one of which (*Delta Wedding*) had sold very well. As the recent stories grew longer and left her with more questions than answers, Welty felt her relationship to Russell, and to authorship, had come full circle—from obscurity to obscurity in seven years, a biblically significant cycle. As rejections came in with the homeless "Music from Spain," Welty suggested to Russell that he send it to "the little magazines," the ranks from which she had climbed, with Russell's help, just a few years earlier. "Moon Lake," she feared, would find no kinder fate.

> I'm so curious to know what you thought of my story called Moon Lake—maybe it left you cold as cold. Also, please will you tell me any ideas this gives you or robs you of, concerning a collection? If I did do a novel, think of all the *work* on these stories to be thrown to the winds—I am enough of a hoarder of energy to be sorry for that. Because I'd have to just start over with a novel. [September 27, 1947]

Before Russell's reply got to San Francisco, Welty had finished another story, "Shower of Gold," in all but the typing. It was written in one day ("What speed, for me! Something is probably wrong with it" [October 1, 1947]) and on its way to New York just a few days later. Typing it, Welty had begun to see all the connections it seemed to sprout toward the others she had already completed and sent away ("The Whole World Knows," "Golden Apples," "Music from Spain," and "Moon Lake"). Prompted by Russell's letters to her, in which he had suggested a collection of interrelated stories to avert the shagginess of a "conglomeration," and mindful of her own suspicion that the long and ruminative stories required a counterpoint, Welty was beginning to give those ruminations some steady and directed guidance. The idea for a suite or portfolio of related stories, rather than the looser omnibus form of the first two collections, began to stir toward clear definition. Some stories, like "A Sketching Trip," seemed "way back in time and feeling" (September 27, 1947), and therefore ineligible for the new book. After "Shower of Gold" had been typed and mailed, Welty took a day or two to formulate the idea of the new book, then wrote to Russell:

> I think now that a novel isn't necessary—that would be, at this point anyway, an artificial way for me to go ahead with the material. So why not just go my own way, writing the stories as short stories, the way they occur to me, but letting them go on and be inter-related, but not inter-dependent, just as they actually are in my head. Just let the material take its natural course with me, and not force anything on it but just have the flexible plan ahead of a number of additional stories with these characters—the stories might move far from Battle Hill, and up and down in their lifetimes, anywhere and any point a story might

> want to take them up. Not have plots and strings tied to them except for the short stories' sakes. But hope that some over-all thing would emerge from the group that might have a significance greater than that of the stories taken one by one—by virtue of accumulation and familiarity and so on. Do you think a book like this would have value, that is beyond a random collection of stories? I believe if I went ahead with this in mind, then the trouble I've had trying to get too much into a single story would lay off me, for I'd know I'd have another story and another chance to get it into their [the characters'] lives if I needed to. And yet wouldn't have the burden of the novel, with all that tying up of threads and preparing for this, that and the other. It sounds like the lazy man's book, but—and maybe it is—but I still think it is the fitting use of the material in my head. I *don't* have the pressure to write a novel, just the pressure to go on with some people that stay in my head. It will be fine to hear from you on the subject. I feel myself that it would interest me. So tell me your feeling. [October 6, 1947]

Antagonism to the novel, which had earlier shown itself as antagonism toward "the publishers," had evolved into a kind of aesthetic position at least partially articulated in "the lecture thing." Novel and plot had become synonymous, and plot meant work as boring to contemplate as to do—"that tying up of threads and preparing for this, that and the other." Plot, as the writer had come to see it, obligated the flow of her imagination, sapped the passion of writing, marred her personal engagement with "some people that stay in my head." Concern with plot, with the necessary but flat equations of fiction, had made some of her recent stories sluggish and overweight, at least in the author's mind; the obligation "to get too much into a single story" had drawn out "Moon Lake" and "Music from Spain" and the others as well, made them "drags" to type, "cold as cold" to read (she feared), and less likely to be sold. If she could just let the obligatory aspects of plot distribute themselves as they would through several stories, then the burden could be gracefully shared and no single story would buckle. Writing would still be work, but not the calculated chore she felt inimical to her creative imagination. This "plan" would leave the finished stories with a sense of immediacy and fresh presentation, as free from strings as the impressions of them that lived in her head.

"The lecture thing" had helped to bring Welty to this summit treaty with plot. Cramming for the lecture, Welty read in Forster's *Aspects of the Novel*, "a book any writer can adore," that the elevation of character above any and all other aspects of the novel is the fiction writer's art. Extending Forster's remarks on character, Welty wrote that "character belongs, connects, in its practical use in stories, to the vastness of our secret life, which is endlessly explorable; whereas situation [plot], no matter how strenuous or intriguing, is without escape superficial. For there seems to be no limit to the resources of bringing human character out into the written word" (*SS*, 24). Plot and situation she identified mostly with the novel, the work of obligation; character and the revelation of the secret resources of human life she reserved for the short story.

The short stories she had recently completed, she told Russell, gave her trouble insofar as they pitted situation *against* character. She had acknowledged that a certain amount of practical weight must be supported by any story; but the story achieved finish, excellence, and passion in proportion as it held the practical to the minimum. A story was a way to make the secret life visible and shareable; it was the only means available to mortal beings who desired "complete revealing" (*SS*, 24). Virgie Rainey, who emerges in the finished stories as the eventual recipient of a totally revealed self—her immersion in the river in "The Wanderers" seems to signify her rebirth as a person reconciled to the full knowledge of herself—seems to be the figure for which the writer's imagination strove: always on the move, not so much toward a set objective as just moving for the sake of life, Virgie embodies the writer's will to revelation over representation.

Welty tried writing without conscious awareness of plan, and had to get along without much public praise. Brickell's remarks in the preface to the 1947 O. Henry collection verged on unpleasant surveillance. The lack of notice, as long as she was satisfied that her writing was going somewhere, troubled her less than it had in the past. "So I keep getting rejected," she wrote to Russell in late October

1947. "That's all right. I'm going right ahead as I please, even if all the stories come back—not very good for *you*— So far I haven't done any further work on the stories, on paper, but maybe after I get a hand in the dirt at home it will give me new thoughts."

Welty left California around November 1, 1947, and after a stop-over at the Grand Canyon, impressive for its pure age (rocks that had millennia ago lost all qualities and had become "just matter"), arrived home in Mississippi to a remarkable autumn and some reminder of the business end of her career.

> Here I am in Mississippi, and thanks for the letters here and I got the two big checks [one from *The Atlantic* for "A Sketching Trip," the other unidentified]. You are probably having a holiday today and maybe the lilies had come and you got them in the ground. How are the azaleas looking? Yes, if the camellia doesn't act right this year, burn it. It has gone far enough. I came back and looked over some of the antics of mine while I was away, and think the whole tribe should be taught a lesson. Maybe they can hear this low rumble of discontent if we practice it around them, and will heed, fearing the guillotine.
>
> The Italian Wide Net—how much better is the Mediterranean title of Primo Amore—is here and I didn't know I could write so beautifully, I opened the book and loved the way it seemed to sound. So admire myself in other languages. [November 12, 1947]

•

She and Russell quickly struck an agreement with the Levee Press of Greenville, Mississippi, an enterprise owned by Hodding Carter, author and editor of the *Delta Democrat-Times* in Greenville; Ben Wasson, author and collector; and others, to print "Music from Spain" in a limited edition. Russell had surrendered none of his prejudice against special editions voiced when Doubleday had proposed such a format for *A Curtain of Green*, but the story had bounced back from so many places that he relented and allowed Levee Press to have it.

"The speech" was about to be sent on its rounds, and Welty was skeptical of its chances. Russell chose *The Atlantic* for the first stop. Welty washed her hands of literary criticism: "[Let] Mr. Weeks do whatever he wants if he wants to, but I don't want to do a thing more to it, I'm tired of it and don't know any more *to* do with it at the moment" (November 17, 1947). Weeks did eventually buy the essay, edited it into two parts, and published it in *The Atlantic* in February and March 1949. Welty's indifference to criticism was only temporary; she and John Robinson had floated the idea of an anthology of short fiction (Allen Tate and Caroline Gordon had asked for a story for their anthology, *The House of Fiction*) for which the essay would be the introduction. After several postponements, the Robinson/Welty plan expired.

Work on the stories was suspended too; Welty estimated she could get back to them after Christmas. Household work, logjammed since her departure for Seattle in the summer, was brightened by one unexpected piece of news. Admiration in England continued; Elizabeth Bowen, a writer whom Welty admired, had written a complimentary review of the English edition of *Delta Wedding* (The Bodley Head, 1947) and Russell had had a copy typed and mailed to Jackson. Bowen had found Welty's stories "flying particles of genius" and predicted that *Delta Wedding* would "in time come to be recognised as a classic" (*Tatler and Bystander*, August 6, 1947). When some voices, like Brickell's, asked where the writer was hiding, it was reassuring to hear others, from whatever distance, acknowledge that she was still among the living.

Nineteen forty-eight came in with arctic cold fronts. It was too cold to type. "Maybe with spring things will turn out better," she wrote to Russell from the depths of a cold blast that had frozen her camellias "stiff as glass, poor things" (February 8, 1948). He wrote back that it would be a better idea to finish the collection a bit sooner, cold or not. And Welty, taking the hint, made her way to the typewriter by the middle of February.

Her first chore was to finish a clean copy of "Music from Spain" for the Levee Press printers. Usually the work of retyping a story that was already finished in her mind was a daily grind that she measured in pages and hours. Retyping "Music from Spain," however, was the occasion for a rare dividend, an unexpected communication from the postponed plan for a collection of interrelated stories. She had expressed the hope to Russell, in her letter from San Francisco, that some of the *future* stories "might move far from Battle Hill" (October 6, 1947). Now one of the finished stories turned out to be from there.

> Yes, I agree that what I'd better do is finish my book. In fact I felt cheered by your letter and maybe that's why at 11 o'clock last night I began writing a new story and finished it up right then in bed. I'd already typed solidly all day getting Music from S. ready for Levee (wrote the whole damn thing just about over—but really I think *this* time I got it right—and the key is, you'd never guess, the little man in it is from Battle Hill and who he is is one of the MacLain twins—don't faint. Cleared everything up.) [February 18, 1948]

Russell did not faint, but he was worried; at first he could not see the San Francisco story as part of the Battle Hill collection. He had always known it as "the San Francisco story." He was concerned, too, that Welty, in her long mood of blithe unconcern for plot, had become too prone to take the "lazy man's" exit. But she tried to assuage his concerns.

> Don't be worried about the story being one of the series, for maybe I'll have *two* books of them—anyway, if enough good stories turn up in the series to make a book of them, we can certainly go ahead without Music. And if enough don't turn up or they ain't good, then we'd have to wait anyway. I should have foreseen it would be part of the others, because what worried me about the leading character in all the work I'd done was his lack of any taproot. All there was to do was put two and two together, him and my little group, and I had him by the tail, or was closer. [February 28, 1948]

There was, suddenly, good reason for the confidence. Weeks had expressed serious interest in "the lecture thing" and even more serious interest in "Shower of Gold" (a check for $600). "Sir Rabbit," after a solid day of typing on "Music from Spain," had come as another dividend from Yeats, by way of "Leda and the Swan." The decision to trust her own fancy and pace seemed finally to be reaching a real destination, one that had always satisfied her and now seemed to be placating editors.

As each new story was finished, Welty had put off thoughts about the whole. But readers on the outside were more and more insistent; few could see any obstacles to finishing a collection in the spring of 1948, with more to follow. Lambert Davis at Harcourt had even suggested a volume of criticism with "the lecture thing" leading off. Welty wrote to Russell with some last-ditch reservations:

> About the stories and Lambert, yes, I'd just as soon leave all that until I have to. Don't know yet what I will do with the book—and don't need the money particularly. But I don't think I'd let him get the idea there's anything novelish about the book, for I'm pretty certain he'd be misled—I intend to go on as fancy takes me and maybe the nucleus of the stories still to come, so what I've done so far doesn't define it. [March 14, 1948]

Her campaign of patience continued. Welty was content to wait for the nucleus to appear rather than force it by imposing a plan: that would be too much like a novel. A month later, she wrote to a patient Russell, "Haven't written a word."

Most of the early summer was spent in New York and Jackson working with Hildegard Dolson on a revue to be called *Bye Bye Brevoort*. Russell, Welty knew by now, was just a little impatient with her, for he was immune to the attractions of the theater and Welty had always been charmed. She meant to enjoy the interlude, however, and tried to keep her agent's frowns to a minimum.

> Dear Diarmuid, don't you and Henry feel bad about not liking those skits—I felt that I came away leaving us all sad and hot sitting there. It's really helpful to know what seems funny or not at this point—and situations and lines must both be funny, or neither will be, really. I'm going to finish the rest of the stuff, best I can, and after that go back

> to the first ones—meanwhile seeing if the Little Theater people can bring any enlightenment by speaking and doing some of it for me. Anyway, it all being such a shot in the dark, everything helps and we'll all just hope that somewhere along the line the stuff will get useably funny. [n.d.; early June 1948]

The revue was never produced, although one sketch was salvaged and staged in New York during the same theater season *The Ponder Heart* played on Broadway.

When Welty returned South, the stories started working in her imagination again. She knew the collection would be good, she wrote to Russell when she got home, no more like the revue than the train is like the landscape it crosses.

> Well, I'm working on a story, just couldn't help it—started coming in my head so fast while I was riding along one day I was writing with one hand and driving with the other, and I was so glad to see it—hope to send it to you in the week—it may, too, connect too closely with the others—and somehow, now, I'm more pleased with the idea of the book of the stories than I was. Maybe prematurely. You might when you see this make a little composition of them all in your head and see how it looks, I mean an over-all picture? [n.d.; June 1948]

For the rest of the summer, revue and stories alternately claimed the writer's time. The revue was allocated strictly limited blocks of time, "3 weeks only . . . and be done with it," while the stories "started coming in my head so fast" that they made a shambles of all agendas. By midsummer the pattern of interrelated stories was set, and a new one came complete with connections to the others (early July 1948). This story was to be finished by late September and called "The Hummingbirds"; it wove together the dramatis personae of the collection at the funeral of Katie Rainey, the teller of "Shower of Gold." By the time Welty sent this story off to Russell, she was sure, more or less, of the "over-all picture the stories make" and waited only for the energy and the time to bring the whole together (September 24, 1948).

Through October the writer kept her distance from the stories. *The Hudson Review*, for whom she did a review of Faulkner's *Intruder in the Dust* (she had met him in May: "the best writer going today," she wrote to Russell [n.d.; May 1948]), was considering "Sir Rabbit" and accepted the story in November; *Harper's Bazaar*, one pole of the Russell-Aswell alliance, was just about to take "The Hummingbirds" in spite of its length. But Welty was not ready to bring herself into the work of pulling the potential whole together. "It's simply that I hate reading over my own work—" she explained to Russell, "throws me into a low state and I postpone any proof reading, etc." (October 18, 1948). By mid-November she still had not started, and Russell had to remind her that time waits for no writer, man or woman. The "poor old tired revue" still obliged her to work on it; she took some time to apply for a Guggenheim and wrote a letter to *The New Yorker* objecting to the obtuseness of Edmund Wilson in his review of *Intruder in the Dust*.

> I answered Edmund Wilson's New Yorker review the other day but don't imagine Mr. W. will answer *me*. I waited a little while to get cool enough and maybe I waited *too* long—maybe *too* cool. I felt like heating it up again. But did you see it! Believe I'll send you my answer just for to show you, I kept a copy and would you send it back? I felt you would agree. Must get to work. [n.d.; mid-November 1948]

Russell did agree and spoke a word to Gustave Lobrano at *The New Yorker*, who scheduled the letter for publication in "Department of Amplification" in the New Year's Day, 1949, issue of the magazine. Ironically, Welty entered the pages of *The New Yorker* (January 1, 1949), as a critic rather than as a story writer.

Levee Press finally got "Music from Spain" into print and into circulation. Welty had dedicated the volume to Herschel Brickell, who had wondered about her writing fate while she was working on the story. Charles Poore's New Year's Day (1949) review in "Books of the Times" made only one embarrassing point: the musical phrases used as running heads on each page could not be played. The little book attracted not just collectors and devoted readers willing to pay more for one story ($3.65) than they would for *The Golden Apples* ($3.00) when it was published eight months later. Maurice Evans and Eddie Dowling, two established Broadway actor-producers, both expressed interest in "Music from Spain"; for a moment there were visions of large sums in option sales. Welty was rooting for Dowling; she had admired his production of *The Glass Menagerie* with Laurette Taylor. "Old stodgy Maurice Evans bores me to death on the stage, so grand and *fixed*, might as well be a statue," she wrote to Russell (February 18, 1949). Neither deal came to fruition, but the signals were clear that Welty's fiction and the stage were converging.

The semiofficial sabbatical of the fall and winter of 1948 was abruptly called off when Harcourt asked for the manuscript of the story collection by March 1. Russell had made a good deal, an advance of $5,000 and the usual royalty rate, even though Welty had not had a book published for more than two years. It was hell-for-leather getting the stories cleaned up and retyped. As usual, Welty wanted to rewrite them all, but she held herself to concentrating only on the longer stories. She had help in the typing: her sister-in law and John Robinson, who was in Mississippi between moves in a nomadic life that was to take him to Mexico and eventually to Italy, took shifts. Even with the extra hands she had to have more time. Russell got an extension of the deadline, and the manuscript finally was dispatched to New York in mid-March 1949 for a mid-August publication date.

By the time the whole of *The Golden Apples* (the title, as usual, had not yet been determined in March) was bound and sent off, Welty's sense of what the book was *not* was clearer than her sense of what it was. She wrote to Russell with a position to pass on to Harcourt, who she had the impression wished to advertise *The Golden Apples* as a novel. Having just struggled through the stories themselves and through a long essay staking her claim to the short story, she was unwilling to give all that up for what she considered a sales convenience. Though pleased that Russell had obtained a handsome advance, she asked him now to stand up for her on what seemed to be Harcourt's condition for publication:

> I'll turn it down if that's the catch and maybe they'll turn back the book but nothing changes the book into a novel or play or poem, if it's a book of related stories, then it is. (Maybe we could call it something like "Variations on a Portfolio" or something from the other arts where such groupings are more common?) [March 28, 1949]

Harcourt, Russell, and the author had no need of a summit meeting over the genre of *The Golden Apples*. They simply avoided the issue, at least in all the advertising, by billing the book as a "chronicle" of the Mississippi town of Morgana.

Most of the issues of contents, arrangement, titles, and production schedule were settled by early April 1949. Much had been completed in a very short time. "And they gave me a Guggenheim!" Welty exclaimed to Russell (April 3, 1949). With her second fellowship (worth $2,500 this time) and the advance from Harcourt, Welty felt "positively and horridly rich."

Her favorite among her books (Prenshaw, 42) stands as the tangible symbol of almost three years of peripatetic writing that—except for the speech and the revue—was more exciting than any she had done at such a stretch before, of a period of her life spent circulating among many friends without the confining sense of appointments to keep; of recognition from two English writers (Forster and Bowen) whom she admired highly; of once more overcoming the appearance of fading powers and weak marketability. As the reviews of *The Golden Apples* would testify, Welty was no longer a "promising" writer; she was well on the way to becoming a "master."

EIGHT

The Three Lives of The Ponder Heart

Until the tribe of producers, playwrights, play doctors, theater reviewers, actors, and other show folk homed in on *The Ponder Heart*, author and agent had enjoyed a relatively sane existence in the world of letters. They had had only the familiar eccentricities of the literary world to deal with. Only infrequently, and at a comparatively low insanity level, had the would-be adapter petitioned for options on Welty's work. Russell, at first, handled all the requests from individuals and teams with plans to adapt his client's work for another medium. In the late 1940s there had been one such female team, dubbed "the girls" by Russell and Welty, who toiled at a dramatic version of *The Robber Bridegroom* but had brought forth nothing when their option expired. Welty and John Robinson had worked on a screenplay of "the fantasy," hoping to interest a Hollywood studio, perhaps Disney Productions. Henry Volkening, Russell's partner, who had Hollywood connections, was ready to handle the negotiations. Not until 1974, when the Acting Company successfully mounted a musical version of *The Robber Bridegroom*, with book and lyrics by Alfred Uhry, did "the fantasy" finally reach the Broadway stage. When the hoopla over *The Ponder Heart* started, even before publication in 1954, author and agent were not totally prepared for the madness of success.

Welty, by her own confession, cherished an incurable love for the curtain going up on anything. Her memoir, *One Writer's Beginnings*, depicts a childhood highlighted by movies and stage plays; while a student at Columbia, she had spent enough time in New York theaters to know several of the buildings by heart. She had, in her mind's eye, seen popular actors and actresses in her own stories. But the close connection of theater and story had always gone deeper in the writer's imagination than, say, reading Jamie Lockhart, the bandit-hero of *The Robber Bridegroom*, and seeing Danny Kaye. In *One Writer's Beginnings*, Welty couples "the dramatic instinct" with the storyteller's lifework:

> It was taken entirely for granted that there wasn't any lying in our family, and I was advanced in adolescence before I realized that in plenty of homes where I played with schoolmates and went to their parties, children lied to their parents and parents lied to their children and to each other. It took me a long time to realize that these very same everyday lies, and the stratagems and jokes and tricks and dares that went with them, were in fact the basis of the *scenes* I so well loved to hear about and hoped for and treasured in the conversation of adults.
>
> My instinct—the dramatic instinct—was to lead me, eventually, on the right track for a storyteller: the *scene* was full of hints, pointers, suggestions, and promises of things to find out and know about human beings. [14–15]

It is revealing, in the context of the Broadway experience with *The Ponder Heart*, that, although Welty closely connected lies, tricks, jokes, and stratagems (all unsavory activities) with the theater, she bore no moral prejudice against it or the people involved—until they had actually done something lowdown to her, her work, or her friends. Her partner, Diarmuid Russell, seems not to have been so lenient.

Welty was fascinated by the artificiality, the fantasy, the intimacy, and the communal (and temporary) alliance within a cast and between cast and audience. She could not see herself as performer; she disliked delivering papers and public readings from a sense that center stage was an inappropriate spot for her. Writers should be invisible; actors were another breed. But she could write for a cast of actors, and could vicariously share their hectic, uncertain effort. One of her earliest letters to Russell in 1940 mentions a play she would like to complete.

Diarmuid Russell, on the other hand, had, as Henry Volkening put it wryly, something of an aversion to the stage.

> What'll we *do* with Diarmuid, by the way, back stage. He has a thing, as you know, on theatre people. . . . Of course, I feel the same way, though less shall we say fervently. Still it'll be a hell of a lot of fun, dear (after all, we must fall into the lingo), and thanks very much for offering me a part-time job as a Peacock. From that vantage point I can count the house right through my beak. [HV to EW, January 7, 1954]

Russell entered the "strange world" of the theater with ingrained circumspection and reluctance. His past as son and deputy to A.E. suggests a few reasons for his suspicion of theater folk. He had no cause to remember his father's contacts with the theater fondly.

Russell's father had had a serious falling out with Yeats over the direction and character of the Irish theater under the pressure of Irish nationalism. Their differences lingered even after A.E.'s death; Yeats could not be persuaded to deliver the eulogy at A.E.'s funeral, even though Diarmuid, in one of his last duties as son, had tried to prevail upon him. A.E.'s own play, *Deirdre,* did not achieve much fame, and in fact brought upon him a sort of condescending scorn from younger and more realistic dramatists. One of the dissenters from the consensus on A.E.'s lordly sway in Irish letters was such a playwright: Sean O'Casey. Privately and publicly, O'Casey had no great regard for A.E. Whereas A.E.'s admirers found him wise, good, and genuine, O'Casey, in a private letter of 1951, called him "the richest humbug I have known" (*Letters*, II, 815). To drama critic George Jean Nathan, O'Casey wrote:

> To me, A.E. has less of the poet in him even than Clarence Mangan. . . . I hardly think anyone has read A.E.'s poems [more] often than I; and I've always thought very little of them. [*Letters*, II, 925]

Publicly, the nastiness between O'Casey and A.E. broke out in 1930. Diarmuid Russell had left Ireland and *The Irish Statesman* by then and was in America, but the controversy followed him from Dublin. O'Casey took aim at A.E. in retaliation for the latter's negative opinions of modern art. A.E. had, O'Casey alleged, let it be known that he thought painters such as Matisse and Picasso and Cézanne should be suppressed for their corrosive effect on younger artists, an opinion that put A.E. head-on against the prevailing winds of modernism. A.E. held, and his son Diarmuid (in such statements as his to Welty on the fallacy of believing that the gratuitous stroke ever brings unity, see pp. 70–72) concurred, that painters ought to operate by natural "laws" derived from the real world. Matisse, Cézanne, and Picasso had, to A.E.'s mimetic eye, swaggered into the history of art proclaiming exemption from the laws of realistic representation. O'Casey upheld the rebels and sniped at A.E., charging him with the rankest form of patriarchal censorship, and said as much (and more) in letters to *The Irish Statesman*, of which A.E. was editor. When A.E. declined to continue the exchange of letters in the *Statesman*, O'Casey sent copies to *The New York Times* (February 6, 1930; March 20, 1930), thus opening up an American front in his revolt against A.E.

The public clash was revived in 1949 (not too many years before the Broadway career of *The Ponder Heart*) with the publication of one volume of O'Casey's autobiography, *Innishfallen Fare Thee Well* (1949). O'Casey repeated his bill of indictment, labeling A.E. "Dublin's Glittering Guy," neither artist nor original political wise man. As close to the publishing world as Diarmuid Russell was, he must have been aware of O'Casey's attacks. The attacks came from a playwright; playwrights worked in the theater; the theater should be held at some distance and in some contempt.

Russell also—and perhaps more fundamentally—distrusted the collaborative nature of theatrical "works." From what he knew of Broadway he had distilled a negative opinion of "adapters," producers, directors, stars, theatrical agents, and the legion of hangers-on. Adapters he thought little better than editors of anthologies: both strove to get rich on the work of *real* writers. Adapters, to their limited benefit, paid more for the privilege and so drew less of Russell's contempt. Of producers and directors, he confessed to his client when the negotiations for *The Ponder Heart* grew serious, he knew too little. All he did know he had picked up from reading squibs in the *Times*. He did not read *Variety* until *The Ponder Heart* was in production and generating box office receipts. Rather than serve his client ill in such business, Russell engaged from the start a co-agent from the Society of Authors' Representatives to handle things from the Broadway side. Of stars he knew only what he read in the papers, and seems to have subscribed to the belief that any adult who acted on the stage was psychologically arrested or flawed. Russell was, when *The Ponder Heart* began to head to Broadway, admittedly unprepared for and temperamentally biased against the "strange world" he and his client were about to enter. On the verge of glitz, the agent still insisted that one must reach a "personal estimate" of the character of the person with whom one struck agreements. At least two complications were inherent in that position: Russell carried, dissolved in his being, elements of a bias against theater people as a tribe; and the collaborative nature of theater made it necessary for him to reach satisfactory personal estimates of several individuals in each deal, some of whom he was never to meet. Although he became, almost in spite of himself, enthusiastic for his friend and client's play once it seemed a viable event, Russell never felt comfortable with stage business, and expected cast, crew, sets, receipts, and the theater itself to evaporate at any moment.

The roller coaster started slowly, almost imperceptibly. After *The Golden Apples*, Welty's career resumed its established pattern. One of the first stories she "finished" and sent to Russell after her return from Europe was "The Burning." "The Burning," still evolving in early September 1950, seemed to Welty to be "funny, maybe" (September 8, 1950). Mary Lou Aswell, who had not yet returned to *Bazaar* after a leave, had been reading an early version (September 20, 1950) that, Welty confessed, might be a "sinner in obscurity." Obscurity, however, was no longer a sin that made the author cower in her study. Welty finished typing and revising "The Burning" about three weeks later and sent the story up to Russell with a revised opinion; now it impressed her as "not *that* funny—wish it were" (October 11, 1950). She had used the story, she told Russell in her next letter, to make a point about symbolism.

> I got the story back safely and have been doing work on it—mostly organizing and deleting, but of course I went and added something. I came right out and said my say about symbols, in the story—that things are symbolic—not the author. A mirror's very nature is a symbol. Then I cleared up Phinny I hope, and thereby by both things made my African slave the complete savage—Phinny made a kind of rite for all the characters but in the end it was the slave who carried it out. [n.d.; October 1950]

Russell liked "The Burning," though, in spite of the symbol talk, which, he reiterated in one of his last letters to Welty (February 2, 1973), always gave him "the willies." He did not deny symbolism; he just thought it lay too close to the actual life-giving heart of art to be safely discussed: "It exists but really unconscious of the writer, like a quality of voice."

He immediately sent "The Burning" to Mary Lou Aswell, back at work at *Bazaar*, who liked it too and signed it up for the magazine. Payment, up now to around $700 a story, would "be along in the usual slow Hearst manner" (DR to EW, October 24, 1950). In the meantime, Welty reported to her agent, she had had another letter from a "theatrical man" inquiring about the availability of options on her works. She forwarded the letter to Russell for his advice. It was succinct:

> Sure, tell the theatrical man that you've often thought of a play, but don't make any more commitment than that about the play or to him especially. Maybe the whole American stage will be asking you about plays and there's nothing like a little competition. [September 22, 1950]

The inquiry had come from William Archibald, who was curious about the state of the rights to *The Robber Bridegroom*, a book he found full of " 'natural' poetry." He was interested in adapting the fantasy as a musical (he had had some success on Broadway in that line) and wanted Welty to collaborate on the book. The offer seemed sufficiently serious to Russell that he investigated.

> I have made inquiries and find that Mr. A. is quite reputable and well-known. He had a play on Broadway recently THE INNOCENTS which ran for some five months and before that he has had other plays and musicals on Broadway. So he's what might be called a professional rather than an amateur playwright and must be assumed to have a fair amount of competence. [December 14, 1950]

For Russell to call Archibald a professional was a grudging acknowledgment from the skeptic. *The Innocents*, Archibald's stage adaptation of Henry James's *The Turn of the Screw*, had opened the previous February (1950) to respectable reviews. Brooks Atkinson had called it "one of the distinguished events of the season" and had ranked it "with the best things on the stage" (*NYT*, February 12, 1950). Although a five-month run was not a gold mine, it was a decent financial showing. Russell decided that cautious progress was in order.

Russell, in December 1950, was satisfied that he and his client could go ahead with the request for an option. He needed only one additional piece of information—the all-important "personal estimate of the person we will be dealing with"—for he knew he was on the outskirts of strange territory "where troubles and disagreements are apt to arise" (December 14, 1950). Russell, however, was careful to spell out for his client what she might expect from "collaboration" of the sort Archibald had requested. His suspicion and his interest in preserving the work of his client were uppermost.

> P.S. On this point [the request that Welty work on the book with Archibald] if you were to decide you wanted to give him a free hand it would have to be *free*. You would have no control over the final

script. You would be allowed to see it to make what [?] you might have. But they could be rejected and you could not reject or veto any script because people of Mr. A.'s standing would not enter into an agreement if in the end all the work they did could be thrown aside.

The last option on *The Robber Bridegroom*, taken by two amateur dramatists, had failed to produce a viable script, but Welty was instructed to remember that the failed script had in several ways also failed to represent her book faithfully. The pain of seeing her work misrepresented in a public theater had been avoided. Russell was scrupulous to point out that Archibald was in a different league, and that dealings with such professionals would not be literary business-as-usual.

Welty, because of her fascination with the theater, was less cautious. She was inclined to see the adventure rather than the complications.

I think it might be fun to have him do the play, as far as I'm concerned he can take it away. I don't think I'm a good collaborator to begin with, and Robber's old with me, and then he must be an able person and he seems to have his ideas already; so I shouldn't meddle. Oh I'd like a look at things he does, just to see, and if you think him a nice man I'd take a chance on his respecting my feelings to some extent. Let me know what you think of him and what happens. [n.d.; mid-December 1950]

Such a trusting attitude would, when the professional attention shifted to *The Ponder Heart*, suffer an initiation by anguish. In late 1950, there were no warning signs. In any case, the author had distant, speculative hopes for another trip to England and Ireland in the spring—"a nice dream"—and inquired about the money that might come her way from the deal. Her dreams, though, were close to the earth: "I don't refer to when it's a hit on B'way!"

Option money did not pay Welty's passage to England in March 1951; a $1,250 advance from Harcourt on an untitled book of unnamed stories did, but left less per diem than the comparative Farouk-style riches of her previous trip. Welty had "Circe" and "The Burning" finished and earmarked for the promised book. One long story estimated at ten thousand words and two shorter ones were in the works; she had taken notes and rough manuscripts of the three with her. She finished one, "The Bride of the Innisfallen," in England and sent it over to Russell. "If you can't sell it don't worry," she wrote from London. She was already at work on the other two, between stretches of travel from the Cotswolds to Brighton and back to London, where she had a flat from June 1 through mid-July, when it would be time to think of coming home. Serious writing would have to wait until she set up in the London flat.

Russell liked "The Bride of the Innisfallen," and wrote back that he was going to *The New Yorker* with it. He was confident that, with support from Gustave Lobrano and William Maxwell, he could finally get this story through the legendary inquisitions set up by Harold Ross. Welty wrote an alternate ending for the story, thinking that several paragraphs about Ireland at the close of the story sounded too much like travelogue, and the story went to Ross. For the present, travel and writing in England and waiting to hear from *The New Yorker* displaced all thoughts about theatrical gold.

"The Bride of the Innisfallen" came back to Russell from Ross, not exactly rejected, but covered with the "annotations" for which he was widely known. Welty was faced with a transatlantic dilemma. A fat check from Ross (the story eventually sold for $2,760) could make her trip more enjoyable. Still, she vaguely resented the Rossian manner and, also vaguely, felt uneasy with what *The New Yorker* as an institution had come to stand for in the literary world.

> Thanks for the letter reporting on Maestro Ross. I suppose I could look at the story with his annotations, just for the ride anyhow. It is a temptation about the money, which I could use, but I feel badly also about Mary Lou's not having it if she likes it, since she's printed what she calls more "difficult" stories and now here is one that would maybe not cause a battle on her part to get printed. . . . I do think their [*The New Yorker*'s] stories stink so—it sort of prejudices me, but I shall try to look at it dispassionately. [June 5, 1951]

To further complicate the matter was the real opportunity—the first one—to win a big commission for Russell & Volkening. In the confines of Bowen's Court, where she had gone at the invitation of Elizabeth Bowen, Welty wrote with a sort of Celtic gloom and resignation to her agent:

> I got your nice letter here today and was interested that we both felt the same about the New Yorker and the story. I also had a feeling influencing me that this would be—if the story did go to and sell to the New Yorker—the only time I ever brought in a decent commission to my agents—I don't even know how decent! But probably something will stop it—probably me, if and when I see Mr. Ross's questions— He is coming up extra hard against something he couldn't know, wouldn't care about either—that it's my favorite story I ever happened to write so I am specially sensitive and tender on the subject. (Will you see about the questions?) About the worst person to advise somebody like me on snagging the money, whether or no, is somebody like you— We will neither one ever end up rich. [June 13, 1951]

The anticipated problems with the editorial ax of *The New Yorker* filtered away with the intercession of William Maxwell. By mid-July Welty was back home, where the temperature seemed permanently parked over 100 degrees Fahrenheit. But there were compensatory events: "That stupefying New Yorker check came. . . . You were right about it—it was big" (n.d.; August/September 1951). Welty wrote from an air-conditioned hotel room in New Orleans (the Monteleone), where she had gone seeking refuge from the heat. She could sleep and write in comfort there. After Bowen's Court, the plunge into a Mississippi summer was a drastic shock. The temperature did not moderate until the fall.

By October Russell had his own dramatic news of a sort. He had been asked by Dodd, Mead to select and edit "a monstrous selection" from the prose works of George Bernard Shaw. Before consenting, Russell wisely made an estimate of the project: "I went in to check how much prose there was and he certainly must have been the most prolific writer of the last couple of hundred years. . . . He must have had a quite frightening energy" (October 11, 1951). There was Russell's Irish literary pride, his natural admiration for a man who could remain so steadily and dauntlessly at work, and the necessity of financing a child at boarding school in the coming year. He took on the massive reading and editing project. Welty now switched roles and became the agent's constant supporter. Her letters voiced encouragement, and she returned to Shaw's plays to put herself in a helpful mode. The heavy dose of drama conveniently prepared both writer and agent for the excursion into show biz that was waiting in the future.

Prose fiction, however, still occupied Welty's immediate attention. A "long story" she had begun in England, transferred to New Orleans in the heat, and brought back to Jackson was still unruly and mysterious. In mid-October it seemed to her "a *novel*—but short, I pray—which involves me in *plot* at this late date— Just a heap of yellow pages looking at me now" (n.d; mid-October 1951). Before the mass of material could disclose its nature any further, Welty had a visit, over Thanksgiving, from Elizabeth Bowen, in the United States for a lecture tour. Bowen arrived in Jackson after being "stranded in, of all desolate places, Butte, Montana" (n.d.; late November 1951). Her flight did not arrive until after midnight Thanksgiving night. Welty traveled with her to New Orleans and to Shreveport, Louisiana, where Bowen gave literary lectures. Welty calculated that her friend had given about fifty such lectures over the length and breadth of North America: "I don't see where all the energy comes from, but she's got it." Both agent and author had firsthand examples of indefatigable Irish literary energy, and they both felt as lazy as slugs. Bowen's visit was capped when the two went up to Chicago for a lecture, and Welty's Irish story, "The Bride of the Innisfallen," partly written and revised at Bowen's Court, was published in the December 1, 1951, issue of *The New Yorker*.

When Bowen left, Welty could once again turn to the burgeoning long story, still hoping "this story stays within bounds of a long story and never is a novel" (n.d.; November/December 1951). The plan as she saw it, close to Christmas, was to finish in one "little stretch of manual labor," then let it cure while she worked on one or two other stories. Russell, steeping himself in Shaw, thought her plan a sensible one. They had both pledged to work harder with the recent examples of industry before them.

The "little stretch of manual labor" stretched on into the new year, 1952, and pushed hard up against spring. But Welty was happy with the story.

> I've been doing nothing but work, work, work, but I love this thing I'm on. Still don't know what it may be, but it's really a story extended everywhere though compressed a good deal too. It's in pins and scratch-work now, but soon the typing-up can start. Say it's about a hundred pages long—a guess—will it go sensibly into a book with The Innisfallen, Burning, and that little one about Circe if I use that? That will sure be the long and short of it. [n.d.; mid-January 1952]

Interruptions came first with Robert Penn Warren's visit to Jackson—the first in-person meeting between the two. They found immediate common ground in a shared fascination with the *annus mirabilis* of Mississippi frontier history, 1811. Welty had written "First Love" with the miraculous winter as background; Warren used it similarly for *Brother to Dragons*. Katherine Anne Porter came to town to lecture next, and stayed for about a week. Welty still kept May as the target for a New York visit with completed work in hand.

Another story—"a little tangent-one"—came before the long one was finished. And some commission work for *Bazaar*, "The Abode of Summer," shouldered its way into the schedule by paying "a noble sum" (April 30, 1952). "Kin," the surprise, was mailed up to New York about a week or two before Welty herself made the trip. As usual she was worried about the length—not so short as she had estimated, but it seemed "good" as she let it go. Russell dispatched it right away to *The New Yorker*, where William Maxwell took it in hand.

Since Mary Lou Aswell had left *Bazaar* in the editorial shake-up following Hearst's death (in the early fall of 1951, before a decision on "The Bride of the Innisfallen" could be made at the magazine), the Russell-Aswell alliance was crippled. Fortunately, William Maxwell and *The New Yorker* appeared on the scene. Welty's long and difficult stories found a new ally where she was inclined to suspect a cold eye. While the author was in New York, in May 1952, she took "Kin" to Maxwell's office for an editorial conference. Only when she was back on home ground did Welty decide for certain that the *New Yorker* editing had been for the good.

> I read over the story the next morning after I got it [with editorial notes and suggested changes], in the relative cool before the vapors of heat rose up, and thought it sounded all right—the changes made that long day in Bill Maxwell's office were to the good and for clarity, and the first part's better packed in now. [June 23, 1952]

During the early 1950s, when Welty was feeling her relationship with Harcourt Brace "not too sympathetic" (November 5, 1949), Maxwell entered and, for the several stories published in *The New Yorker* ("The Bride of the Innisfallen," "No Place for You, My Love," "Kin," and "The Ponder Heart"), picked up the editorial trust that Aswell had had to relinquish and that no one at Harcourt (since Woodburn's departure several years earlier) had earned. Brendan Gill, Maxwell's colleague at the magazine, acknowledged Maxwell's editorial genius, "the means by which he makes other writers' stories more nearly their own than they know how to make them" (162). About William Shawn, Ross's successor in 1952, Welty was a bit more fearful, always suspecting that he plotted, as a permanent habit of his editorial mind, to cut stories. Not in the case of "Kin," however; it was accepted, after the session with Maxwell, "length and all." Another "fabulous" check ($695) dropped like manna from heaven (June 16, 1952).

Encouraged by the success of "Kin" and unscathed by the fiery furnace of *New Yorker* editing, Welty felt comfortable deciding that the long story on which she had been working for so long had to be dropped. "Some of the writing's all right, the work's honest, but the impulse behind it was in a mistaken direction or something. I don't mind throwing it away. I ought to know by now to think better before I write—anyway nothing's lost—discovered rather, maybe, I don't believe I ever failed quite that badly" (June 23, 1952). Russell gently interceded and Welty postponed burning the "failed" work. A few weeks later, she had begun to think it might be a "cluster of separate stories" after all (n.d.; June/July 1952). She returned to it, but only in her spare time, for she was hard at work on two other stories, "one funny and one strange." By July 20 the strange one, a "sort of ghost story" ("No Place for You, My Love"), was through the typewriter and on its way to the agent.

Russell was quick to respond:

> I thought this new story quite lovely, and sort of mysterious, both in the heat and the ride, a curious dreamlike affair with the effect on me that something was hovering in my mind ready to be said. But it is good and holds together wonderfully, just right. I'm sending it off to Bill Maxwell to secure, if we can, some of the money from their coffers, for I'd like to get your coffers built up some before we send any stories elsewhere where the money will be lesser. Yet, later on, with your permission, when you are comfortably padded I would like to forgo some of The New Yorker's big money to have some stories appear elsewhere. And, of course if The N.Y'er do want this new story you must be suitably adamant about changes. I can't believe they will often offer suggestions to make things better, just little minor things. [July 23, 1952]

Once again *The New Yorker* coffers opened: a "huge, fantastic check" ($1,610) came in return for "No Place for You, My Love." There was no anxiety over cutting or other changes (August 27, 1952).

With the "ghost story" successfully placed, Welty concentrated on the "funny" one through the fall and winter of 1952. Monthly checks from Archibald and his collaborator, Baldwin Bergerson, continued to come in, but there were no actual progress reports on their adaptation of *The Robber Bridegroom*. "Do you think they're working on that thing, or just throwing their money away? Still, I'm not their aunt," Welty asked Russell just before Christmas, 1952. Russell's selection of the Shaw prose was published that fall, and one review in particular infuriated Welty.

> Although he [Russell] keeps to biographical data or the kind of observations anyone who can read Shaw can surely make for himself, his comments are inept and his writing amateurish. (*NYT*, December 7, 1952, p. 34)

Now the writer turned partisan. "The dog," she wrote to Russell; "the idea of his just setting about to do you harm" (n.d.; mid-December 1952). Russell seems to have been unperturbed; perhaps he expected no better so close to the "strange world" of the theater. The renewed memories of the O'Casey bitterness were only three years old.

Coincidentally, the immersion in Shaw had prepared Welty and Russell—although neither could have known it—for the impending theatrical roller-coaster ride with *The Ponder Heart*. Shaw, Russell noted in the introduction so haughtily dismissed by the cur of a reviewer, was the consummate professional dramatist: "He was a practicing playwright himself, involved in the whole business of writing plays, casting them, aiding in the production and, since Shaw was a first-rate business man, interested in the whole financial background" (*Selected Prose of George Bernard Shaw*, p. 11). Russell would feel a yearning for such expertise in the years ahead.

His client closed out the year with a surprising pop of political involvement. The fall of 1952 had been an election season, nationally and in Mississippi. There was a referendum on whiskey in the state and the first Eisenhower-Stevenson campaign in the national headlines while Welty was working on the funny story about Uncle Daniel, later to be called *The Ponder Heart*. In December, the editors of *The New Republic* asked Welty to contribute to a collection of New Year's greetings to the defeated Democratic candidate. Others asked to contribute were John Steinbeck, Lewis Mumford, Elmer Rice, Marshall Field, and Mark Van Doren. "I'm the only lady," Welty observed, "and where did they get me?" She responded with a three-page letter to Stevenson, of which *The New Republic* printed only the final three paragraphs (January 5, 1953). In the unused part of her letter Welty confessed to a political ignorance unchanged until Stevenson's campaign:

> The moving fact emerged for us that the voice of the passionate intelligence speaks to the whole range of the mind—in politics as well as in poetry. This intelligence so charged to communicate, so shaped in responsibility and impelled with learning and curiosity, so alight with imagination, from the start couldn't be denied for what it is; it could be resisted only—another form of recognition. It challenges still, and what was said in the campaign remains said, clear to and beyond the finish of any race.

It is tempting to believe, but ultimately perhaps only coincidental, that Adlai Stevenson and Uncle Daniel found similar defeats in Welty's imagination at about the same time.

The author made a January trip to New York—rare for one who loathed the cold as much as she did—with the Uncle Daniel story in her suitcase. The central purpose of the trip was to confer with Russell on the next book. She was concerned to erase the $1,250 advance from Harcourt on the book of stories. All proposals for a miscellaneous collection, however, left her colder than the weather outside. Welty had, in uncollected stories at her disposal, "Circe," "The Burning," "The Bride of the Innisfallen," "Kin," "No Place for You, My Love," and the Uncle Daniel story. All combinations and permutations seemed to her to create flaws in the ensemble. She wanted, she wrote to Russell before leaving the city, to flank the Uncle Daniel story with others. But which others?

> I've been sitting here [a hotel room in New York] making books out of stories—will you think over the combinations and tell me Friday what you think of them? Yes, they're all alternatives to publishing Uncle Daniel as a separate book—which—I can't help it—is against some

> story-writer instinct of mine. Maybe it's just the feeling that the Daniel story needs companions on either side to make its balance—I know you're right about the money. [January 27, 1953]

"Money" in this context denoted the debt to Harcourt Brace and the income potential of two publications: a collection and the separate publication of the Uncle Daniel story. If it were not for the debt, Welty wrote, she would not consider the time right for a book at all.

The question was put in abeyance for a few months while Welty, back in Mississippi, mulled over the various tables of contents of the proposed collection and worked on a new story. "Spring" went up to Russell in late April. "I think it's a lovely story—and it's written, so it seems to me, as if you were painting, which gives it an odd sort of character, but a thoroughly nice one" (April 30, 1953). Without knowing it, Russell was echoing his response to an earlier painterly April story, "Livvie." Welty concurred. "It was visible every minute" she was working on it (May 4, 1953). Another story, "The Mother of Us All," rooted in memories of her first voyage to Europe, her sailing to Italy on her Guggenheim in 1949, was so close to completion that it needed only to be typed. Welty was hopeful that these two stories would break the impasse over the new book.

Russell, however, was hatching another plan, a plan in which the proposed collection would only be a secondary feature. Welty had read the unfinished version of *The Ponder Heart* to Maxwell during her January New York trip. The open editorial session on "Kin" had worked so well she felt encouraged to try again with the Uncle Daniel story. Maxwell remembers the reading:

> We were living on the top floor of a Murray Hill brownstone and I see Eudora standing by the window with the manuscript in her hands. It went on all morning and all afternoon, as I remember, with time out for lunch. As a reader Eudora is better than a whole company of actors and when I am moved to laughter, it is often accompanied by tears of amusement. I shed them all through the first half of the book but was dry-eyed during the second half, not because it wasn't funny, but

> because the tear glands gave up. [Maxwell to author, November 16, 1988]

Russell had promised *The New Yorker* "first look" when the story was deemed ready for circulation. Maxwell had not yet called in that pledge, nor had Russell told Welty that the story had been promised. He had to tell her all, however, when Mary Lou Aswell, now an independent editor, made an offer to take the story to Ian Ballantine, who was inaugurating a new and controversial line of paperback originals.

Ballantine was known as an innovator in the publishing business. Bantam Books, one of the earliest paperback houses to be organized, was founded in 1945, when Ballantine and a few of the officers of Penguin left that house to start their own firm. In 1952 Ballantine, in turn, left Bantam and, with his wife, set up Ballantine Books. His plan was to simultaneously publish titles in hard- and softcover, distributing the former through the traditional retail outlets and the latter through a network modeled on the one used for magazines: drugstores, rail and bus station kiosks, etc. It was a new idea in 1952, and it riled the book business. Older and more conservative publishers were convinced that hardcover sales would be sacrificed to the cheaper editions. Only a few houses went with Ballantine's idea. Houghton Mifflin issued the first title in the scheme in November 1952, and Farrar, Straus & Young followed. Both titles turned respectable profits; to the surprise of the doubters, hardcover sales were not dented (Tebbel, IV, 395 ff.).

Russell, however, was of the conservative party, as indeed he always had been on the issue of literary tradition and quality.

> I got your letter and Mary Lou's about THE PONDER HEART and it puts me into considerable perplexity. To start off with a proposition, this Ballantine venture is either book or magazine publication. As a book then Harcourt have you under option. As a magazine I promised Bill Maxwell first look, which he asked for immediately after you had read the story to him. Financially Ballantine has nothing to offer comparable to what would be got elsewhere. Now in the end as you know it is

you who must say what will be done and if you say no matter what you want Mary Lou to have it I can try to work out some arrangement—but no matter what the arrangement it would have to be as a magazine use.

Speaking to you plain business-like I don't like the proposition at all. These original publication paper books come and go and the work in them gets lost after a while just as it would in the back copy of a magazine. They are all right for reprint business [Russell quickly made a deal with Dell after *The Ponder Heart* was published in hardcover] but at this stage original publication seems to me to be a shoddy affair. So from the point of view of plain utility, of having one's work available to people, it does not fill the bill at the moment.

I do wish this had not arisen for I like Mary Lou a lot but if she had spoken to me I would have said No firmly for there is no possible aspect of publication this way that can help you—and that is what I will have to say to her when she comes back and speaks to me. The only way out of it is for you to order me to try to work out something with her—provided it won't cut athwart legal obligations to Harcourt. ([P.S.] What a horrible letter to have to write—but I'd be plainly dishonest if I wrote any other way.) [May 18, 1953]

Perhaps no other single moment in Russell's stewardship so succinctly dramatizes his position as agent. From the perspective of the 1990s, when the top literary agents boast of advances in the millions for books not yet imagined, Russell's stern position seems antique. As the 1950s progressed, a decade of great change in American book publishing, Russell began to chafe at the new ways and new people in the business. He had much more in common with writers like Walker Percy and Bernard Malamud (the latter his client), who preferred to postpone talk of the contract until the book was finished (McDowell, 22). So crucial were the ramifications of the anti-Ballantine plan to Russell that he wrote a follow-up letter the next day, revealing more of his plan:

The fact that I had to write such a letter yesterday made me irritable all evening and made me end up with a headache. You must know that from personal feelings alone I would wish to assent. I would stretch a good many points for either you or Mary Lou.

Leaving aside the matter as to whether it is legally proper there are two points as to which I think this Ballantine offer very unsatisfactory. The money I know would count very little with you but you are making Mr. Ballantine a gift which I reckon at the minimum to be $7000 and at the maximum $20,000. I feel sure I can sell this to a magazine and done as a separate book Harcourt will put up $5000 as an advance—and as a book done this way I think it would stand a good chance of being a dual choice for the BOM which would mean another $15,000 or so—of course this latter is problematical but I would think the chances very good and that chance can't exist in the way Ballantine does the work. Mary Lou herself would be extremely unhappy about this situation.

The other matter is what I dwelt on yesterday. I plain don't like the appearance of the story in this kind of publishing. It's a cheap and shoddy way of doing things, the editions are cheap and shoddy, there is not permanence to it and I don't think it would do you good.

As I say you can do what you wish, and I know how much you would like to give Mary Lou help—as I would myself—but I wish you could feel able to leave the matter in my hands and let me talk to Mary Lou about it. I'm sorry to be so tiresome but I'm rather keen about THE PONDER HEART and have been resting a lot of hope in what might be done with it. [May 19, 1953]

Russell's publishing campaign for *The Ponder Heart* was the most elaborate—and potentially the most remunerative—that he had as yet incubated for Welty. If he could pull it off, he could succeed in bringing his client the money he had always hoped to forward to her, and would solidify her reputation among editors and readers. Aswell's Ballantine deal only forced him to reveal the plan sooner than he had anticipated.

Welty was staggered. She had not been fully aware of the "fabulous" arrangements Russell had painstakingly designed. She promised to raise the matter with Aswell, who was vacationing with her on the Mississippi Gulf Coast. It was a delicate matter, as Welty realized: "I think we all have been going in a circle feeling badly for one another—only I'm the one that profits" (May 24, 1953), but a delicate matter in which the agent's commercial decisions took precedence over friendship. Russell worked hard to keep the alliance together.

> Yes, I am glad that Mary Lou feels the same way so that no one's feelings have been hurt. Guess perhaps I caused it by being so restrained in the beginning. I seldom say something is more than good work, which is probably too cool—but then I never want to get an author's expectations all roused up so that they go around in a glow, hoping for all things. [May 27, 1953]

The Ballantine imbroglio had caused Russell an uncharacteristic moment of confession.

Welty stood aside and let the agent do his work. The mini-drama had made her think about the publishing of her work in a new light: "The Ballantines don't look pretty to me either. . . . Is it old-fashioned to feel that all books worth printing ought to keep? Then I am. About the money, I do care, and think a lot would be just wonderful, though won't it be a masterpiece of selling? Only it cheers me most, more than I can say, that you think highly of a story, and in that way the money doesn't matter" (May 24, 1953).

Russell waited until July to begin the implementation of his "masterpiece of selling"; Welty needed that much time to complete the revision and retyping of the final version, with the "flawed" ending. She was having misgivings about Uncle Daniel finishing Bonnie Dee off at the end. Russell was more satisfied. At lunch with Eugene Reynal, a senior editor at Harcourt, Russell carried out part one of his plan. Reynal agreed to a $5,000 advance on *The Ponder Heart* (July 15, 1953). He spoke for the house, he wrote to the author a few days later, when he pronounced the book a "masterpiece." Publication was set for the first Thursday in January 1954. By August, an illustrator had been signed on. Almost as an afterthought, Russell reported that *The New Yorker* was taking the story too, at $7,700, for December publication, "length or no length" (July 17, 1953). Only the Book-of-the-

Month Club part of the plan had not come through. Russell had to be satisfied with partial victory on that front. The BOMC editors, meeting in August, declined *The Ponder Heart* before publication. After publication they belatedly took it as an alternate selection for May 1954, at a sum of $4,000, half of which went to Harcourt.

The author was as pleased for the agent's victory as for her own success.

> It really is just marvelous news and dazzles my head when I try to think about it till I'm not sure I've taken it in. It was a feat you did—for sure—I'm more pleased than anything that it worked out exactly as it came to you it might. I can believe you did it better than I can believe what it was. It was a double feat—and don't be cast down even the least if it isn't triple, that's getting too miraculous—this is miraculous now. [July 20, 1953]

Russell was truly pleased to inform his client, who had made less than $5,000 in writing income the previous year, that she might have to look into ways of deferring some of her *Ponder* riches into 1954—no use giving too much to the Internal Revenue.

The Ponder Heart had not finished producing miracles; what riches did not spill from the coffers of the Book-of-the-Month Club seemed, immediately after *The New Yorker* published the story on December 5, 1953, to be forthcoming from the deep pockets of theatrical producers. Here was a surprise development Russell had not quite foreseen.

The first to call was Herman Levin, in Russell's words "a really reputable and well-heeled producer" (December 11, 1953). Very quickly, Russell, whose experience in the theatrical business was limited, implemented the lesson of his Shaw editing and engaged as co-agent a member of the Society of Authors' Representatives, John Rumsey, to manage the Broadway side of the negotiations. Russell's knowledge of show business was imperfect, even though he worked in Manhattan. But even the most cursory investigation told him that

Levin was a man to respect. He was the producer of *Call Me Mister* (1946) and *Gentlemen Prefer Blondes* (1949)—a title Russell consistently reversed: *Blondes Prefer Gentlemen*. He was to produce both the London and New York versions of *My Fair Lady* (1956). Trained as an attorney, Levin served as the president of the League of New York Theaters in 1955–57 and 1962–63. He impressed Russell as quite unlike the vagabond theatrical types he had always imagined.

Some of the background on Levin, and on others in the theater interested in Welty's works, came from Lehman Engel, a fellow Jacksonian and high-school friend of Welty's, who lived in New York and worked in the theater as composer, conductor, and occasional co-producer. Engel, who knew and respected Levin, added his recommendation and a caveat, which Welty passed on to Russell:

> L. agrees he's an astute producer, has taste, and is very much interested in the money though not to the exclusion of something he really wants to put on regardless. But he thinks generally speaking it's starting wrong end first to get a producer before a writer, and says if the right writers do a show they can take their pick of producers, and seems Joe Fields and partner are such a pair. (Can't remember that partner's name [Jerome Chodorov] though seems they're well known.) Lehman describes them as gentle people, very smart, sympathetic and knowledgeable. So I don't know what you think of it but he suggested that if and when Mr. Levin comes forward it might be a good idea to tell him I'd been approached now from the writers' end and that we'd be happy to have him consider the play along with others when the time comes. (Lehman said Joe Fields also spoke of the story's having offbeat movie possibilities, but didn't comment on that.) Oh well, nothing's likely to come up before the new year, but I'm passing all this along for what use it might be—Lehman is fond of the story and also knows all concerned, has worked with them all, so he can look at it from both sides. He thinks I'd have to help *anybody* on the dialogue at some point, and seems that's what Fields wants. Just now I couldn't put a single word in any character's mouth if life depended, with apprehensions about the book coming out and people reading it. [n.d.; mid-December 1953]

Joseph Fields and Jerome Chodorov had just won a New York Drama Critics Circle Award for their musical *Wonderful Town* (1953). Their interest in *The Ponder Heart* promised to be more successful than the Archibald-Bergerson collaboration on *The Robber Bridegroom*—that team had not come forth with a script in the several months of their option. Engel's Broadway grapevine also reported that John Patrick, who had won a Pulitzer, a Tony, and a New York Drama Critics Circle Award for *Teahouse of the August Moon* (1953), and Ruth and Augustus Goetz, who had successfully adapted Henry James's *Washington Square* for the stage as *The Heiress* (which appeared coincidentally in the same season as Archibald's *The Innocents*), were also interested. Offers, inquiries, and gossip came thick and fast. "Dashed if I know which is the right way to get these things started," Russell wrote.

> We have had a lot that started with a play-writer interest and none of them worked out—either they didn't do a play or if they did they couldn't interest a producer. I gather that Mr. Levin is so good and substantial that within limits he can have his pick of dramatists—if they are free—because they know there will be a producer. At any rate he seems to have a clear idea of what should be done with Ponder and his problem is to pick the right dramatist. Evidently very well-known dramatists, the Goetzes, want to do it—but Mr. L. isn't sure they have the right touch. I hope that Mr. L. will find someone and that sometime we will have a roaring success on our hands. [December 23, 1953]

The third life of *The Ponder Heart*—on the stage—had already started. Controlling its growth was to be the problem.

By January 6, 1954, the day before *The Ponder Heart* was to be officially published, Henry Volkening sent the option agreement with Levin to Welty for her signature; Russell was at home with a bad cold. Volkening was quite amused about the Broadway hullabaloo and looked forward to the project. He also knew that his partner would be equally reluctant to fall into the show-biz mode. Russell ignored all predictions of his obstreperousness, however, and wrote to his client with predictions of Aladdin-like riches. "Here's the option money—$500 less 10%. [Levin had agreed to a six-month option, at

$500 a month.] And now we can all sit down and pray that Mr. Levin finds some good dramatist who will make a good play—and then we can roll in money" (January 12, 1954).

There was to be no immediate rollicking in show-biz bucks. In fact, *The Ponder Heart* was to bring in more money as a book than as a play for almost two years. By February 25, Russell happily reported sales of 10,883, by far the best-selling single book Welty had ever had.

Literature, not drama, kept Welty's attention throughout the year. In March she was nominated to go to Cambridge University to deliver a series of three short lectures and two panel discussions on literature under the auspices, and at the expense, of the Fulbright program. Remembering the ordeal of "the lecture thing" at the Pacific Northwest Writers' Conference in 1947, she wrote to Russell: "It's like saying I would have to fly five times across the room. But you know I would agree to try almost anything for a trip, and this would be a free one" (March 29, 1954). Welty was soon thereafter formally invited to participate, and the speech she wrote for Cambridge, "Place in Fiction," proved just as difficult to write, to revise, and to place in publication as "The Reading and Writing of Short Stories" had been.

Welty was also engaged in revising and assembling the stories for the next collection, postponed to make way for *The Ponder Heart*. By late April the retyping had been completed. "Circe" had been rewritten, and the author was unsure whether it ought to be included in the collection at all. *The Bride of the Innisfallen and Other Stories* was scheduled for publication the following April (1955). All this work had to be finished before she sailed for England in early July.

The sailing date came and still there was no truckload of theatrical riches. Levin's option was soon to expire and he had not chosen a playwright. Russell felt his deep-seated suspicion of theatrical folk returning: "These theatrical people are very casual, taking options and then often doing nothing and though Mr. L. has a first class reputation as a producer I'm still not counting on him—we've had so many options taken up and let go" (March 12, 1954). He reminded his client that the collection was due soon—better to work on that than to count stage money.

Another Broadway production team, the Frederick Brisson–Robert

Griffith–Hal Prince partnership responsible for the hit *The Pajama Game*, approached with an idea to transform *The Ponder Heart* into a musical. Welty felt committed to Levin while his option was in force; she had even promised to think about writing all or part of an act on speculation for Levin to show prospective playwrights. Moss Hart's name was mentioned. Welty was, however, cooler and cooler toward the idea of collaboration. "As for my preference between a straight play by Levin and a musical . . . I don't know a thing . . . so couldn't say yet, but on the whole, after having samples of how people in N.Y.C. interpret Ponder, I believe a light-hearted musical would do less harm to it" (June 18, 1954). The theatrical world, closer than ever before, was beginning to seem a land of folly as well as a land of fun. Welty sailed for England, preferring to suffer the slings and arrows of writing literary criticism rather than collaborate on a play with people she scarcely knew.

She returned to the States in October. By late the following month, she had signed an eighteen-month option with Joseph Fields and Jerome Chodorov, who proposed to write a play based on *The Ponder Heart*. The Levin option had come to nought; he could not find a playwright or convince Welty to collaborate on one act as a speculation. Lehman Engel's prediction of almost a year earlier had come to pass; he had foretold that it was better to begin with a playwright. By signing with Fields and Chodorov, Russell and Welty were resuming the Broadway saga from another starting point. If the would-be producer could not find a playwright, maybe the would-be playwrights could find a producer. Russell was no more than neutrally willing to close the deal; dreams of great bonanzas had been scattered: "It seems like a good deal to me because both these people are well-known. I guess Lehman [Engel] had talked to them about the book" (November 4, 1954). It is altogether likely that he had, for Engel had conducted the orchestra for the run of *Wonderful Town*. *Wonderful Town* had excellent credentials: music by Leonard Bernstein and lyrics by Betty Comden and Adolph Green. Fields and Chodorov, as authors, did indeed appear to be a good deal, and Engel's recommendation smoothed the way. Welty had, however, learned some of the harsher lessons of show biz by that time: "I haven't the slightest illusion that the play, by any Broadway writer, will have any inner resemblance to my story," she wrote to Russell (November 26, 1954). Russell did not try to soften that lesson.

> I fancy the two playwrights don't want any interference from you whatsoever. They might want you to look over the play when it's finished, to verify atmosphere or speech or something of that order, just to see that they haven't run off the tracks in making people say or do something they wouldn't do in the South. [November 30, 1954]

New Year's news was mixed. Welty's writing income was more than double what it had been in 1954. The downside of that report was that the writer owed a sizable sum to the tax collector. Sales of *The Ponder Heart* in England were almost nil. Welty felt badly for James Hamilton, of Hamish Hamilton, who had won a bidding skirmish for the British rights to publish her work the year before. Welty was at work on the early draft of a long story, already stretching out to sixty pages. The length, as always, was not good news, but she thought the story, when finished, could be pruned without much harm (January 25, 1955). Her mother's eyesight, a long-standing problem, had worsened so that Mrs. Welty could not "read much any more or see the new shoots coming up in the garden" (n.d.; mid-February 1955). Doctors had advised an operation, and soon. Since recuperation from cataract surgery, in the days before lasers, was known to be protracted, Welty wrote to Russell that her annual May visit to New York might have to be postponed.

By early March, events had taken over. Her mother's operation was approaching. A promised visit to Duke University, for a reading of "Place in Fiction," was scheduled for the week before. The unnamed long story grew even longer. Fields and Chodorov wanted to come down to Jackson: "They are looking for local color—don't know where that is" (n.d.; early March 1955). Russell was sympathetic, and cautioned Welty to prepare herself for the play: "Glad the playwrights are active and nice and wonder what kind of play they will write—probably something quite unlike the book but I guess you may be expecting that" (March 7, 1955).

For the present, Welty was not expecting anything. Her mother's eye operation took place early in March, and by St. Patrick's Day Mrs. Welty was back at home. Experts promised some functional vision in the left eye, but no doctor could or would be more optimistic. The bad eye had deteriorated under a "traumatic cataract of 30 years standing" and the "good" eye was due for cataract surgery in the near future. The playwrights had a script for Welty to read, but there was little time for her to get to it. Most of her time was rerouted to household chores, gardening, reading to her mother. Welty asked for recommendations of detective novels; Russell was an avid reader of the genre—like his father, who was said to have read ten per week.

Russell also kept her current on New York news and gossip, since it seemed unlikely that she would be able to make her annual visit. This client was falling by the wayside; that one was still promising. Tremors at Harcourt: Robert Giroux, the editor in chief, was leaving to join the firm that became Farrar, Straus & Giroux. Denver Lindley, whom Giroux had hired some years earlier, was to be the new editor in chief. Russell liked Lindley. The man at the epicenter of the tremors was not mentioned: newly elected president William Jovanovich. His time would come. Welty was grateful for all the news, but could manage time for little more than a postcard in reply. It carried an ominous postscript: "Read play—am confused" (n.d.; early April 1955).

Russell remained patient:

> I'll be interested to hear in more detail what you think of the play. Chances are it's not in the least like the book but I think this was inevitable with any playwright for all of them would pick and choose what suited their own tastes. Still drop me a word as to how it confused you. [April 4, 1955]

But the play changed as rapidly as the spring weather. By the time Welty could tell Russell her opinion of the first version, the playwrights had completed a fourth, which Lehman Engel had to read and on which he reported to Welty. As for version #1, Welty thought it "lacked texture, made the characters much too calculating and too self-explanatory (Uncle Daniel couldn't say he's an innocent), and didn't make the town love Uncle Daniel—they were sort of cynical instead. Of course I'm a seismograph—I wrote them [Fields and Chodorov] this and they replied kindly but didn't send new version. Probably we don't do each other any good" (n.d.; mid-April 1955). Welty was right, but when she finally met the team on their visit to Jackson, she quickly learned that they were oblivious to being liked by authors: "Oh, listen, everybody hates us," they reassured her.

Later in the month Welty had retreated from her initial alarm to a safer distance. "I regard the whole thing as Wyrd," Welty wrote, "who goeth whither she is bound (though I forget how you spell her)" (n.d.; late April 1955). Part of the reason for her new mood was that the agent had read a version of the script and was less upset. Russell thought the version of the play he had read

> . . . probably would go off well on stage, though it has not at all got the same feelings as the book. But that I expected, that the magnets inside Messrs. C. and F. would pull out of the book what appealed to them. . . . This is rather down to earth slapstick—misses your wild sense of humor and conveys nothing of Miss Edna. All it means is someday you'll have to write your own play. This may do well and make you some money, all the same. [May 6, 1955]

By late July it was too late to do anything but try to find some comfort in the money. The New York papers began to bubble with hype. David Wayne, according to sources in Beverly Hills, was "eager to act in 'The Ponder Heart.'" The local grapevine reported that David Merrick, fresh from *Fanny*, wanted to "acquire the Jerome Chodorov–Joseph Fields variation of Eudora Welty's novel" (*NYT*, July 22, 1955). Opening night was scheduled for late November, just in time to draw the holiday crowds. Fields had written to Welty with more news and amplification: Merrick was indeed the producer of the moment, by virtue of a $3,500 advance, and he had flown somewhere "to see if he can get Josh Logan to direct" (n.d.; late July 1955). Logan had directed *Fanny* for Merrick. When such news from the principals got slim, Lehman Engel supplied more reconnaissance; he had seen them all, playwrights and producer, in a New York restaurant, so all must be going well (August 8, 1955). Mrs. Welty was still recovering, but slowly: "It's like that frog climbing out of a well, up three and back two—but just so we get out" (August 8, 1955). And the "long story about the country [was] running in [Welty's] mind" (April 16, 1955) to keep her busy with writing in the odd free hours.

By late summer Russell was a little nettled at the way theater people conducted business in the press. He had been reading of the progress of the production in the *Times*, but no one had been in contact with him about a contract for the play. One anecdote he did remember about the New York theater involved a producer who had absconded with box office receipts; the story seemed to him a sort of foundation myth. In mid-September the press reported a snag. Russell inquired at MCA, under whose auspices the negotiations were supposedly taking place, about an item in the newspaper reporting that Merrick and the playwrights had had a falling out. "Mr. M. wanting all sorts of things for himself that weren't customary," he relayed to Welty. "And I'm told the new deal is financially much better and that the process of casting is going on, so it looks as if there's some movement. But we'll have to wait and see for the theatrical world is changeable and bewildering" (September 15, 1955). Merrick was out and Roger Stevens was in, as producer. Welty had had a note from Fields and Chodorov; the two were in England working on another show. "Well," she commiserated, "we can be prepared for anything at all—they may yet put it On Ice—everybody skating" (n.d.; late September 1955).

The first sign that the new deal was indeed financially better was the arrival of a check in the amount of $1,050, Welty's share of the advance paid by the new producer, Roger L. Stevens of The Playwrights Company, a production company whose most famous play at the time was *Cat on a Hot Tin Roof*. She was puzzled since the money had come from the Dramatists' Guild, not from Russell & Volkening. Russell ruefully explained the strange ways of money management in the world of show biz:

> No, the sum is all yours. In the theatrical business agents don't seem to be trusted as they are in the literary business so the money goes to The Dramatists Guild who deduct the agent's commission and send it to him and send the author the money direct. At least they do at this stage and dashed if I know what happens later. The theatre is a mysterious place where mirages blow up in a second and pop a second later. Who knows what will happen and when—not me or not you and probably not the agent either. I think things happen at some favorable conjunction of the planets and maybe an astrologer is needed to say when the time is right. [September 30, 1955]

Russell settled himself for the theatrical ride with cushions of irony; he had little or no faith in the pilots or the maps they used. The theater was a world of illusions in which no one trusted anyone else. One person was probably an embezzler, the next a wizard. Welty was rueful and resigned as well. Craziness seemed to be popping up everywhere under the wand of Broadway. Almost hopelessly she asked Russell to keep his eyes peeled for news of an actual opening night: some Jackson friends were seriously talking about "something from Jackson called the Ponder Plane, full of my pals" and headed for New York. Only no one knew when to schedule a takeoff (n.d.; early October 1955).

The director, Robert Douglas (not Josh Logan, another mirage), passed through Jackson on his way from Hollywood to New York in mid-October. Welty found him very nonchalant for a director who had not yet seen his cast and was aiming for an opening night in New Haven in late December. Douglas, born in England in 1910, had acting credits in England and in America on his résumé in 1955. He had directed for major Hollywood studios, principally M-G-M and Warner Brothers, and was to go on to a steady career as a journeyman actor and director of movies and television. He acted in or directed several of the Warner Brothers television serials in the 1960s: *Maverick* and *77 Sunset Strip*. In October 1955, he was a visitor from the strange land of theatrical production, who told Welty that he had never directed a play in America. He was in the South to look and to listen. She found him nice (she lent him her car) but a little too smooth.

> I don't exactly know what he thinks of the script, but what I think of it is it's woeful and at the lowest ebb of vulgarity and taste ever, but Douglas tells me still another version waits on him in New York, so my comments on the one I read won't do much good—they won't anyway, but I felt upset on seeing my little story turned into a sort of bedroom dilemma with gags, and no characterization remaining—the lines are interchangeable—well, I won't beset you with it, but you would hate it. They have removed the very parts I'd have thought were of any dramatic significance—giving away the money, the ball of fire, to name two—and Mr. Douglas asked if I'd try to fix up what's left so it would make a plot—I said I wouldn't touch it with a 10-foot pole. [October 22, 1955]

Russell could do little more than wish his client a sort of lukewarm comfort; the play was out of their hands now.

> That script does sound dismaying and I guess is several versions later than the one I saw months and months ago. I was told the boys were on the slapstick side and it sounds as if they were outdoing themselves—and I guess all one can do is to look grim and bear it. Anyway no one can know what goes on in the theatre and there's still plenty of time for all sorts of things to happen. [October 26, 1955]

As the season wore on, Russell sent bulletins from the theatrical front. Always the news was uncertain or contradictory. "The theatre," he wrote, "is just the other end from philosophy which is always trying to find the eternal certainties; it is always finding delay, hesitation, uncertainty, replacements and the Lord knows what. Hold on to your hat" (November 3, 1955). The latest dispatches indicated an out-of-town opening January 2, 1956.

Publicity types found the author as the opening drew near. One from The Playwrights Company relayed an invitation from the *Herald Tribune* for Welty to write about anything connected with *The Ponder Heart*—except the play itself. She declined. "It really is a nutty world"

(November 16, 1955). Later the same month both author and agent were shocked to learn that the title had been changed to *The Prize in the Crackerjack Box*. To Welty, "Ponder as a play [was] getting more gruesome by the hour" (December 1, 1955). She had made it a point to see David Wayne in the film *The Tender Trap* and came away convinced that he was going to be wasted in something called *The Prize in the Crackerjack Box*. But by Christmas it was too late to stop; a road schedule of New Haven, Boston, and Philadelphia was already set. The New York opening was scheduled for February 6, if a theater could be found; as yet no house had been rented. The point of no return had been met and passed before author and agent heard the news. They were alien visitors on a planet in its own orbit.

Russell's wife, Rose, went up to Boston to catch the premiere there on January 4. Welty was even then not sure she wanted to be in the audience for the Broadway opening—if such an opening should ever take place. "I don't want to spend all that money to come for one night and see 'The Prize in the Crackerjack Box,' if prize it still is, go to pieces before our eyes." She was, however, still anxious for Rose Russell's report: ". . . tell Rose please to write me what the play was like, if it was like anything on earth, I'd be spurred on" (January 4, 1956).

Russell did not—perhaps in spite of himself he could not—wait to relay the report from Boston:

> Rosie . . . reports that the play is almost certain to be a hit, one of the funniest [she has] ever seen (and heard many in the lobby saying the same thing), with a marvelous performance by Wayne. They say the second act is perfect as is but that the first act needs some cutting and tightening up, a matter of repetitious stuff. I guess their diagnosis is right for Dolly [Rosa Farrar Wells, a friend and fellow Mississippian who lived and worked in New York] tells me the New Haven reviews say the same things and I enclose a note from today's Times which also says the same thing. . . . So maybe this is all going to be fun and profitable and you'll end up with enough money to buy pieds-à-terre in various parts of the world. [January 6, 1956]

Success on the road meant that a Broadway theater could finally be rented, and the *Times* reported that *The Ponder Heart,* the old name restored, would move into the Music Box as soon as *Bus Stop* moved out. (Weirdly, Joshua Logan turned up here: he was to direct the movie version of *Bus Stop.*) The date would be either February 7 or February 16.

"The ticket business will drive us all crazy," Russell fretted (January 9, 1956). He could get only six tickets through The Playwrights Company in Welty's name; he needed at least another six to accommodate everyone they, author and agent, wanted in the opening-night party. Still, there was no fixed opening date, so other plans (where to eat, where to drink) had to be left in limbo. "I think they [theater folk] all like this element of uncertainty and I will keep on trying to find out something definite," Russell wrote, mildly exasperated (January 9, 1956). He thought the cast might have to stay on the road like a band of gypsies until an opening date could be finally set. By January 12, though, the uncertainty had been cleared away. The various theater parties had been assembled, tickets reserved, and train and hotel arrangements made. The show would open February 16, and appeared to Russell to be a solid hit. "Anticipation is getting to a fever heat," he wrote, and closed with more ebullience than was customary: "Can't wait. Can't wait. Can't wait" (January 12, 1956).

Welty too was anxious to see what had been wrought, but was intrigued by the coincidence that the play that *would* have opened at the Music Box, had it not (temporarily) closed out of town, was "that Beckett thing, 'Waiting for Godot' " (January 12, 1956). Later in the 1956 season *Waiting for Godot* (finally on Broadway) would spark one of the most active debates in modern theatrical history, a debate that sent Brooks Atkinson to review the show twice, and to insist in the face of severe audience disapproval that Beckett's play was "not a fake."

Russell was less concerned about the theatrical coincidence than about his client's financial fate. He was happy to report that box office receipts for the Philadelphia run had covered the advance, and that weekly royalty checks would be coming in shortly. As author of the novel, Welty was to receive 10 percent of the play's receipts. The theater seemed to pay handsomely for all the aggravation.

Money was not center stage in the author's mind. A note from Lehman Engel, who had seen the show in Philadelphia, had triggered an old anxiety. He had told her she "must be prepared to have great control over my most personal feelings. . . . He says it's all slick and adroit, with a whole new scheme being worked out for the first act, and getting further and further and further away from the real McCoy" (January 19, 1956). Right up to the opening, tinkering was the rule of the game. Engel's music for the play had been dumped—according to reports in the press—so that Dorothy Fields, Joseph Fields's sister, could write a song to entice Paramount and Bing Crosby to buy the play as a vehicle for the star. *The Ponder Heart* was to be retitled after the song "The Happy Heart." There was, however, nary a nibble from Bing or Paramount. Welty tried to keep track of it all: "I really can't wait to see what in the name of goodness they've got," she wrote, with a mixture of curiosity and dread (n.d.; late January 1956). Russell volunteered to do a juggling act, if called upon; "the theater is certainly wonderful" (January 27, 1956).

The opening and early run of *The Ponder Heart* turned out, in actual fact, not to be so horrible. In spite of a flare-up of her mother's eye trouble early in the month, Welty made the trip in February, saw the play on opening night, congratulated the cast backstage, and enjoyed a taste of the celebrity life. *The Ponder Heart* got off to a good start; author's royalties for the partial opening week in New York and the tail end of the road tour totaled $1,400. Russell hoped that his client could bank such sums, perhaps even larger ones, every week for the next two years (February 29, 1956). He even attempted to give a little financial advice (bonds), although it was Henry Volkening who was the partner with the aficionado's knowledge of investments.

Signs predicted a comfortably long run. *Life* featured the play in its "Theater" section with nine pictures of the production and praise for David Wayne (March 5, 1956). With her eye for context, Welty noted to Russell that that issue of *Life* also carried William Faulkner's "A Letter to the North." Beckett and Faulkner provided a context for the play that was not lost on the author of the story. "Hobe's" *Variety* review (February 22, 1956) noted, for the professionals, that *The Ponder Heart* had opened at a time when Broadway shows were on the financial skids. Dramatically, "Hobe" found that the play's appeal dwindled after initial charm and energy: "It seems a questionable bet for box office popularity, but could conceivably be picture material, subject to careful revision and superior production." The only sour note among the reviews was Eric Bentley's in *The New Republic* (March 12, 1956); he was on a rampage against most literature, decried the loss of the comic spirit, and called for comic writers to take their example from Joseph Conrad. Welty thought it "pretentiously off-beam" (March 12, 1956). She was so encouraged, though, in the first flush of success, that, she told Russell, she had begun to contemplate two ideas for original plays.

The early success of *The Ponder Heart* was only one reason. Works by Welty were on stage at two New York theaters during the 1956 theater season, and *The Robber Bridegroom* was stirring again as a theatrical property. The Phoenix Theater, off Broadway, opened with *The Littlest Revue* on May 22; it included the "Bye, Bye Brevoort" sketch that Welty had worked on in 1949. There was also material by Ogden Nash, Nat Hiken, and others; the actors included Larry Storch, Tammy Grimes, and Joel Grey. Atkinson found Welty's contribution "wry and enjoyable," but *The Littlest Revue* never made it uptown (*NYT*, May 23, 1956, p. 37). And Zachary Scott, who was appearing in a three-week engagement of *The King and I*—he wore an earring but did not shave his head—wanted an option on *The Robber Bridegroom*. Welty, having learned from the episode of *The Ponder Heart* of the "anguish" connected with adaptations, agreed with Russell that everyone concerned in this request had better be thoroughly investigated before any agreement might be signed (March 22, 1956).

By June *The Ponder Heart* was already in its final weeks. There had been clues to its demise earlier in May when, as the correspondent for the *World-Telegram* reported, the "bubble-gum set" were filling the seats in ever larger numbers (May 2, 1956, p. 33). No show could hope to survive long on a teenage audience. *Variety* had foretold, on the eve of the opening, that the play would have to gross $16,000 a week to break even. Although grosses for the first few weeks exceeded the break-even number (*Variety*, February 15, 1956), by late spring the receipts hovered around $16,000; by June the weekly take was well below the mark. *Variety* estimated a deficit on the production of $100,000 when the show closed (June 27, 1956).

David Wayne did a few performances in summer stock around New England; then he and the rest of the cast went on to other work. All royalties for the final two weeks of the Broadway run were cut by half in an effort to offset overall losses of $93,000 on the production. Russell asked Welty if she wanted to protest the reduction, but she did not: "I don't see any reason to make a to-do about this, all being at the end of things" (n.d.; late June 1956).

She was not particularly disappointed. *The Ponder Heart* had been the vehicle of a weird and rapid ride, if not always a happy one. She had managed to make one more New York trip, in May, with her mother; both saw the show and met Wayne. Mrs. Welty had also been able to meet Russell and his family. Welty's work had finally netted some money for the agents who had loyally worked for her for fifteen years, and she was pleased for the shared good fortune. Her own accounts were more flush than they had ever been in her career. She learned in January 1957 that as quickly as the manna could fall it could also disappear; just as she was beginning to think of the play profits as hers, she had to pay a large chunk of them to "the Eisenhower gov't" (n.d.; January 1957). Everything associated with the theater seemed evanescent, even the money.

Welty returned to the long story about the country that had been running in her mind for quite some time, at least since April 1955 (April 16, 1955); it was now over one hundred pages. Russell had always been anxious to see it, but the Broadway whirl had diverted his attention. He was put off once again after the run of the play. In September 1956, he suffered a heart attack on his way home from taking his son to school in Massachusetts and could not resume regular literary business until November. With her mother slowly recuperating, and now her agent slowed down and proven mortal when he was only fifty-four, Welty felt drawn back to earth with a rough jolt.

NINE

The Long Association

Diarmuid Russell was not sentimental about himself and his work. He rarely looked to the past for comfort, and he knew that longevity in the profession of literary representation did not automatically confer honor on the agent. Nevertheless, the passage of time could be educational, and on the eve of thirty years of representing Eudora Welty, Russell became curious about the lessons.

> I've been digging into old records and old letters—dear me what a long association it has been. It was May 31, 1940, when you first wrote saying "be your agent" and what a long happy time it has been for me and I look with amazement at the old cards and how many people and places turned your work down—and what they said. You remark that at Breadloaf the opinion was unanimous that nobody would want POWERHOUSE and that STORY was always writing "This is almost it, but not quite." They don't talk like this now. [January 9, 1969]

There had been no miracles, just consistent hard work by agent and client, some rewards, and the lesson that one thing published did not necessarily make the next one either easy to write or a cinch to sell.

And no one had gotten rich. That was never more true than in 1969, almost fifteen years since the publication of his client's last book, *The Bride of the Innisfallen and Other Stories* (1955).

Absence, especially an absence of fifteen years, had not made the publisher's heart fonder, and Russell knew that changes of major importance had reshaped the business since his last contract negotiations on behalf of a book by Eudora Welty. Circumstances, as always, would not be the same; no one knew just how difficult the new climate would be. Moreover, Russell had not yet put his hands on, much less read "at one scoop," the long comic novel that had been running in Welty's head at least since 1955, alighting in actual paper fragments on several perches around her workroom. When *Time* announced, in its inimitable prose, that "Eudora Welty, the soft-voiced but enduring prose mistress of Mississippi, is bringing out her first novel in 15 years" (January 3, 1969), Russell was pleased to have the publicity, but would have been more pleased had he read (at that moment) more than Part Two of a novel for which he had not yet obtained a contract.

If Welty had seemed to *Time* to have stepped out of the literary public eye for fifteen years, the business of publishing had not been on hold. Circumstances in publishing seemed, on the eve of the 1970s, to have altered all the familiar rules of the game: books, editors, publishers, agents seemed drastically unlike anything they had been just ten years earlier. John Cushman, an agent himself, wrote in *Publishers Weekly* (April 10, 1972) an elegy for the "cottage days" of American book publishing. A new tribe had infiltrated the old profession, and their presence was not always a comfort:

> However, when we move to the large firm [after the merger with the outside industrial giant] the factory, then the money men, the accountants, and the lawyers eventually have a larger role and a louder voice than all the brilliant editors. The clever advertising, promotion, and publicity people, the gifted salesmen, and even the record-breaking subsidiary rights sellers . . . Is publishing still an occupation for a gentleman, or has it become a fertile field for the manager?

Circumstances in private life had changed as well; both author and agent had grown older, family members and close friends had grown ill and died, presenting the lesson of change and mortality. What was the meaning of art and work amid intimations of mortality? The author, even before the *Ponder* follies had slowed down and eventually stopped, had been faced with her mother's eye trouble, and her two brothers, Edward and Walter, both suffered from rheumatoid arthritis. Family health conditions grew worse—or in the long run no better—and other maladies set in, occupying the writer's (and daughter's) time physically and emotionally for more than a decade. Author and agent debated the meaning and importance of work against obligations to kin, and arrived at no restful solution.

It is a small miracle that the comic country novel maintained any momentum or coherence at all when it was shunted aside by so many contingencies for more than a decade. In free moments Welty wrote pieces of the story on scraps of paper and tossed all the scraps into a box. There was never time to get to the box. Russell recovered from his heart attack but grumbled at his other physical ailments: bursitis, arthritis, suspected gall-bladder trouble, the lung cancer that eventually hurried on his retirement from the agency in 1973. His friends and acquaintances fell ill and died. Eventually Russell's advice to his friend and client echoed Mr. Ramsey's in Virginia Woolf's *To the Lighthouse* ("We perish each alone"), for he saw no way for mortals to reverse fate itself. Except, perhaps, with literature. Bad and disordered as the world was, both close up and far away, Russell wrote after finally securing a contract for *Losing Battles*, it might still straighten up and recognize a marvelous book: "It *will* end up all right. It's a most marvelous book, and bad as the world is, it will still recognize" (June 25, 1969). Literature was his best and only hope.

Circumstances and personal feelings braided themselves into the agent's and writer's work during the fifteen years between *The Bride of the Innisfallen* and *Losing Battles*. By the time the manuscript of *Losing Battles* was ready for Russell to read from beginning to end, it had become symbolic of his client's power to draw a masterpiece out of personal and family hardship and of his own growing uneasiness with a changed profession.

Whatever the possible innovations to the agent's role during "the great change" in American publishing, one fundamental duty did not change. An agent still had to encourage his client to keep on writing during hardship, passages of doubt, and inexplicable silence brought on by those periodic clampings of the brain, and this responsibility Russell did not shirk. As early as April 1955, as the querulous reviews of *The Bride of the Innisfallen* were appearing, Russell knew about a new story in which country people talked nonstop about things that threatened to add up to nothing coherent according to the requirements of storytelling. This story, his client wrote, oscillated between fiction and drama. As time put the *Ponder* follies farther in the past, however, the country story settled into fiction. By the summer of 1956, a month after the closing of *The Ponder Heart*, Welty wrote that she was going back to the material of the story—as usual, much too long for publication; working on plays, she added, had taught her many good lessons, not the least of which was how much she knew about the story form:

> I'm about to type up that story I had lying around that was too long, and let it be too long. I was driven to it, because working on a play has showed me how much more I know about the short story. (Only it's too long.) What you'll do with it I don't know. [n.d.; late July/August 1956]

Welty had considered sending "this unholy long thing" up to Russell for a surgical opinion in the late summer (1956); she hoped he could tell her where and how much to "whack" out. The agent was willing, even anxious, to sharpen his editorial technique, "for [it has been] too long a time since we've had some mss. from you" (August 2, 1956). Before Welty could get the pages to him, however, Russell had suffered his heart attack. It was not a time to take such events lightly, to push them complacently to the margins of one's life story. The previous March, Gustave Lobrano, a partisan of Welty's stories at *The New Yorker* who had launched her career there by publishing her letter of rebuke to Edmund Wilson, had died of cancer at the age of fifty-three. Welty's mother was still recuperating from cataract surgery, and one of her brothers, Walter, was ill with an arthritic condition very difficult to treat. Russell celebrated his fifty-fourth birthday that November recuperating from his heart attack.

By the new year, 1957, with Russell in his office every day, it was again possible for author and agent to think about the long country story.

> It seems a lot more cheerful for some reason to think of you as there not every other day, but every day. . . . It would be good to talk over these floating fragments of things on my desk, my table, my bookcase and my chairs. It all looks too active to put away, so I leave it to wait on me—then spread it all out on the floor or the bed and look at it. Some days it appears all ready to shoot in the typewriter, other days it looks like just "material." What I need of course is some *consecutive* time. This would be possible at night, only I'm not a night person. Anyway, what I feel tempted to do—when you've caught up with all that was waiting on you, and things aren't too demanding—is send up one of the fragments. An opening section of a story. . . . [n.d.; early January 1957]

The days were filled with household work. Her mother's eye, healing slowly because of recurrent infections, needed treatment with wonder drugs. No one yet knew which drugs or which dosage would work the wonders. The "great burden of a ms." was too great and miscellaneous to send to New York; she would have to bring it in person on her annual spring visit.

> It's the worst for length yet, I don't dare back up to read it over. If it ever goes into the movies (it wouldn't fit a stage) only Cecil B. DeMille could direct it, he is used to a large cast. [n.d.; mid-April 1957]

Russell avidly read what she did bring up and encouraged her to finish. His cheerleading, however, worked only momentarily.

> Haven't done any work yet (story) but am about ready to get it out. Thank you again for reading the unfinished thing—it helped to know it was good enough to finish. Sometimes it had seemed likely that it was just my habit to write, the way it was the habit of Sir Rabbit to dance in the wood, not necessarily well. [May 28, 1957]

The agent's good words had come at an impasse, when the writer was feeling that her writing had become mere habit, not something extraordinary, nothing more than exercise or reflex. William Maxwell had also read the working draft; to him it became the story of "the sparrows" (September 25, 1957), for the family at its reunion seemed to him to behave like a flock of birds. That two trusted "jurors" were convinced of the story's quality was bright good news; still, even as the doctor schedule became more reasonable and home arrangements were adjusted into a semblance of regularity, the years seemed to be flying away. Little or no work on the manuscript was done. The writer's feelings for her duty to her work clashed with her duty to her family

> So I have no excuse at all for not working now that the doctor-going schedule is reduced and all seems under control better. I'm so ashamed of not producing anything. I should think all my friends would have given me up. So I hope I'll be sending you this thing before too long. I've cut it some. Thank you for so much patience. [June 26, 1957]

In a divided psychological state, the writer suffered acutely from events such as the racial upheaval in Little Rock. "I feel like emigrating from the whole country. Bayonets!" (September 25, 1957). Her family concern, moreover, had deepened with the hospitalization of Walter—who, at forty, was six years younger than she—for heart problems linked to his arthritis. For the rest of the year, work on fiction was slow and often interrupted. Her friends would need even more patience than they had already shown. Russell was solicitous.

> That's too bad and worrying about your brother. He had some deal like this before, didn't he, but I had gathered from you that it wasn't to be taken too seriously—and let's hope neither will this attack. All the same I wish all these things didn't pile on you, your mother and now your brother. I do think you ought to try to get away and have a rest and some pleasure. . . .
>
> Saw in Pub. Weekly that you are now a consultant to the Library of Congress. Doesn't this mean that you will have to take trips to Washington—and of course then on up to New York. [January 20, 1958]

Medical complications did not abate, and there was no time for the trips Russell had prescribed. In January 1958 her brother suffered a setback and eventually that spring had to make an arduous trip to New Orleans for consultation with a specialist. Welty helped look after her nieces while their parents were away. Russell himself was not well. Symptoms seemed to indicate a second but very mild heart attack, but no one was sure.

> My local doc. has been making me take a lot of tests to see if that attack was a heart deal or could be something else. Net result inconclusive. They think something's wrong with my gall bladder, but aren't recommending that it be whacked out so long as I feel well. But if I should run into another deal I think they'll want it removed. [February 18, 1958]

He was not so ill as to neglect his duty as an agent to encourage, cajole, and provoke his client into writing. William Maxwell, Russell mentioned by way of closing his account of his medical woes, had been inquiring after new stories, "and all [Russell] could do was wail and lament. You wouldn't want me to keep on doing this" (February 18, 1958). The pressure was subtle but not unfelt. "I work a little every day now," Welty wrote back (February 24, 1958), ". . . I want to get it finished more than I can say—for the work's sake itself, or it will be all worn out and stale and the life out of it. Don't think my conscience doesn't hurt." She was never so glad to see the spring, she wrote to the agent on St. Patrick's Day. The winter and the worry had frozen her in her tracks; she felt no good for writing or for helping the sick.

But the thaw did not completely free her from all obligations and circumstances. Although her brother's condition did not deteriorate through the spring and summer, it did not improve much either. Welty had to continue some care for her nieces, for her mother, and for the house. Time for writing, or for thinking about writing, shrunk to nothing. Russell was more than mildly concerned, and the depth of his patience seemed to change. He began to worry that his client had allowed her feeling for her family responsibility to overwhelm her duty to her work. He wanted more balance. His customary blunt and direct attitude toward the mortality of the human race became even more blunt and direct.

> Do hope that things will go right so that you can get some work done. It's a long time [more than three years since *The Bride of the Innisfallen*] and being what you are you will always be doing things for other people. But I do think that somehow you ought to reserve some time for yourself and your own work. Bill Maxwell and others have been talking to me about this and I must say I do agree—and at this point I think others should be doing something for you, to make you freer (is that right or should it have a third E). . . . [June 5, 1958]

But neither mother nor brother improved to the point of taking care of themselves, and there were no others to do the caring except paid outsiders, and Welty was unwilling to go to strangers in the summer of 1958. Her writing "family" vied with her blood family in strophe and anti-strophe, and blood had the final word. Walter Welty died in January 1959, at the age of forty-three.

Welty persevered in the work of sorting, assembling, and typing the long story during intervals of caring for the sick and managing the household. She was seldom confident that the work was worth the time. The long manuscript always seemed on the brink of futility, ready to become another "Where Angels Fear," a long story she had destroyed in 1953 while working simultaneously on *The Ponder Heart*. She leaned on Russell almost exclusively for encouragement and practical guidance, and in April 1959 he had finished reading something like a story, too long for most magazines except *Ladies' Home Journal*, which he thought ready for circulation. He sent it to the *Journal* hoping for a big sale.

> Have just tied up the ms. to send back via First Class Registered Mail. But in the letter I enclose with the ms. I forgot to say that I will need two copies of the ms.—one for the publishers and one for magazines. This, it seems to me, is far too long for the New Yorker to use as a whole (Bill [Maxwell] talked to me about this a couple of months ago)—they could only take excerpts if they could find them. So before they see it [it] seems to me it ought to be shown to the big magazines like the Journal and so on for it doesn't seem at all impossible to me that they would like it (at this stage I don't see how anyone could fail to like it). They might have to cut to use—as the Atlantic had to do with Delta Wedding—but I know if they have to do this they let authors see the cut version. [April 27, 1959]

The two copies of the manuscript, however, were long delayed. Throughout the summer and fall, "household obligations" kept the author deprived of the "consecutive time" she needed to bring the manuscript into satisfactory shape. Russell became increasingly concerned that Mrs. Welty's illness (lately she had begun to suffer "blackouts" for which doctors could find no cause) was fast becoming an undue, unfair burden on the writer—or that the writer was assuming too much responsibility, obligating herself to a quality of care she could not humanly manage to deliver. One solution, of course, was paid professional help, but without book and magazine revenue, the writer could not afford it. Book reviews for *The New York Times* brought in some extra income, and starting in the early 1960s, frequent press runs of paperback editions of her books generated what Russell called "snippets" of money. But demand (for money) outran supply.

Russell nominated Welty for a Ford Foundation fellowship in a program that would pay successful applicants $7,500 for one year spent "in close touch with the theater." Russell knew his client was trying to finish fiction, but his desire that she have some free time for writing blurred that objection; he was sure that, should she win the fellowship, she would clear up the manuscript before undertaking any new work. Above all, he wanted to dislodge her from the family jam as soon and as effectively as possible.

> Now I'd like to put your name in because you love the theatre and I can't think of anyone who would have more fun out of this and who would be more likely to derive information. I know your mother's position must make you uncertain to take on commitments—but I get very worried about you because I think the burden on you is very great and even though you might not wish it any other way I feel strongly that somehow or other you must be enabled to have a rest and time for yourself. So I hope you will allow me to put your name in and cogitate over ways—which must exist—of taking care of your mother in some other way than with your constant attendance. [August 4, 1959]

Besides, Russell added in a wry afterthought, the Ford Foundation had dispensed money to persons (names he withheld) they both knew of who were no more, and probably much less, deserving than she of corporate largess. Welty filled out the papers.

Russell was also concerned about changes in the publishing business, and it is reasonable to assume that worry in one direction—about his client—exacerbated worry in the other—about the industry in which he conducted the author's business. The two concerns were merging in the manuscript on which his client tried to work. One reason Russell was so anxious to have a copy for presentation to Harcourt was his premonition that changes there did not bode well for business as usual. A few years earlier, in 1955, as the *Ponder* follies were gathering momentum, William Jovanovich had been elected president of the firm when neither the Harcourt nor the Brace faction could successfully install its choice.

Russell was concerned at the upheaval. One of his practical reasons for urging Welty to finish the reunion story was that he wanted a tangible book to offer the new management of Harcourt so that he could determine for himself just how the Jovanovich regime would treat his client. He was particularly anxious to get the negotiations under way in October 1959, when he thought a finished manuscript was about to arrive from Mississippi any day.

> And I am glad you're able to get back to the typing. I do want to see that finished and the decks cleared—and yes, I intend to see that you get a lot of money for it, as much as the traffic can bear. . . . This time I am not going to let Harcourt have an option on the next book—I want to wait and see what happens. There evidently have been some other convulsions in the firm, I don't think affecting the editors but people of some consequence in other branches of the trade department and there are other minor odds and ends that make me uneasy. So I intend to be quite firm (a polite word for tough) about the contract.
>
> Also I'm hoping that that Ford outfit will make that grant to you—they should—but this might mean you'd have to spend some time up here in contact with the theatre—all the same you wouldn't necessarily have to spend the entire time, for what they say they hope for is a play and you would be able to turn to that after the present time and presumably do a fair amount at home, so that if this all came through there would be $7500. But of course there is no certainty about this though the place is dopey if they don't give it to you and I would be quite angry with them. All this expense was one of the things that were worrying me which was partly the reason why I wanted the work finished—to be honest it was mostly for my own pleasure but I also thought that there might be a drain on finances and I further thought that something so long delayed might become a niggle in the mind. [October 1, 1959]

Russell's uneasiness with Harcourt was, he wrote to his client, not yet attributable to a specific source. He wanted to initiate a strategy that would obtain the most favorable financial terms for his client *and* ascertain for himself the new character of the publishing business at Harcourt.

> Now one business item for you to brood about. I'm becoming increasingly uneasy about Harcourt—hard to put a finger on—and no particular fault to find with usage of your past books (if no great praise). But I have this feeling they are moved mostly by business and it comes to me in so many small ways, perhaps easily explained, that it would be hard to take up with them. I think we have talked mildly about this in the past, and with you feeling no strong pull toward another publisher, or person in the business (which might make you want to break) and with me feeling one publisher is very much like another (as they do) no reason for me to cause a break.
>
> But now, in the 18 months or more since Denver Lindley [an editor whom Russell liked and whom Jovanovich fired in the spring of 1958] left, I feel uneasy—and as I say hard to put a finger on. So when your ms. comes in, both because of your needs and my feelings, I'm going to exact a stiff deal from them (and one I feel sure I could get elsewhere in many places). [October 15, 1959]

Russell was reacting to changes in the publishing business that were as radical and far-reaching as any in the twentieth century, and certainly the biggest changes in his years in the business. Observers and historians of the publishing industry have agreed that the business exploded after World War II with a force few existing houses could contain. One particular change was the marketing sophistication of paperback publishers and their success in changing the public view of the paperback book. As one writer put it: "As more and more paperback publishers shrug off their feelings of inferiority, publishing more originals and backing them with serious promotion and first-rate publicity campaigns, and as the consumer press becomes more aware of the need to pay review attention to the paperback originals, authors are recognizing this outlet as a reputable, even prestigious way to reach their readers" (Lottman, 96–97).

Once a temporary or makeshift arrangement—more than a magazine but less than a book—the paperback became a familiar fixture in the drugstores and train depots of the 1950s. Soon paperback reprint deals often involved sums previously unheard of in publishing. Russell was uneasy about the madcap progress toward heights where money seemed the sole measure of literary worth. This was the temperament underlying his skepticism of "business" as the new engine moving the profession he thought he knew. He had, of course, always been aware that profit-and-loss impinged on publishing decisions. Welty had come to him in 1940 with a history of rejections of her book of short stories on (the publishers') grounds that such a book would not turn a profit. More than twenty-five years later Russell was to run into the same dollar barrier with a volume of stories by a newer client, Reynolds Price, according to Hiram Haydn in *Words and Faces*. Russell also knew that one major reason for the short supply of his beloved detective novels was that publishers simply (and benightedly, he had argued) decided on limited press runs and small profit margins for books in that genre (*NYTBR*, June 17, 1945, p. 7). But the state of things in 1959 seemed crucially different—unfamiliar decisions were being made by a different sort of person.

Money was the octane in the system; never before had it seemed, to the agent, so powerfully combustible. Postwar expansion in the publishing industry created a frantic need for capital. In the late 1950s that need became acute and remained sharp through the 1970s. The primary means for gaining capital were mergers and "going public," the public issuing of stock. John Tebbel, whose history of book publishing in the United States covers the period from colonial times to 1980, numbers no fewer than 307 mergers between the years 1958 and 1970. Mergers and partnerships were not entirely new in American publishing. Most of the mergers, however, had occurred between firms in the same industry—a stronger house taking over a weaker or smaller one (as, for example, Harcourt taking over parts of Reynal & Hitchcock in the early 1950s, or Doubleday merging with Doran in the 1920s). A few of the mergers were more threatening, however, because they seemed to be invasions from the outside—RCA's successful bid for Random House in 1965, for example. Whatever the particular circumstances, however, the general and common thrust was the drive for a business advantage: more capital for expansion, for enhanced competitiveness in new bidding wars for the next megabook, for the convenient tax losses a publishing subsidiary might afford a fat conglomerate.

The relatively sudden transformation of book publishing from a so-called gentlemen's club (in the eyes of Wall Street, at least) into a growth industry caused myriad changes in the way the business was handled. Russell sensed these changes all over, but especially at Harcourt Brace, where William Jovanovich personified the new wave.

Jovanovich could be amused by the sudden collision of the traditional ways of old-line publishing with the new men of Wall Street (cf. "Going Downtown" in *Now, Barabbas*), but he was himself "new" enough in the 1950s to play the game rather than be played by it. When it became abundantly clear to him, for example, that corporate takeovers might erase the autonomy of the old house for which he worked, Jovanovich seized the initiative and took Harcourt Brace into the conglomerate business as a predator rather than as prey. Beginning in the early 1960s, he bought "marine parks [Sea World], a chain of seafood restaurants, television stations, trade journals, newsletters, a management consulting organization, an insurance firm, and a psychological testing and school supply company" (Tebbel, IV, 175). He was determined not to let Harcourt Brace become a mere "tax loss" for a flush oil company. In the view of his friend and co-publisher Hiram Haydn, Jovanovich was an able, prescient, proud, and tough executive when he took over the presidency of Harcourt. Moreover, he was always driven to "do more" (Haydn, 142–43); this often meant "push more." One might also call Jovanovich "firm"—that polite synonym for tough that Russell had used. Jovanovich's toughness had, for himself, an almost mythical significance, for he has repeatedly linked it with his Montenegrin ancestors on his father's side. He has written very proudly of the fighting history of the Montenegrins from the fourteenth century to the twentieth. He saw himself as an active participant in that legacy; business, not war, became his ordeal of arms. He is quoted as telling Denver Lindley, on the occasion of the dispute that terminated Lindley's association with Harcourt in 1958,

"You forget, Denver, that I am a proud Montenegrin" (Tebbel, IV, 176–77). In hindsight, one cannot err in predicting a clash between the son of a proud Montenegrin and the son of an Irish mystic and poet.

Toughness conditioned in the guerrilla battles of the new corporate jungle, then, charged to the fore as the recommended virtue for survival in the new world of publishing. Its corollary was a cool, almost arctic, avoidance of the ideal in professional behavior or rhetoric. One of the new men in publishing, Michael Korda, then editor in chief at Simon & Schuster, was quoted as making perhaps the quintessential cool manifesto in 1979: "We sell books, other people sell shoes. What's the difference? Publishing isn't the highest art" (Schwartz, 9). Korda's boss at Simon & Schuster, Richard Snyder, echoed the tough policy: "Publishing is an act of commerce" (9). Jovanovich was not so aggressively unsentimental, but his published attitudes have more in common with the new commercial straightforwardness than they have with the sort of idealistic attitudes and examples Russell experienced in the editorial offices of his father. In *Now, Barabbas* Jovanovich wrote:

> Of publishers it may be said that like the English as a race they are incapable of philosophy. They deal in particulars and adhere easily to Sydney Smith's dictum that one should take short views, hope for the best, and trust God. Their days are filled with royalty rates, accounts and discounts, last printings and first remainders, and it is reasonable to ask even of Malraux or Faulkner how many copies of his previous book were sold. [7]

"What have you done for me lately," as the governing motto of a publisher, was perhaps the worst Diarmuid Russell could imagine, for his whole career as a literary agent had derived from the first principle that books and writers were vital to civilization—more vital than ships or shoes or sealing wax. When he sensed, in the ripples from the "convulsions" at Harcourt Brace, that "business" was at the controls, he sensed accurately. He knew that Welty's new book would not be received in the old way, and he was impatient to get to the showdown.

Russell continued, with a double motive, to encourage the author to finish her manuscript. When good tidings came from the Ford Foundation in February 1960, Russell was quick to remind her to finish the long story before embarking on any new work. This spur to finish had been in his plans all along. A second reminder followed in March; finishing the story, then testing it at Harcourt became more clearly linked.

> There'll be no trouble at all in getting a drop of money (a large drop) if you can send me a slab of the ms., the more of course the better. I rather intend to whack Harcourt on this. And I am so glad you are going on in spite of delays and difficulties because I think you need to. So ship what you have ready to show whenever you like. [March 21, 1960]

As regular as the calendar, Russell reported news from the front and urged Welty to finish the story. A lunch with Bennett Cerf of Random House brought an inquiry about Welty's attachment to Harcourt Brace. Russell knew that the upheavals of Jovanovich's regime were attracting other publishers, who cruised the troubled waters hoping to snatch a few choice survivors.

> Here's a little matter for you to brood over. I had lunch today with Bennett Cerf and during the lunch he asked about you and what were the chances of Random being your publisher (I think many publishers ask about Harcourt authors on account of so many changes). At any rate I just said that I didn't think you had any very strong feelings about Harcourt, and that I thought you might not have any very strong feelings about any publisher. In my idle and nasty fashion I asked what kind of deal he was thinking of and after a little talk it turned out to be a $12,000 advance. So I said I would report this, not knowing how you felt about Random or any publisher.
>
> But with your need of money, owing to your mother's illness, I think this is something we ought to think about. I don't quite know how you feel about any publisher, supposing a move from Harcourt is in order—I have more and more come to feel it is, I feel very uneasy about some

aspects of that firm. But if a move is in order I don't know how you feel about Random. You might want to be somewhere else.

At any rate you might brood over this and give me your thoughts. [April 11, 1960]

Still, family worries delayed the manuscript and any decision on whether or not to leave Harcourt. Mrs. Welty's illness had gone beyond complications from cataract surgery: she was suffering from a broken hip and a stroke. Russell had his own worries as well. His daughter, Pamela, was to be married in June 1960, and the event, though happy, reminded him sorely that his finances—for a man of fifty-eight, after twenty years in his profession—were no cause for boasting. His landlord of nearly twenty years had sold the house Russell rented, and he and his wife were faced with finding and possibly buying a house when he did not feel young enough for long-range deals such as mortgages (July 22, 1960). Several purchase agreements fell through in the next months; Russell never knew for certain where or how he would be living, but he suspected that new arrangements would of necessity mean a reduction. His own uncertainty seemed to concentrate his concern on his client's predicament.

I keep thinking of you all the time, sad that you are having such a wretched fretting time of it—and yet nothing for anyone to do, as far as I can see.

I still feel strongly you ought, willy nilly, to set aside time to write, something your own—but this, I know, depends on circumstances and one's feelings. But I know in the long run we are all dependent on ourselves and that to be committed to others wholly is not right—either for others or ourselves. [July 15, 1960]

He repeatedly argued hard-edged practicality against Welty's tacit sense of obligation and sacrifice. As Mrs. Welty's condition deteriorated, Russell argued that the elderly as a class needed far more professional care than family members as a rule could give—or easily afford—and that the prolonged wear on the writer's nerves might curtail her career.

> I feel desolated that matters aren't really any better—knowing, as I do, that your whole purpose is to do the best you can with a good heart, and at that better than almost anyone could do. So you must get away again—and let me know. The terrible thing here is to be in relation with someone always loved—who is not what they were. Harassing to everyone—but more to you. I don't know what to advise, save we all love you, worry and feel that you are the one to be cared for. You are doing all, and more, than your mother needs. [January 30, 1961]

The reunion story was in jeopardy; Russell pleaded that it be released from limbo as soon as possible. He believed in the quality of the writing, the need for the writer to appear again in print, and in his own need to determine the new interests of the publisher. William Maxwell, Russell added, had read an interim copy (which Maxwell had arranged for *The New Yorker* to type at no cost and with no strings on publication) and was anxious to get in touch for a discussion of publication possibilities (April 5, 1961). Harcourt wanted to use an excerpt for their annual Christmas booklet, but Russell was reluctant to give them permission inasmuch as they had offered no contract on the entire book. As agent and friend he was acutely aware of the financial and emotional pressures on the writer and tried to persuade her to reach a balance between a daughter's responsibility and a writer's work. That balance was maddeningly difficult to achieve in the early 1960s. Whenever Mrs. Welty seemed stabilized in one illness, another would occur. Nursing homes proved too expensive or unsuitable. Circumstances were so hectic that Welty had to request a postponement of the Ford grant she had won. Then the roof was damaged in Hurricane Camille (October 9, 1962).

Russell squeezed every dollar he could from readings of Welty's work by others, from reprints, from excerpts, from paperback editions. In better times, he often wrote, he would have given such permissions gratis; but every twenty-five dollars helped (February 18, 1963). An agent had to be Scrooge sometimes.

Circumstances continued to postpone the book, even after Welty, following Russell's advice, had finally found an acceptable convalescent home for her mother a fifty-mile drive away (April 1, 1963). But Mrs. Welty's stay was measured in weeks. Welty, not ready to let the reunion story go, wrote instead a children's book, *Pepe*, later retitled *The Shoe Bird*. The children's book was not the manuscript Russell wanted to take into the arena with Harcourt, and he was not altogether certain that Harcourt wanted it wholeheartedly either (April 17, 1963). But he also knew that turning down *Pepe* would mean "H.B. loses you" (April 22, 1963). He expected Jovanovich to enter the deliberations in person by accepting the manuscript just to keep Welty on his list. He was correct; Russell got a $5,000 advance, a 15 percent royalty, and a no-option clause on the next book—a contract he believed put Harcourt "on notice to perform" (July 1, 1963). Neither Russell nor Welty, however, was comfortable with the revived relationship with Harcourt.

The assassination of Medgar Evers in Jackson in the summer of 1963 spurred Welty to write "Where Is the Voice Coming From?" almost immediately, proving that as a writer she was better at home struggling to understand the crisis of civil rights than "emigrating from the whole country," her reaction to the Little Rock crisis. Russell was impressed.

> The story I like, filled as it is with scorn and anger—but I don't know what magazines will feel, since it so closely follows Evers, and since a man is going to be put on trial for this murder, and publication might in law be regarded as prejudicial. But we'll see.
>
> I gather your mother is home, or coming home, since you say you have got two nurses. I do wish this had been delayed till you had come up here, for when you come you will fret. It's getting hot now and I start thinking of Maine, still five weeks away. [June 25, 1963]

William Maxwell and *The New Yorker* were equally impressed and unperturbed by potential legal difficulties; Russell reported:

> Bill must have called you to say how wonderful they all thought the story was and that they are pulling an issue apart to get it in. Cheers! [June 26, 1963]

The notoriety was less than cheerful, for it became another factor keeping Welty away from the reunion story. Mrs. Welty tried the nursing home one more time, but returned to her daughter's care that fall. Russell began to worry over his client's heavy burden: "But you must get off, Eudora, for the wear and tear of life at home is going to break you down, and this makes no value to anyone" (October 8, 1963). For the rest of the year this concern for a "more stable arrangement" (December 3, 1963) nagged at Russell. He was relieved when Mrs. Welty returned yet again to a professional facility: "There are situations in life where what is most desirable is impossible—and all one can do is what is possible" (December 9, 1963). The one-hundred-mile-per-day drives did not make writing any easier. Most of 1964 was made up of these visits and Welty's work as writer-in-residence at Millsaps College in Jackson to help pay expenses.

In the backwash from the Evers story, Welty wrote "Must the Novelist Crusade?"—a question she answered in the negative. She realized, however, that a simple, public *no* would not suffice; a public position on the civil rights turmoil would be the topic of every other question for the foreseeable future. She then became reluctant to release the reunion story out of apprehension that reviewers would find it "inconsequential" since she had not showcased the racial theme. Don't worry about "black white turmoil" or possible reviews, Russell answered; the book (of which he had read only Part Two at this time) was "enchanting" and cried out for completion (April 5, 1965; April 15, 1965).

Russell had rejoiced that the novel would be done by midsummer 1964. It was delayed. In January 1965, the agent looked forward again to March. By April, once again true to the Persephone cycle, a section called Part Two seemed to him ready for circulation to magazines. Parts One and Three were in the offing. Word began to circulate among the cognoscenti that Welty had a new novel. Cerf contacted Russell with an offer of a $35,000 advance if Welty would bring the new work to Random House (July 7, 1965). Russell knew it was time to approach Harcourt Brace and ascertain their position; the Cerf offer was the fallback cushion he had needed. He would schedule a lunch, he briefed his client by letter, mention that a large offer (with no additional details) had been tendered, and gauge the Harcourt response (July 13, 1965). Still, there was no completed manuscript, but Russell felt ready to proceed. Mrs. Welty weakened seriously in the fall and winter of 1965; the author's brother Edward suffered a relapse in the fall as well. Welty had time for concentration only on short fiction and wrote "The Demonstrators." She sent it up to Russell in November 1965, and it was taken by *The New Yorker* within a few weeks. The story was published, however, almost a year later. "The Demonstrators" won the O. Henry Prize for 1966. Whereas the monetary payoffs in other categories of publishing had shot through the roof in the 1960s, short-story prize money had not. "The Demonstrators" gained only $300; in the early 1940s Welty's prize-winning stories had brought in $200.

Chestina Andrews Welty died January 20, 1966; the author's brother Edward died unexpectedly four days later. Russell knew that the shock of two such losses in quick succession would interrupt any writer's work. He only hoped that the interruption would not be permanent. By May he was heartened to hear that Welty was back at work on the novel; in July he was still waiting. His vigil was to be prolonged yet again, for Welty set the reunion novel aside to write, from start to finish, a new long story early in 1967. She promised the new story for February; by late April, as consistent as ever with her Persephone-like creative cycle, "Poor Eyes" had been read by the agent. By mid-May Maxwell had also read it, and thought it so good it would swamp any collection in which it might appear. He urged separate publication; Welty demurred, thinking that a story so closely grounded in autobiographical events would get undue attention unless it was camouflaged by other stories. With the form of publication in abeyance, Welty and Maxwell worked together on the revision and reshaping of "Poor Eyes." Maxwell eventually won almost an entire issue of *The New Yorker* (March 15, 1969) for "The Optimist's Daughter," the title of the story when finally published. Maxwell thought the story so fine, a two-year wait was tolerable; it had been set in galleys as early as June 1967. Then, by deep-grooved habit, it was back to the novel.

Waiting for the novel, Russell began to think of consolidating the work of his client's career as a way of conferring what order he could on an association of nearly thirty years. Just at that moment, in the late 1960s, the need for order seemed acute. There were, of course, the clear signs of mutability in his personal orbit—the disturbance of relocating a household, and extensive gardens, after decades in the same place; the troubling suddenness and frequency of death among one's friends and acquaintances (Mrs. Welty and her son in January 1966; Charles Morton, a friend of Russell's and associate editor of *The Atlantic*, in 1967; client Hubert Creekmore in May 1966; in 1964 both R. N. Linscott, who had been at Houghton Mifflin in 1938 when Welty had tried a novel, and Hamilton Basso, friendly reviewer of *Delta Wedding*). Russell's own litany of "dentists, doctors, hospitals" seemed to "erupt" with nasty frequency as he grew older (December 5, 1966; December 9, 1966). There was also unrest in the more distant orbit of national politics. Both author and agent were disturbed by the racial violence all over the country, and by the violence at the Democratic convention in Chicago in the summer of 1968. During this season of circumstances and turmoil, Russell began to collect copyright assignments on all his client's non-fiction (April 25, 1968). He also began to view the impending dealings with Harcourt Brace (or with Random House) over the new novel as crucial for imparting some order to the financial future of the writer; he wanted a deal that would "leave [Welty] reasonably free and untroubled for some time" (November 22, 1968). Russell was sixty-six years old in 1968; he could see the end of his days in the literary agency, but not the end of the fifty-nine-year-old writer. He wrote to Welty that same month, November 1968: "I . . . think the job of the writer is to look at a confused world and to draw from it some sort of order—maybe wrong but still one's own ideal as to what things might, or ought, to be" (November 1, 1968). Just before the presidential election, then, Russell thought it likely that things-as-they-were had overwhelmed things-as-they-ought-to-be, and he wished this particular writer to have the freedom to begin the renovation.

Later that winter Russell's ruminations on time and circumstance were given more direction by a request from James Boatwright, editor of *Shenandoah*, to contribute a brief essay on the early years of his client's career to a special issue of the journal. Russell took to the work with characteristic brusqueness about his own part in the story: "I am not going to say anything about myself—I don't think agents are important, just convenient, and no more than that" (January 15, 1969). His design was to assemble the names and dates of every rejection of every story before publication of *A Curtain of Green*, hoping the data "might be interesting—and I trust heartening to many authors and I hope rebuking to many publishers" (January 15, 1969). The immense and swift changes in publishing in the intervening years since 1940 had sharpened the edge of Russell's rebuke. When news that the novel might be arriving any day (February 7, 1969) was followed by the even better news that it was finished and actually on its way, to be followed closely by the author in person (April 25, 1969), the agent was in a mood to see his client's career as a sustained struggle for deserved recognition from blockheaded publishers who had to be reminded every day of the importance of literature and the relative unimportance of their work as facilitators of its publication and distribution.

When *Losing Battles*, as the novel was eventually titled, met a less than proper reception (by the agent's standards) at Harcourt, the inevitable rending occurred. By mentioning editing and cutting in ways that Russell deemed disrespectful to the novel and the author, Jovanovich and his staff had found the fuse. Russell drafted a terse letter withdrawing the manuscript from Harcourt:

> I had lunch with Eudora to-day to talk over your letter and for her to tell me about her lunch with Dan Wickenden [the editor chosen for *Losing Battles*]. I'm afraid we both came to the conclusion there is no enthusiasm shown by Harcourt for the new novel, nothing save demands for changes, and that the only thing to do is to have the ms. returned to me.
>
> I am sorry about this, as is Eudora, for we are both reluctant about change. Still it is manifest this new work leads to no liking on the part of Harcourt and Eudora would not wish to be published, or to deal with, people whose attitude is unsympathetic.
>
> I wish I did not have to write this parting letter but it's probably better so. It's clear the novel has no great appeal for your firm and it

> should be obvious that Eudora, a greatly distinguished writer, is not going to have her work edited in the manner you describe. It has to be her work, liked or disliked as may happen, but run as written. [Draft, Russell to William Jovanovich, May 22, 1969]

Jovanovich was, understandably, alarmed, and wrote immediately to Welty, who was in New York. He made the tactical error of enclosing a copy of Russell's letter to him, assuming perhaps that the author and the agent were or could be divided. But after three decades, their loyalty could not have been more solid. Welty's letter to Jovanovich sealed the departure from Harcourt:

> My letter to you and yours to me crossed, and I suppose they each suffered for a reply to the other, but I would feel better if something of an acknowledgment were made, so I'll write it.
>
> Diarmuid Russell does not need my testimonial to his integrity, and I did not need the xerox of his letter to you. He and I had talked over your letter to him; and I read him my letter to you and he then wrote and showed me his letter to you before either was sent you. Both were direct expressions of what I thought about your suggestions; Diarmuid was in full agreement with me; and I don't see how you could really disbelieve that I didn't want to "collaborate" with anybody in cutting or changing my novel, and didn't want my new long story "The Optimist's Daughter" given its book publication as one of a collection of old stories. To get your letter—the one written to me—and the roses in combination was a sort of shock. But you were told the truth about everything and I am sorry to think it wasn't both evident and understandable. I'm sorry about the upset and unhappy feelings. And I'm sorry about the departure with my novel. But it can't be helped. In saying goodbye, I do also want to say I have valued my long association with Harcourt Brace and am grateful for all that the firm has done on my behalf. [Draft, Welty to Jovanovich, June 3, 1969]

The son of Montenegrin warriors, who would not hesitate to ask "even of Malraux or Faulkner how many copies of his previous book were sold," and the son of the Irish poet had had their showdown.

Ironically, whereas "business" had doomed any cooperative relationship between Russell and Harcourt Brace on the book, it facilitated his agreement with the eventual publisher, Random House. That Albert Erskine was to be the editor for the book did not impede the deal. Erskine had been married to Katherine Anne Porter and had known Welty and her work since the days of *The Southern Review* in the early 1940s. The presence of such a friend at Random House made the move easier. Both Atheneum and Farrar, Straus & Giroux wanted the book but could not muster the capital to stay in the bidding. Russell swiftly closed a favorable deal with Random House; totaling advance, royalties over the advance, the author's share of paperback rights, and a belated sale to the Book-of-the-Month Club, the author reaped close to $100,000 for *Losing Battles*, enough to pave the near future smoothly. Averaged over the previous decade, the years of actual work, the sum does not seem so extravagant.

Russell did not remain in the literary agency business long after the publication of *Losing Battles*. He had not lost his verve or his commitment to literature; the spirit was willing, but the flesh gave out. In May 1970, just as *Losing Battles* was making its way into the best-seller lists, Henry Volkening's wife died of cancer. Volkening himself went into the hospital for a routine of tests and surgery the following January 1971. His recovery—long, painful, eventually unsuccessful—left doubled work for Russell. The agent's own health was not robust: arthritis, a bad back, the history of heart trouble. In October 1972, he had bad news to report:

> Hate to tell you I got not very good news from my doctor—lung cancer, and I go into the hospital this Thursday for some tests Friday, am told I may be let home for the weekend and then go back to have the operation Wednesday. Dunno how long I will be out of action. . . . I feel surprisingly philosophic about it all and only sorry that Rosie and friends have to worry too. [October 3, 1972]

Russell knew, when he came back to work in January 1973, that he would have to retire soon; he thought he could make it through June. It was, however, much too arduous simply to get through the routine of an ordinary day. In February he wrote to his client that he would retire at the end of March, confident that her interests would be faithfully looked after by Timothy Seldes, who had taken over Russell & Volkening.

Enforced leisure paid at least one dividend: after more than thirty years of association, Russell was finally to visit his client in Mississippi. Lean finances had always kept him and his wife, Rose, from returning Welty's many visits to their Westchester home, but the proclamation of "Eudora Welty Day in Mississippi," May 2, 1973, brought them to Jackson. Physically drawn and easily tired, Russell nevertheless seems to have relished the invitation and the opportunity to party with so many friends and clients. The celebration of Welty's work, held in the midst of damaging rains in Mississippi and the Watergate scandals in Washington, seems to have been special. Nona Balakian, who had been assistant to the editor of *The New York Times Book Review* in 1943 when Welty began to write reviews, was in Jackson as associate editor in 1973 and wrote of the celebration:

> For the visitor from the East, the "celebration" had a fairy-tale quality. Writers in America are not supposed to be famous and happy at the same time: the "literary life" so often engenders tense, semi-tragic figures with glossy fronts that cover up a multitude of frustrations. Yet here was a writer perfectly attuned to her milieu, the lilt in her voice and simplicity of her manner giving her away as no words could. No gloss. No front. Only a sharp, intense responsiveness, a feeling of comradeship.

One can only guess at the reaction of the singularly un-sentimental Russell. If he looked up at the United States Air Force precision flying team, the Thunderbirds, roaring in the heavens over Jackson, he might have wondered if his client's fame had been carried a bit too far. But the fighters were for the Mississippi Arts Festival, not just for Eudora Welty.

His client was, however, the center of a kind of literary worship. After her reading from *Losing Battles* in the Old Capitol, where Jefferson Davis had declared the secession of Mississippi from the Union, Welty endured a receiving line for more than an hour, signing "autographs on napkins, on the backs of certificates given some of the winners in the festival literary competition, on various festival programs, and on any surface offered, often having to use a saucer to write on" (Skelton, 20A). It would not be the last.

For a couple of days Welty was the center of local and national attention. Russell could not keep up with all of it. He was the center of another celebration, for Welty had the Russells as her house guests and was careful to show him as many gardens and wildflowers as the environs of Jackson could muster. She visited the Russells at least one more time after the Mississippi celebration and before Russell's death in December. On one of those visits Diarmuid gave Welty all her letters to him, beginning with the first one, of May 1940.

Diarmuid Russell died December 16, 1973; obituary notices in *The New York Times* and *Publishers Weekly*, totaling about four hundred words, noted the barest facts of his life and work. It is likely that Diarmuid Russell would have thought four hundred words too many for a "convenience." Unlike his father, who dispatched a farewell letter to friends in America in which he wrote that he had no regrets at the door of death and was reconciled to the fact that although he had striven to move the world toward "the heavenly city" it had obstinately declined to budge, Diarmuid Russell did not participate in the Celtic flair for farewells. He would have deemed the two spare death notices unavoidable; he would no doubt have disapproved of a book in which he shared the foreground with any author, especially with one whose gift was the treasure of his professional career.

But he had created a presence in the author's life and work that transcended the word "convenience"; he had become the reader on the other end (Prenshaw, 193), whose real presence was an integral part of all that Welty wrote from the summer of 1940 on. He was as solid in business as he was in literary opinion. If Welty has survived against the odds of literary America, Russell deserves much of the credit.

> But, you know, his terms were not uncertain; you knew how well he liked something or how well he didn't. I just can't tell you what it meant to me to have him there. His integrity, his understanding, his instincts—everything was something I trusted. [Prenshaw, 185]

List of Sources

Obviously the principal source for this book is the collection of letters between Eudora Welty and Diarmuid Russell covering the years 1940 through 1973. I am deeply grateful to Miss Welty and to Pamela Russell Jessup and her brother William Russell for permission to use these letters freely.

A. E. *The Candle of Vision*. London: Macmillan, 1928.

———. *Imaginations and Reveries*. Dublin and London: Maunsel and Company, 1915.

Ascher, Barbara Lazear. "The Color of the Air: A Conversation with Eudora Welty." *Saturday Review*, November/December 1984, 31–35.

Aswell, Mary Louise, ed. *It's a Woman's World: A Collection of Stories from "Harper's Bazaar."* New York: Whittlesey House, 1944.

——— and Frederic Wertham, eds. *The World Within: Fiction Illuminating Neuroses of Our Time*. New York: Whittlesey House, 1947.

Atkinson, Brooks. Review of "The Innocents." *The New York Times*, February 12, 1950, section II, 1.

———. "Mystery Wrapped in Enigma at Golden." Review of *Waiting for Godot*. *The New York Times*, April 20, 1956, 21.

———. "'Godot' Is No Hoax." *The New York Times*, April 29, 1956, section II, 1.

———. Review of *Littlest Revue*. *The New York Times*, May 23, 1956, 37.

Balakian, Nona. "A Day of One's Own." *The New York Times Book Review*, May 27, 1973, 27.

Basso, Hamilton. Review of *Delta Wedding*. *The New Yorker*, May 11, 1946, 89+.

Bentley, Eric. "Theatre." *The New Republic*, March 12, 1956, 29.

Berg, A. Scott. *Max Perkins: Editor of Genius*. New York: Dutton, 1978.

Blackmur, R. P. "The Economy of the American Writer." *Sewanee Review*, 53 (April–June 1945), 175–85.

Brickell, Herschel. "Introduction," *Prize Stories of 1947: The O. Henry Awards*. Garden City, N.Y.: Doubleday, 1947.

Cohn, David. "The Deep South: An Editorial." *Saturday Review of Literature*, September 19, 1942, 3.

Colum, Mary. *Life and the Dream*. Garden City, N.Y.: Doubleday, 1947.

Cushman, John. "The Literary Agent and Book Publishing." *Publishers Weekly*, 201 (April 10, 1972), Pt. II, 112–14.

Donald, David Herbert. *Look Homeward: A Life of Thomas Wolfe*. Boston: Little, Brown, 1987.

Engel, Lehman. *This Bright Day: An Autobiography*. New York: Macmillan, 1974.

Engle, Paul. Review of *Delta Wedding*. *Chicago Tribune*, April 14, 1946, 12.

Feld, Rose. Review of *A Curtain of Green and Other Stories*. *Herald Tribune Books*, November 16, 1941, 10–12.

Gabriel, Trip. "Call My Agent!" *The New York Times Magazine*, February 19, 1989, 44+.

Gibbons, Monk, ed. *The Living Torch*. London: Macmillan, 1937.

Gill, Brendan. *Here at the New Yorker*. New York: Random House, 1975.

Haydn, Hiram. *Words and Faces*. New York: Harcourt Brace Jovanovich, 1974.

Henry, Augustine. *Forest, Woods, and Trees in Relation to Hygiene*. London: Constable, 1919.

Hills, L. Rust. "The Structure of the American Literary Establishment." *Esquire*, July 1963, 41. [Two-page literary chart, pp. 42–43.]

"Hobe." Review of *The Ponder Heart*. *Variety*, February 22, 1956, 22.

Jovanovich, William. *Now, Barabbas*. New York: Harper & Row, 1964.

Joyce, James. *Ulysses*. New York: Random House, 1934.

Kane, Harnett. Review of *Delta Wedding*. *Herald Tribune Books*, April 14, 1946, 1.

Lottman, Eileen. "Paperbacks: The Illegitimate Child Comes of Age." *Publishers Weekly*, 201 (April 10, 1972), Pt. II, 96–99.

McDowell, Edwin. "Ideas and Trends." *The New York Times*, May 20, 1990, 22.

Marrs, Suzanne. "The Making of *Losing Battles*: Plot Revision," *Southern Literary Journal*, 18 (Fall 1985), 40–49.

———. *The Welty Collection: A Guide to the Eudora Welty Manuscripts and Documents at the Mississippi Department of Archives and History*. Jackson: University Press of Mississippi, 1988.

Miller, Joe. "Counterpoint." *Seattle Post-Intelligencer*, August 3, 1947, n.p.

Mirrielees, Edith Ronald. "The American Short Story," *The Atlantic Monthly*, 167 (June 1941), 714–22.

The New York Times. "Russell Goes Home After Weary Visit." March 2, 1935, 32.

———. December 30, 1934, IV, 4. (Visit of A.E. to United States.)

———. July 18, 1935, 19. (Obituary of A.E.)

———. December 18, 1973. (Obituary of Diarmuid Russell.)

North, Sterling. "Miss Welty Needs to Be Untangled." Review of *Delta Wedding*. *Atlanta Constitution*, April 21, 1946, section B, 10.

O'Casey, Sean. *Innishfallen Fare Thee Well*. New York: Macmillan, 1949.

———. *The Letters of Sean O'Casey*, edited by David Krause. New York: Macmillan, 1975.

Peper, William. Untitled. *New York World-Telegram*. May 2, 1956, 33.

Poore, Charles. Review of *Delta Wedding*. *The New York Times Book Review*, April 11, 1946, 1+.

———. Review of *Music from Spain*. *The New York Times*, January 1, 1949, 11.

Prenshaw, Peggy W., ed. *Conversation with Eudora Welty*. Jackson: University Press of Mississippi, 1984.

Prescott, Orville. "Books of the Times." *The New York Times*, April 17, 1946.

Publishers Weekly. "On the Future of the Trade: William Jovanovich." 201 (April 10, 1972), Pt. II, 66–78.

———. January 14, 1974, 62. (Obituary of Diarmuid Russell.)

Rickett, H. W. *Wildflowers of America*. New York: Crown, 1953. (This book does not bear Russell's name, yet it is the book of which he was probably most proud; he organized and supervised the committee which raised the considerable amount of money needed to underwrite publication.)

Robinson, John. "Room in Algiers." *The New Yorker*, October 19, 1946, 82+.

———. "'. . . All This Juice and All This Joy.'" *Horizon* (London), 18 (November 1948), 341–47.

———. "The Inspector." *Harper's Magazine*, 200 (June 1950), 96–101.

Rosenfeld, Isaac. "Double Standard." *The New Republic*, April 29, 1946, 633–34.

Rugoff, Milton. Review of *Selected Prose of George Bernard Shaw*. *The New York Times*, December 7, 1952, 34.

Russell, Diarmuid. "An Experiment with the Imagination." *Harper's Magazine*, 185 (September 1942), 428–31.

———. "AE (George William Russell)." *The Atlantic Monthly*, 171 (February 1943), 51–57.

———. "Let the Children Read What They Want." *Good Housekeeping*, 118 (March 1944), 23+.

———. "The Art of Conversation." *Good Housekeeping*, 118 (May 1944), 43+.

———. "The Literature of Utility." *Tomorrow*, IV (March 1945), 34–35.

———. "The Memorial Tree." *Good Housekeeping*, 120 (March 1945), 43+.

———. Review of *The Long Goodbye* by Raymond Chandler. *The New York Times Book Review*, June 17, 1945, 7.

———. *The Portable Irish Reader*. New York: Viking, 1946.

———. *Selected Prose of George Bernard Shaw*. New York: Dodd, Mead, 1952.

———. "First Work," *Shenandoah*, 20 (Spring 1969), 16–19.

Schwartz, Tony. "A Publisher Who Sells Books." *The New York Times Book Review*, December 9, 1979, 9, 28–29.

Skelton, Billy. "State Pays Eudora Welty Tribute." *Jackson Clarion-Ledger*, May 3, 1973, 1A, 20A.

Spender, Stephen. "The Situation of the American Writer." *Horizon* (London), 29 (March 1949), 162–79.

Tebbel, John. *A History of Book Publishing in the United States*: Volume III, *The Golden Age Between Two Wars, 1920–1940*. New York: R. R. Bowker, 1978.

———. *A History of Book Publishing in the United States*: Volume IV, *The Great Change, 1940–1980*. New York: R. R. Bowker, 1981.

Time. Review of *A Curtain of Green and Other Stories*. November 24, 1941.

———. Review of *The Wide Net*. September 27, 1943, 100–1.

———. Comment on publishing prospects, 1969. January 3, 1969, 66.

Trilling, Diana. "Fiction in Review." *The Nation*, May 11, 1946, 578.

Variety. Comment on *The Ponder Heart*. February 15, 1956, 17.

———. Comment on *The Ponder Heart*. June 6, 1956, 37.

———. Comment on *The Ponder Heart*. June 27, 1956, 41.

Waldron, Ann. *Close Connections: Caroline Gordon and the Southern Renaissance*. New York: G. P. Putnam's Sons, 1987.

Weeks, Edward. "The Atlantic Bookshelf." *The Atlantic Monthly*, 173 (January 1944), 121.

———. "The Atlantic Bookshelf." 174 (November 1944), 131–33.

Welty, Eudora. *A Curtain of Green and Other Stories*. Garden City, N.Y.: Doubleday, Doran, 1941.

———. *The Robber Bridegroom*. Garden City, N.Y.: Doubleday, Doran, 1942.

———. *The Wide Net and Other Stories*. New York: Harcourt Brace, 1943.

———. "Mirrors for Reality," Review of *A Haunted House and Other*

Short Stories, by Virginia Woolf. *The New York Times Book Review*, April 16, 1944, 3.

———. *Delta Wedding*. New York: Harcourt Brace, 1946.

———. *Music from Spain*. Greenville, Miss.: Levee Press, 1948.

———. *The Golden Apples*. New York: Harcourt Brace, 1949.

———. *Short Stories*. New York: Harcourt Brace, 1950. Limited edition.

———. "Department of Amplification." *The New Yorker*, January 1, 1949, 50–51.

———. "The Ponder Heart." *The New Yorker*. December 5, 1953, 47+.

———. *The Ponder Heart*. New York: Harcourt Brace, 1954.

———. *The Bride of the Innisfallen and Other Stories*. New York: Harcourt Brace, 1955.

———. *The Shoe Bird*. New York: Harcourt Brace, 1964.

———. "The Optimist's Daughter." *The New Yorker*, March 15, 1969, 37+.

———. *Losing Battles*. New York: Random House, 1970.

———. *The Optimist's Daughter*. New York: Random House, 1972.

———. "Find the Connections." In Ralph Sipper, ed. *Inward Journey: Ross Macdonald*. Santa Barbara, Calif.: Cordelia Editions, 1984.

———. *One Writer's Beginnings*. Cambridge: Harvard University Press, 1984.

Zolotow, Sam. "Actor Gives Nod to 'Ponder Heart.'" *The New York Times*, July 22, 1955, 27.